Praise for
UNCREATIVE WRITING

"Multimedia artist and executive manager of words, Goldsmith offers a provocative manifesto for writing in the digital era, with a treasure trove of ideas, techniques, and examples that allow us to make it new—again!"

—MARCUS BOON, author of *In Praise of Copying*

"What Goldsmith argues has significant implications for the world of poetry, poetics, and pedagogy. His book contains brilliant moments of exegesis and archival documentation, and its keen attention to, knowledge about, and currency in artistic practice makes it as much a user's manual as a scholar's tome."

—ADALAIDE MORRIS, The University of Iowa

"In these witty, intelligent essays, Goldsmith brings his encyclopedic knowledge of radical artistic practice to bear on how the rise of the Internet has irrevocably changed, or should irrevocably change, our existing conceptions of writing. Goldsmith's practice as artist and critic is deeply interesting. His book is sure to generate lively debate among writers, artists, literary historians, and media theorists."

—SIANNE NGAI, University of California, Los Angeles

"Goldsmith offers brilliant and elegant insight into the exact relation of contemporary literary practices and broader cultural changes, explaining how the technologies of distributed digital media exemplified by the World Wide Web have made possible the flourishing of a particular type of literature."

—CRAIG DWORKIN, author of *The Consequence of Innovation: Twenty-First-Century Poetics*

UNCREATIVE WRITING

Managing Language in the Digital Age

Kenneth Goldsmith

 COLUMBIA UNIVERSITY PRESS   New York

Columbia University Press
Publishers Since 1893
New York Chichester, West Sussex
Copyright © 2011 Columbia University Press
All rights reserved
Library of Congress Cataloging-in-Publication Data
Goldsmith, Kenneth.
    Uncreative writing: managing language in the digital age / Kenneth Goldsmith.
        p. cm.
    Includes bibliographical references and index.
    ISBN 978-0-231-14990-7 (cloth: acid-free paper)—ISBN 978-0-231-14991-4
    (pbk.: acid-free paper)—ISBN 978-0-231-50472-0 (e-book)
        1. Literature and technology.   2. Creation (Literary, artistic, etc.)
    3. Creative writing—Data processing.   4. Creative writing—Study and
    teaching.   5. Authors—Effect of technological innovations on.   6. Literature
    and the Internet.   7. Modernism (Literature)—History and criticism.
    8. Poetics.   I. Title.
    PN1031.G638 2011
    808.00285'4678—dc23

2011003302

References to Internet Web sites (URLs) were accurate at the time of writing.
Neither the author nor Columbia University Press is responsible for Web sites that
may have expired or changed since the book was prepared.

i had always had mixed feelings about being considered a poet
if robert lowell is a poet   i dont want to be a poet
if robert frost was a poet   i dont want to be a poet
if socrates was a poet   ill consider it

—DAVID ANTIN

CONTENTS

ACKNOWLEDGMENTS

Several of the essays in this book were inspired by pieces initially commissioned by the Poetry Foundation, where they appeared as a weeklong journal on their site in January 2007; other ideas were developed on their blog, Harriet. I'd like to thank Emily Warn, who after hearing my talk at Marjorie Perloff's MLA Presidential Panel in 2006, offered to publish it on the foundation's site, which has resulted in a long and happy collaboration. My thanks also to Don Share, Christian Wiman, Cathy Halley, and Travis Nichols for their open-mindedness and continuing support.

Portions of "Language as Material" appeared in *New Media Poetics* (Cambridge: MIT, 2006) and was first written for the New Media Poetry Conference in October 2002 at the University of Iowa. Other parts of the chapter were given at Digital Poetics at SUNY Buffalo in 2000. "Infallible Processes: What Writing Can Learn from Visual Art" evolved from two gallery talks commissioned by Dia:Beacon in 2008 and 2009. An early version of "Why Appropriation?" was given for the "untitled:speculations," a CalArts conference held in 2008 at the Disney REDcat Theatre and again at Cabinet Space in 2009 in Brooklyn.

Originally this book began as a project on sampling with Marcus Boon, but ended up splitting into two separate books, *Uncreative*

Writing and Boon's great *In Praise of Copying*. Although the two books map different territories, they both stem from the same ten days between Christmas and New Years almost a decade ago.

This book developed over years of conversation with my peers, many of whom I write about here. Without this decade-and-a-half-long ongoing discourse, this book in its present form would not exist.

Thanks the University of Pennsylvania for allowing these words to be put into practice. In particular, I'm grateful for the support of Al Filreis and Charles Bernstein at the Center for Programs in Contemporary Writing and to Claudia Gould and Ingrid Schaffner at the Institute of Contemporary Art.

I'd like to acknowledge Princeton University's Department of American Studies for granting me their Anschutz Distinguished Professorship in the winter of 2009, which provided the support and environment where these ideas could take root. Thanks to Princeton's Hendrik Hartog and Susan Braun.

At Columbia University Press, the careful efforts of Susan Pensak made this a stronger book. And I can't thank my editor, Philip Leventhal, enough for reading this book closer than it deserved to be read, for shaping it, saving it, and for giving me the opportunity to see it into print. His challenges and provocations pushed this book to places I'd never imagined.

The patience and devotion of my wife Cheryl Donegan, along with the feisty playfulness of my sons Finnegan and Cassius, made for a rock-solid writing environment over the years it took to pen this.

Special thanks to Marjorie Perloff for her continuing support to the most extraordinary degree. My admiration and gratitude for her work never ceases.

And finally, this book is dedicated to the "six guys, all in a line, all basically the same age, same stocky build, same bad haicuts [*sic*], and black T-shits [*sic*]." You know who you are.

UNCREATIVE WRITING

INTRODUCTION

In 1969 the conceptual artist Douglas Huebler wrote, "The world is full of objects, more or less interesting; I do not wish to add any more."[1] I've come to embrace Huebler's ideas, though it might be retooled as "The world is full of texts, more or less interesting; I do not wish to add any more." It seems an appropriate response to a new condition in writing today: faced with an unprecedented amount of available text, the problem is not needing to write more of it; instead, we must learn to negotiate the vast quantity that exists. How I make my way through this thicket of information—how I manage it, how I parse it, how I organize and distribute it—is what distinguishes my writing from yours.

The literary critic Marjorie Perloff has recently begun using the term *unoriginal genius* to describe this tendency emerging in literature. Her idea is that, because of changes brought on by technology and the Internet, our notion of genius—a romantic isolated figure—is outdated. An updated notion of genius would have to center around one's mastery of information and its dissemination. Perloff has coined a term, *moving information*, to signify both the act of pushing language around as well as the act of being emotionally moved by that process. She posits that today's writer resembles more a programmer than a tortured genius, brilliantly conceptualizing, constructing, executing, and maintaining a writing machine.

Perloff's notion of unoriginal genius should not be seen merely as a theoretical conceit but rather as a realized writing practice, one that dates back to the early part of the twentieth century, embodying an ethos where the construction or conception of a text is as important as what the text says or does: Think, for example, of the collated, note-taking practice of Walter Benjamin's *Arcades Project* or the mathematically driven constraint-based works by the Oulipo. Today, technology has exacerbated these mechanistic tendencies in writing (there are, for instance, several Web-based versions of Raymond Queneau's 1961 laboriously hand-constructed *Hundred Thousand Billion Poems*), inciting younger writers to take their cues from the workings of technology and the Web as ways of constructing literature. As a result, writers are exploring ways of writing that have been thought, traditionally, to be outside the scope of literary practice: word processing, databasing, recycling, appropriation, intentional plagiarism, identity ciphering, and intensive programming, to name but a few.

In 2007 Jonathan Lethem published a pro-plagiarism, plagiarized essay in *Harper's* entitled, "The Ecstasy of Influence: A Plagiarism." It's a lengthy defense and history of how ideas in literature have been shared, riffed, culled, reused, recycled, swiped, stolen, quoted, lifted, duplicated, gifted, appropriated, mimicked, and pirated for as long as literature has existed. In it he reminds us of how gift economies, open source cultures, and public commons have been vital for the creation of new works, with themes from older works forming the basis for new ones. Echoing the cries of free culture advocates such as Lawrence Lessig and Cory Doctorow, he eloquently rails against current copyright law as a threat to the lifeblood of creativity. From Martin Luther King Jr.'s sermons to Muddy Waters's blues tunes, he showcases the rich fruits of shared culture. He even cites examples of what he had assumed were his own "original" thoughts, only later to realize—usually by Googling—that he had unconsciously absorbed someone else's ideas that he then claimed as his own.

It's a great essay. Too bad he didn't "write" it. The punchline? Nearly very word and idea was borrowed from somewhere else—either appropriated in its entirety or rewritten by Lethem. Lethem's essay is an example of *patchwriting*, a way of weaving together various shards of other people's words into a tonally cohesive whole. It's a trick that students use all the time, rephrasing, say, a Wikipedia entry into their own words. And, if they're caught, it's trouble: In academia, patchwriting is considered an offense equal to that of plagiarism. If Lethem submitted this as a senior thesis or dissertation chapter, he'd be shown the door. Yet few would argue that he hasn't constructed a brilliant work of art—as well as writing a pointed essay—entirely by using the words of others. It's the way in which he conceptualized and executed his writing machine—surgically choosing what to borrow, arranging those words in a skillful way—that wins us over. Lethem's piece is a self-reflexive, demonstrative work of unoriginal genius.

Lethem's provocation belies a trend among younger writers who take his exercise one step further by boldly appropriating the work of others *without* citation, disposing of the artful and seamless integration of Lethem's patchwriting. For them, the act of writing is literally moving language from one place to another, boldly proclaiming that *context is the new content*. While pastiche and collage have long been part and parcel of writing, with the rise of the Internet, plagiaristic intensity has been raised to extreme levels. Over the past five years we have seen works such as a retyping of Jack Kerouac's *On the Road* in its entirety, a page a day, every day, on a blog for a year; an appropriation of the complete text of a day's copy of the *New York Times* published as a nine-hundred-page book; a list poem that is nothing more than reframing a listing of stores from a shopping mall directory into a poetic form; an impoverished writer who has taken every credit card application sent to him and bound them into an eight-hundred-page print-on-demand book so costly that even he can't afford a copy; a poet who has parsed the text of an entire nineteenth-century book on grammar according to its own methods, even down to the book's index; a lawyer who re-presents the legal briefs of her day job as poetry in their entirety without changing a word; another writer who spends her days at the British Library copying down the first verse of Dante's *Inferno* from every English translation that the library possesses, one after another, page after page, until she exhausts the library's supply; a writing team who scoops status updates off social networking sites and assigns them to names of deceased writers ("Jonathan Swift has got tix to the Wranglers game tonight"), creating an epic, never-ending work of poetry that rewrites itself as frequently as Facebook pages are updated; and an entire movement of writing, called Flarf, that is based on grabbing the *worst* of Google search results: The more offensive, the more ridiculous, the more outrageous the better.

These writers are language hoarders; their projects are epic, mirroring the gargantuan scale of textuality on the Internet. While the works often take an electronic form, there is often a paper version that is circulated in journals and zines, purchased by libraries, and received by, written about, and studied by readers of literature. While this new writing has an electronic gleam in its eyes, its results are distinctly *analog*, taking inspiration from radical modernist ideas and juicing them with twenty-first century technology.

Far from this "uncreative" literature being a nihilistic, begrudging acceptance—or even an outright rejection—of a presumed "technological enslavement," it is a writing imbued with celebration, its eyes ablaze with enthusiasm for the future, embracing this moment as one pregnant with possibility. This joy is evident in the writing itself, in which there are moments of unanticipated beauty, some grammatical, others structural, many philosophical: The wonderful rhythms of repetition, the spectacle of the mundane reframed as literature, a reorientation to the poetics of time, and fresh perspectives on readerliness, but to name a few. And then there's emotion: yes, *emotion*. But far from being coercive or persuasive, this writing delivers emotion obliquely and unpredictably, with sentiments expressed as a result of the writing process rather than by authorial intention.

These writers function more like programmers than traditional writers, taking Sol Lewitt's famous dictum to heart: "When an artist uses a conceptual form of art, it means that all of the planning and decisions are made beforehand and the execution is a perfunctory affair. The idea becomes a machine that makes the art,"[2] raising new possibilities of what writing can be. Poet Craig Dworkin posits:

> What would a non-expressive poetry look like? A poetry of intellect
> rather than emotion? One in which the substitutions at the heart of

metaphor and image were replaced by the direct presentation of language itself, with "spontaneous overflow" supplanted by meticulous procedure and exhaustively logical process? In which the self-regard of the poet's ego were turned back onto the self-reflexive language of the poem itself? So that the test of poetry were no longer whether it could have been done better (the question of the workshop), but whether it could conceivably have been done otherwise.[3]

There's been an explosion of writers employing strategies of copying and appropriation over the past few years, with the computer encouraging writers to mimic its workings. When cutting and pasting are integral to the writing process, it would be mad to imagine that writers wouldn't exploit these functions in extreme ways that weren't intended by their creators.

If we look back at the history of video art—the last time mainstream technology collided with art practices—we'll find several precedents for such gestures. One that stands out is Nam June Paik's 1965 *Magnet TV,* where the artist placed a huge horseshoe magnet atop a black and white television, eloquently turning a space previously reserved for Jack Benny and Ed Sullivan into loopy, organic abstractions. The gesture questioned the one-way flow of information: in Paik's version of TV, you could control what you saw: Spin the magnet and the image changes with it. Up until that point, television's mission was a delivery vehicle for entertainment and crystal clear communication. Yet a simple artist's gesture upended television in ways of which both users and producers were unaware, opening up entirely new vocabularies for the medium while deconstructing myths of power, politics, and distribution that were embedded—but hitherto invisible—in the technology. The cut-and-paste function in computing is being exploited by writers as Paik's magnet was for TV.

While home computers have been around for three decades and people have been cutting and pasting all that time, it's the sheer penetration and saturation of broadband that makes the harvesting of masses of language easy and tempting. On a dialup, although it was possible to copy and paste words, in the beginning (gopherspace), texts were doled out one screen at a time. And, even though it was text, the load time was still considerable. With broadband, the spigot runs 24/7.

By comparison, there was nothing native to the system of typewriting that encouraged the replication of texts. It was incredibly slow and laborious to do so. Later, *after* you finished writing, then you could make all the copies you wanted on a Xerox machine. As a result, there was a tremendous amount of twentieth-century postwriting print-based *detournement*: William S. Burroughs's *cut-ups* and *fold-ins* and Bob Cobbing's distressed mimeographed poems are prominent examples.[4] The previous forms of borrowing in literature, collage and pastiche—taking a word from here, a sentence from there—were partially developed based on the amount of labor involved. Having to manually retype or hand-copy an entire book on a typewriter is one thing; cutting and pasting an entire book with three keystrokes—select all / copy / paste—is another.

Clearly this is setting the stage for a literary revolution.

Or is it? From the looks of it, most writing proceeds as if the Internet had never happened. The literary world still gets regularly scandalized by age-old bouts of fraudulence, plagiarism, and hoaxes in ways that would make, say, the art, music, computing, or science worlds chuckle with disbelief. It's hard to imagine the James Frey or J. T. Leroy scandals upsetting anybody familiar with the sophisticated, purposely fraudulent provocations of Jeff Koons or the rephotographing of advertisements by Richard Prince, who was awarded a Guggenheim retrospective for his plagiaristic tendencies.[5] Koons and Prince began their careers by stating upfront that they were appropriating and intentionally "unoriginal," whereas Frey and Leroy—even after they were caught—were still passing their works off as authentic, sincere, and personal statements to an audience clearly craving such qualities in literature. The ensuing dance is comical. In Frey's case, Random House was sued and forced to pay millions of dollars to readers who felt deceived. Subsequent printings of the book now include a disclaimer informing readers that what they are about to read is, in fact, a work of fiction.[6]

Imagine all the pains that could have been avoided had Frey or Leroy taken a Koonsian tact from the outset and admitted their strategy was one of embellishment with a dashes of inauthenticity, falseness, and unoriginality thrown in. But no. Nearly a century ago, the art world put to rest conventional notions of originality and replication with the gestures of Marcel Duchamp's readymades, Francis Picabia's mechanical drawings, and Walter Benjamin's oft-quoted essay "The Work of Art in the Age of Mechanical Reproduction." Since then, a parade of blue chip artists from Andy Warhol to Matthew Barney have taken these ideas to new levels, resulting in terribly complex ideas about identity, media, and culture. These, of course, have become part and parcel of mainstream art world discourse to the point where counterreactions based on sincerity and representation have emerged. Similarly, in music, sampling—entire tracks constructed from other tracks—has become commonplace. From Napster to gaming, from karaoke to torrent files, the culture appears to be embracing the digital and all the complexity it entails—with the exception of writing, which is still mostly wedded to promoting an authentic and stable identity at all costs.

I'm not saying that such writing should be discarded: Who hasn't been moved by a great memoir? But I'm sensing that literature—infinite in its potential of ranges and expressions—is in a rut, tending to hit the same note again and again, confining itself to the narrowest of spectrums, resulting in a practice that has fallen out of step and unable to take part in arguably the most vital and exciting cultural discourses of our time. I find this to be a profoundly sad moment—and a great lost opportunity for literary creativity to revitalize itself in ways it hasn't imagined.⑦

Perhaps one reason writing is stuck might be the way creative writing is taught. In regard to the many sophisticated ideas concerning media, identity, and sampling developed over the past century, books about how to be a creative writer have completely missed the boat, relying on clichéd notions of what it means to be "creative." These books are peppered with advice, like "A creative writer is an explorer, a ground-breaker. Creative writing allows you to chart your own course and boldly go where no one has gone before." Or, ignoring giants like de Certeau, Cage, and Warhol, they suggest that "creative writing is liberation from the constraints of everyday life." In the early part of the twentieth century, Duchamp and composer Erik Satie both professed the desire to live without memory. For them, it was a way of being present to the wonders of the everyday. Yet it seems every book on creative writing insists that "memory is often the primary source of imaginative experience." The how-to sections of these books strikes me as terribly unsophisticated, generally co-ercing us to prioritize the theatrical over the mundane as the basis for our writings: "Using the first-person point of view, explain how a 55-year old man feels on his wedding day. It is his first marriage."[8] I prefer the ideas of Gertrude Stein who, writing in the third person, tells of her dissatisfaction with such techniques: "She experimented with everything in trying to describe. She tried a bit inventing words but she soon gave that up. The english language was her medium and with the english language the task was to be achieved, the problem solved. The use of fabricated words offended her, it was an escape into imitative emotionalism."[9]

For the past several years, I've taught a class at the University of Pennsylvania called "Uncreative Writing." In it, students are penal-ized for showing any shred of originality and creativity. Instead, they are rewarded for plagiarism, identity theft, repurposing papers, patch-writing, sampling, plundering, and stealing. Not surprisingly, they thrive. Suddenly, what they've surreptitiously become expert at is brought out into the open and explored in a safe environment, re-framed in terms of responsibility instead of recklessness.

We retype documents and transcribe audio clips. We make small changes to Wikipedia pages (changing an *a* to an *an* or inserting an extra space between words). We hold classes in chat rooms, and en-tire semesters are spent exclusively in Second Life. Each semester, for their final paper, I have them purchase a term paper from an online paper mill and sign their name to it, surely the most forbidden ac-tion in all of academia. Each student then must get up and present the paper to the class as if they wrote it themselves, defending it from attacks by the other students. What paper did they choose? Is it pos-sible to defend something you didn't write? Something, perhaps, you don't agree with? Convince us. All this, of course, is technology-driven. When the students arrive in class, they are told that they must have their laptops open and connected. And so we have a glimpse into the future. And after seeing what the spectacular results of this are, how completely engaged and democratic the classroom is, I am more

convinced that I can never go back to a traditional classroom pedagogy. I learn more from them than they can ever learn from me. The
role of the professor now is part party host, part traffic cop, full-time
enabler.

The secret: the suppression of self-expression is impossible. Even
when we do something as seemingly "uncreative" as retyping a few
pages, we express ourselves in a variety of ways. The act of choosing
and reframing tells us as much about ourselves as our story about
our mother's cancer operation. It's just that we've never been taught
to value such choices. After a semester of forcibly suppressing a student's "creativity" by making them plagiarize and transcribe, she will
approach me with a sad face at the end of the semester, telling me
how disappointed she was because, in fact, what we had accom-
plished was not uncreative at all; by not being "creative," she produced the most creative body of work writing in her life. By taking
an opposite approach to creativity—the most trite, overused, and
ill-defined concept in a writer's training—she had emerged renewed
and rejuvenated, on fire and in love again with writing.

Having worked in advertising for many years as a "creative director," I can tell you that, despite what cultural pundits might say,
creativity—as it's been defined by our culture with its endless parade
of formulaic novels, memoirs, and films—is the thing to flee from,
not only as a member of the "creative class" but also as a member of
the "artistic class." Living when technology is changing the rules of
the game in every aspect of our lives, it's time to question and tear
down such clichés and lay them out on the floor in front of us, then
reconstruct these smoldering embers into something new, something contemporary, something—finally—relevant.

Clearly, not everyone agrees. Recently, after I finished giving
a lecture at an Ivy League university, an elderly, well-known poet,
steeped in the modernist tradition, stood up in the back of the audi-
torium and, wagging his finger at me, accused me of nihilism and of
robbing poetry of its joy. He upbraided me for knocking the foundation out from under the most hallowed of grounds, then tore into
me with a line of questioning I've heard many times before: If everything can be transcribed and then presented as literature, then what
makes one work better than another? If it's a matter of simply cutting

and pasting the entire Internet into a Microsoft Word document, where does it end? Once we begin to accept all language as poetry by mere reframing, don't we risk throwing any semblance of judgment and quality out the window? What happens to notions of authorship? How are careers and canons established, and, subsequently, how are they to be evaluated? Are we simply reenacting the death of the author, a figure such theories failed to kill the first time around? Will all texts in the future be authorless and nameless, written by machines for machines? Is the future of literature reducible to mere code?

Valid concerns, I think, for a man who emerged from the battles of the twentieth century victorious. The challenges to his generation were just as formidable. How did they convince traditionalists that disjunctive uses of language conveyed by exploded syntax and compound words could be equally expressive of human emotion as time-tested methods? Or that a story need not be told as strict narrative in order to convey its own logic and sense? And yet, against all odds, they persevered.

The twenty-first century, with its queries so different than that of the last, finds me responding from another angle. If it's a matter of simply cutting and pasting the entire Internet into a Microsoft Word document, then what becomes important is what you—the author—decides to choose. Success lies in knowing what to include and—more important—what to leave out. If all language can be transformed into poetry by merely reframing—an exciting possibility—then she who reframes words in the most charged and convincing way will be judged the best. I agree that the moment we throw judgment and quality out the window we're in trouble. Democracy is fine for You-Tube, but it's generally a recipe for disaster when it comes to art. While all words may be created equal—and thus treated—the way in which they're assembled isn't; it's impossible to suspend judgment and folly to dismiss quality. Mimesis and replication doesn't eradicate authorship, rather they simply place new demands on authors who must take these new conditions into account as part and parcel of the landscape when conceiving of a work of art: if you don't want it copied, don't put it online.

Careers and canons won't be established in traditional ways. I'm not so sure that we'll still have careers in the same way we used to.

Literary works might function the same way that memes do today on the Web, spreading like wildfire for a short period, often unsigned and unauthored, only to be supplanted by the next ripple. While the author won't die, we might begin to view authorship in a more conceptual way: perhaps the best authors of the future will be ones who can write the best programs with which to manipulate, parse and distribute language-based practices. Even if, as Bök claims, poetry in the future will be written by machines for other machines to read, there will be, for the foreseeable future, someone behind the curtain inventing those drones; so that even if literature is reducible to mere code—an intriguing idea—the smartest minds behind them will be considered our greatest authors.

This book is a collection of essays that attempts to map those territories, define terminologies, and create contexts—both historic and contemporary—in which these works can be situated and discussed. The first few chapters are more technically oriented, laying the groundwork, the hows, wheres, and whys of uncreative writing. "Revenge of the Text," focuses on the rise of the Web and the effect digital language has had upon the act of writing itself. The new conditions of abundance and quantity of words are noted and an ecosystem by which to manage it is proposed. "Language as Material" sets the stage for viewing words not only as semantically transparent vehicles of communication but also emphasizing their formal and material properties, a transformation that is essential when writing in a digital environment. Two mid-twentieth-century movements, situationism and concrete poetry, are discussed in relation to contemporary ways of writing on the screen, on the page, and out on the streets. "Anticipating Instability" focuses on issues of contextualization in the digital environment and comments on the fluidity and interchangeability between words and images. "Toward a Poetics of Hyperrealism" grapples with how the always-slippery subject of defining oneself has become even more complicated in the online environment, setting the stage for a postidentity literature in our global consumerist milieu. The chapter concludes with a brief analysis of a work by Vanessa Place, "Statement of Facts, that radically casts uncreative writing as an ethically weightless space where transgressive and mechanistic impulses may be explored without consequence.

Place enacts a documentary poetics, one that subjugates its own moral impulses to preinscribed ethical DNA that comes embedded in appropriated language. Finally, "Why Appropriation?" questions why collage and pastiche have long been acceptable methods of writing while appropriation has rarely been tested. It explores the rich history of appropriation in the visual arts and proposes ways to apply these precedents to literature.

The next essay, "Infallible Processes: What Writing Can Learn from Visual Art," reads the work of these two visual artists through the lens of uncreative writing. Uncreative writing can learn from studying the career and output of Sol LeWitt. So much of what he did and the way he went about doing it in the visual arts can be elegantly applied to writing in the digital age. The second part of the chapter examines the work and life of Warhol as it relates to uncreative writing, viewing his mechanistic tendencies and maniacal production as similar to the way we push digital words around today.

The last section of the book demonstrates how uncreative writing can be put into practice. Generally focused around a single author or work, the essays demonstrate how that work is representative of a specific tendency in uncreative writing. "Retyping *On the Road*" claims that the simple act of retyping a text is enough to constitute a work of literature, thereby raising the craft of the copyist to the same level as the author. It's a utopian critique of labor and value in the valueless space of poetic production. "Parsing the New Illegibility" says that the new writing might be best not read at all: it might be better to think about. Moving away from modernist notions of disjunction and deconstruction, difficulty is now defined by quantity (too much to read) rather than fragmentation (too shattered to read). "Seeding the Data Cloud" examines how short forms—the telegraph, the newspaper headline, and the bold-faced name—have always gone hand in hand with media-based writing, and remarks upon how this impulse continues in the age of Twitter and social networking. "The Inventory and the Ambient" highlights the new and prominent role that archiving has taken in the creation of literary works in an era where the way in which one manages information impacts upon the quality of one's writing.

"Uncreative Writing in the Classroom" is a brief treatise on pedagogy and how the digital environment impacts the way we teach and learn writing in a university setting. A short polemical manifesto-like piece, "Provisional Language," concludes the book, articulating the new condition of language's debasement and temporality in the age of the Web. An afterword speculates on one potential outcome of uncreative writing, "robopoetics," a condition whereby machines write literature meant to be read by other machines, bypassing a human readership entirely.

In 1959 the poet and artist Brion Gysin claimed that writing was fifty years behind painting. And he might still be right: in the art world, since impressionism, the avant-garde has been the mainstream. Innovation and risk taking have been consistently rewarded. But, in spite of the successes of modernism, literature has remained on two parallel tracks, the mainstream and the avant-garde, with the two rarely intersecting. Yet the conditions of digital culture have unexpectedly forced a collision, scrambling the once-sure footing of both camps. Suddenly, we all find ourselves in the same boat grappling with new questions concerning authorship, originality, and the way meaning is forged.

1 REVENGE OF THE TEXT

There is a room in the Musée d'Orsay that I call the "room of possibilities." The museum is roughly set up chronologically, happily wending its way through the nineteenth century, until you hit this one room with a group of painterly responses to the invention of the camera—about a half dozen proposals for the way painting could respond. One that sticks in my mind is a trompe l'oeil solution where a figure is painted literally reaching out of the frame into the "viewer's space." Another incorporates three-dimensional objects atop the canvas. Great attempts, but as we all know, impressionism—and hence modernism—won out. Writing is at such a juncture today.

With the rise of the Web, writing has met its photography. By that, I mean writing has encountered a situation similar to what happened to painting with the invention of photography, a technology so much better at replicating reality that, in order to survive, painting had to alter its course radically. If photography was striving for sharp focus, painting was forced to go soft, hence impressionism. It was a perfect analog to analog correspondence, for nowhere lurking beneath the surface of either painting, photography, or film was a speck of language. Instead, it was image to image, thus setting the stage for an imagistic revolution.

Today, digital media has set the stage for a literary revolution. In 1974 Peter Bürger was still able to make the claim that "because the advent of photography makes possible the precise mechanical reproduction of reality, the mimetic function of the fine arts withers. But the limits of this explanatory model become clear when one calls to mind that it cannot be transferred to literature. For in literature, there is no technical innovation that could have produced an effect comparable to that of photography in the fine arts."[1] Now there is.

If painting reacted to photography by going abstract, it seems unlikely that writing is doing the same in relation to the Internet. It appears that writing's response—taking its cues more from photography than painting—could be mimetic and replicative, primarily involving methods of distribution, while proposing new platforms of receivership and readership. Words very well might not only be written to be read but rather to be shared, moved, and manipulated, sometimes by humans, more often by machines, providing us with an extraordinary opportunity to reconsider what writing is and to define new roles for the writer. While traditional notions of writing are primarily focused on "originality" and "creativity," the digital environment fosters new skill sets that include "manipulation" and "management" of the heaps of already existent and ever-increasing language. While the writer today is challenged by having to "go up" against a proliferation of words and compete for attention, she can use this proliferation in unexpected ways to create works that are as expressive and meaningful as works constructed in more traditional ways.

I'm on my way back to New York from Europe and am gazing wearily at the map charting our plodding progress on the screen sunk into the seatback in front of me. The slick topographic world map is rendered two dimensionally, showing the entire earth, half in darkness, half in light, with us—represented as a small white aircraft—making our way west. The screens change frequently, from graphical maps to a series of blue textual screens announcing our distance to destination—the time, the aircraft's speed, the outside air temperature, and so forth—all rendered in elegant white sans serif type.

Figure 1.1. DOS Startup screen on an airplane.

Watching the plane chart its progress is ambient and relaxing as the beautiful renderings of oceanic plates and exotic names of small towns off the North Atlantic—Gander, Glace Bay, Carbonear—stream by.

Suddenly, as we approach the Grand Banks off the coast of Newfoundland, my screen flickers and goes black. It stays that way for some time, until it illuminates again, this time displaying generic white type on a black screen: the computer is rebooting and all those gorgeous graphics have been replaced by lines of DOS startup text. For a full five minutes, I watch line command descriptions of systems unfurling, fonts loading, and graphic packages decompressing. Finally, the screen goes blue and a progress bar and hourglass appear as the GUI loads, returning me back to the live map just as we hit landfall.

What we take to be graphics, sounds, and motion in our screen world is merely a thin skin under which resides miles and miles of language. Occasionally, as on my flight, the skin is punctured and, like getting a glimpse under the hood, we see that our digital world—our images, our film and video, our sound, our words, our information—is powered by language. And all this binary information—music, video, photographs—is comprised of language, miles and miles of alphanumeric code. If you need evidence of this, think of when you've mistakenly received a .jpg attachment in an e-mail that has been rendered not as image but as code that seems to go on forever. It's all words (though perhaps not in any order that we can understand): The basic material that has propelled writing since its stabilized form is now what all media is created from as well.

Besides functionality, code also possesses literary value. If we frame that code and read it through the lens of literary criticism, we will find that the past hundred years of modernist and postmodernist writing has demonstrated the artistic value of similar seemingly arbitrary arrangements of letters.

Here's a three lines of a .jpg opened in a text editor:

```
^'?Îj€≈ÔI∂fl¥d4˙‡À,†ΩÑÎóªjËqsõëY"Δ"/å)1Í.§ÏÄ@˙'ʃJCGOnaå$ë¶æ
   QÍ"5ô'5å
p#n›=ÁWmÁflÓàüú*Êœi"›_$îÛµ}Tß‹æ"["Ò*ä≠˘
Í=äÖΩ;ĺ'≠Ó ¢ø¥}è&£S˙Æπ›ëÉk©ı=/Á"/"˙ûöÈ>∞ad_ïÉúö˙€Ì—é/Æ∆˙aø6ªÿ-
```

Of course a close reading of the text reveals very little, semantically or narratively. Instead, a conventional glance at the piece reveals a nonsensical collection of letters and symbols, literally a code that might be deciphered into something sensible.

Yet what happens when sense is not foregrounded as being of primary importance? Instead, we need to ask other questions of the text. Below are three lines from a poem by Charles Bernstein called "Lift Off," written in 1979:

```
HH/ ie,s obVrsxr;atjrn dugh seineocpcy i iibalfmgmMw
er,,me"ius ieigorcy¢jeuvine+pee.)a/nat" ihl"n,s
ortnsihcldseløøpitemoBruce-oOiwvewaa39osoanfJ++,r"P²
```

Intentionally bereft of literary tropes and conveyances of human emotion, Bernstein chooses to emphasize the workings of a machine rather than the sentiments of a human. In fact, the piece is what its title says it is: a transcription of everything lifted off a page with a correction tape from a manual typewriter. Bernstein's poem is, in some sense, code posing as a poem: careful reading will reveal bits of words and the occasional full word that was erased. For example, you can see the word "Bruce" on the last line, possibly referring to Bruce Andrews, Bernstein's coeditor of the journal L=A=N=G=U=A=G=E. But such attempts at reassembling won't get us too far: what we're left with are shards of language comprised of errors from unknown documents. In this way Bernstein emphasizes the fragmentary nature of language, reminding us that, even in this shattered state, all morphemes are prescribed with any number of references and contexts; in this case the resultant text is a tissue of quotations drawn from a series of ghost writings.

Bernstein's poem comes at the end of a long line of modernist poetry and prose that sought to foreground the materiality of language while allowing varying levels of emotion or sense to come through, throwing into question traditional notions of authorship. Stéphane Mallarmé's *Un coup de dés jamais n'abolira le hasard* (A throw of the dice will never abolish chance; 1897) is a poem whose words—and their placement on the page—have been subjected to chance, scattering stability, controlled authorship, and prescribed ways of reading to the winds. Words are no longer primarily transparent content carriers; now their material quality must be considered as well. The page becomes a canvas, with the negative spaces between the words taking on as much import as the letters themselves. The text becomes active, begging us to perform it, employing the spaces as silences. Indeed, the author himself reiterates this by claiming that "the paper intervenes each time as an image."[3] Mallarmé asks us to consider the act of reading—whether silent or aloud—as an act of decoding by actualizing and materializing the symbols (in this case letters) on a page.

Mallarmé's letteristic materiality inspires others to explore the same: whether it's Gertrude Stein's columns' eye-tickling repetitions or Ezra Pound's later *Cantos*, writers continued to treat words materially as the century progressed. Parts of Pound's epic are filled with barely decipherable words comprised of dozens of languages jammed together with annotations and references to nonexistent footnotes:

> chih, chih!
> wo chih^3 chih^3
> wo$^{4-5}$ wo$^{4-5}$ ch'o$^{4-5}$ ch'o$^{4-5}$
>   paltry yatter.^{4}

It's a sound poem, a concrete poem, and a lyrical poem all rolled into one. It's both multilingual—bits of Chinese mingle with the "patter" of English—and nonlingual. Pound's constellations hold the page like calligraphic strokes begging to be spoken aloud. This is active language, reminiscent of the sorts of tag clouds that you see today on Web pages, language that begs to be interacted with, to be clicked on, to be highlighted and copied.

James Joyce's thunderclaps are the ten one-hundred-letter words scattered throughout *Finnegans Wake*, a six-hundred-page book of compound words and neologisms, all of which look to the uninitiated like reams of nonsensical code:

> bababadalgharaghtakamminaronnonnbronntonnerronnuonnthunn-
> trobarrhounawnskawntoohoohoordenenthurknuk

Spoken aloud, it's the sound of thunder. This, of course, goes for the rest of *Finnegans Wake*, which, on first sight, is one of the most disorienting books ever written in English. But hearing Joyce read/decode a portion of *Finnegans Wake*, most famously his own recording of the "Anna Livia Plurabelle" section, is a revelation: it all makes sense, coming close to standard English, yet on the page it remains "code." Reading aloud is an act of decoding. Taken one step further, the act of reading itself is an act of decoding, deciphering, and decryption.

Computer code, made up of numbers—1s and 0s—can't possibly have any literary or aesthetic value. Or can it? The twentieth century was brimming with number poems. Take this transcribed excerpt from a series called "Seven Numbers Poems" by British poet Neil Mills, published in 1971:

1,9
1,1,9
1,1,1,9
9
1,1,1,1,9
8,4
1,1,1,1,1,9
8,4
8,4

If you read it aloud, you'll find it transform from a seemingly random bunch of numbers into a complex and beautiful rhythmic poem. Mills states, "I believed that the meaning which emerged in the reading of poetry lay primarily in intonation and rhythm, and only secondarily in semantic content i.e. that what was important was how something was read, rather than what was said—the human voice functioning as musical instrument."[5]

The contemporary Japanese poet Shigeru Matsui writes what he calls "Pure Poems," which come closest to the alphanumeric binaries we find in computer code. Begun in early 2001 and currently numbering in the hundreds, they are based on the 20 x 20 grid of standard Japanese writing paper. Every "Pure Poem" consists of four hundred characters, each a number from one to three. Originally written in Chinese script, which figures the numbers one, two, and three with a single, a double, and triple dash accordingly, later poems are written with roman numerals.

1007~1103
III III I III I III I III III II II I II I I II II II I III
II II III II III II III II II I I III I III III I I I III II
III III II I I I II III I II I II I II II III I III II III
II II I III III III I II III I III I III I I I II III II I II
I I III II II II III I II III II III II III III I II I III I
III I II I III III II II I II III II I I II I III III II I
II III I III II II I I III I II I III III I III II II I III
I II III II I I III III II III I III II II III II I I III II
I III II I I III II II III III II I I I III II I II III II III

III II I III III II I I II I III III III II I III I II I II
II I III II II I III III I III II II II I III II III I III I
I I II I III I II II III II III III III I II I II III I II
III III I III II III I I II I II II II III I III I II III I
II II III II I II III III I III I I I II III II III I II III
I III II I I I II II I II II I III III I III II III III II
III II I III III III I I III I I III II II III II I II II I
II I III II II II III III II III III II I I II I III I I III
III II II I III I I II I II II III I I III III II III I II
II I I III II III III I III I I I II III III II II I II III I
I III III II I II II III II III III I II II I I III I II III

When Matsui reads these poems aloud, they're absolutely precise and hypnotic to listen to.

Read through the lens of these examples, a translation of a common computer icon graphic into its hex code has literary value. Here is the code that's rendered into the *W* that you see in your Web browser's address bar every time you load a Wikipedia page, called a favicon:

0000000	0000	0001	0001	1010	0010	0001	0004	0128
0000010	0000	0016	0000	0028	0000	0010	0000	0020
0000020	0000	0001	0004	0000	0000	0000	0000	0000
0000030	0000	0000	0000	0010	0000	0000	0000	0204
0000040	0004	8384	0084	c7c8	00c8	4748	0048	e8e9
0000050	00e9	6a69	0069	a8a9	00a9	2828	0028	fdfc
0000060	00fc	1819	0019	9898	0098	d9d8	00d8	5857
0000070	0057	7b7a	007a	bab9	00b9	3a3c	003c	8888
0000080	8888	8888	8888	8888	288e	be88	8888	8888
0000090	3b83	5788	8888	8888	7667	778e	8828	8888
00000a0	d6lf	7abd	8818	8888	467c	585f	8814	8188
00000b0	8b06	e8f7	88aa	8388	8b3b	88f3	88bd	e988
00000c0	8a18	880c	e841	c988	b328	6871	688e	958b
00000d0	a948	5862	5884	7e81	3788	1ab4	5a84	3eec
00000e0	3d86	dcb8	5cbb	8888	8888	8888	8888	8888
00000f0	8888	8888	8888	8888	8888	8888	8888	8888
0000100	0000	0000	0000	0000	0000	0000	0000	0000

*

```
0000130  0000  0000  0000  0000  0000  0000  0000
000013e
```

A close reading of the favicon reveals an enormous amount of literary and aesthetic value, rhythmically, visually, and structurally unfolding like a piece of minimalist music. The first column of numbers logically progresses in steps from 0000000 to 0000090, then takes a short derivation into 00000a0—00000f0 before picking back up to 0000100. Patterns occur in the horizontal lines as well, with minute variations on 1s, 0s, 2s, 8s, and 4s in the first four lines, before shifting over to combinations of numbers and letters in the middle section, only to be broken up by several 8888s in the mid to lower portion. Squint your eyes and you can almost discern the *W* embedded within the square of the code. Of course, this isn't poetry, nor was it meant to be, rather it shows us that even seemingly meaningless and random sets of alphanumeric can be infused with poetic qualities. While this language is primarily concerned with transforming from one state to another (from code to icon), those same transformative qualities—language acting upon more language—is the foundation for much of the new writing.

There's a Flickr pool called "The Public Computer Errors Pool" that documents what I experienced on my flight multiplied a hundred.[6] It's a fascinating set of photos. You see a digital elevator button displaying a question mark instead of a number, ATMs in reboot mode, subway advertisement signs with "out of memory" error messages, and flight arrival boards punctured by Windows desktops. My favorite is a larger-than-life size Mrs. Potato Head at an amusement park holding a display with a blue DOS screen filled with cold white letters where clearly something more child-friendly should have been. This photo pool documents the puncturing of the interface covering language.

But don't take my word for it. You can easily create these textual ruptures on your computer. Take any MP3 file—we'll use the prelude from Bach's "Cello Suite No. 1"—and change the filename extension from .mp3 to .txt. Open the document in a text editor, you'll see gobs of nonsensical alphanumeric code/language. Now, take any text—let's say for the sake of consistency, we take Bach's whole Wikipedia entry—and paste it into the middle of that code. Then save it and rename the file with the .mp3 extension. If you double click it and open it your MP3 player, it'll play the file as usual, but when it hits the Wikipedia text, it coughs, glitches, and spits for the duration of time it takes for the player to decode that bit of language before going back to the prelude. With these sorts of manipulations, we find ourselves in new territory: While many types of analog mashups were created in the predigital age—such as the cutting up and gluing together of two separate LP halves or splicing magnetic tapes into collages—there was no language acting upon other language to form such ruptures. With digital media, we're squarely in the world of textual manipulation, which not too long ago was almost the exclusive province of "writing" and "literature."[7]

We can do the same thing with images. Let's take a .jpg of the famous Droeshout engraving from the title page of the 1623 First Folio edition of Shakespeare's plays and change the extension from .jpg to .txt. When we open it in a text editor, we'll see garbled code. Now let's insert his ninety-third sonnet into it, three times at somewhat equal intervals, and save the file and change the extension back to .jpg.

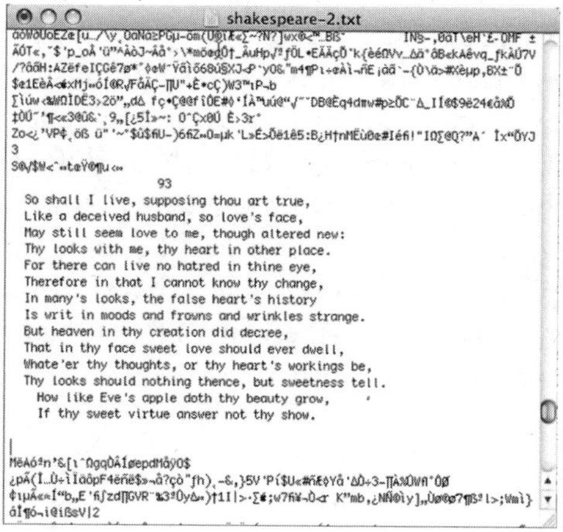

Figure 1.2. Inserting Shakespeare's 93d sonnet three times into the source code of an image.

When we reopen it as an image, the effect that language had upon the image is clear:

Figure 1.3. The Droeshout Engraving before.
Figure 1.4. The Droeshout Engraving, after inserting text.

What we're experiencing for the first time is the ability of language to alter all media, be it images, video, music, or text, something that represents a break with tradition and charts the path for new uses of language. Words are active and affective in concrete ways. You could say that this isn't writing, and, in the traditional sense, you'd be right. But this is where things get interesting: we aren't hammering away on typewriters; instead—focused all day on powerful machines with infinite possibilities, connected to networks with a number of equally infinite possibilities—the writer's role is being significantly challenged, expanded, and updated.

Quantity Is the New Quality

In the face of unprecedented amount of digital text, writing needs to redefine itself in order to adapt to the new environment of textual abundance. What do I mean by textual abundance? A recent study showed that "in 2008, the average American consumed 100,000 words of information in a single day. (By comparison, Leo Tolstoy's *War and Peace* is only about 460,000 words long.) This doesn't mean we read 100,000 words a day—it means that 100,000 words cross our eyes and ears in a single 24-hour period."[8]

I'm inspired by how these studies treat words materially. They're not concerned with what words *mean* but with how much they *weigh*. In fact, when media studies wanted to first quantify language, they used words as their metric, a practice that continues to this day:

> In 1960, digital sources of information were non-existent. Broadcast television was analog, electronic technology used vacuum tubes rather than microchips, computers barely existed and were mainly used by the government and a few very large companies . . . The concept that we now know as *bytes* barely existed. Early efforts to size up the information economy therefore used *words* as the best barometer for understanding consumption of information.
>
> Using words as a metric . . . [it is] estimated that 4,500 trillion words were "consumed" in 1980. We calculate that words consumed grew to 10,845 trillion words in 2008, which works out to about 100,000 words per American per day.[9]

Of course, one can never know what all those words mean or if they have any use whatsoever, but for writers and artists—who often specialize in seeing value in things that most people overlook—this glut of language signifies a dramatic shift in their relationship to words. Since the dawn of media, we've had more on our plates than we could ever consume, but something has radically changed: never before has language had so much *materiality*—fluidity, plasticity, malleability—begging to be actively managed by the writer. Before digital language, words were almost always found imprisoned on a page. How different today when digitized language can be poured into any conceivable container: text typed into a Microsoft Word document can be parsed into a database, visually morphed in Photoshop, animated in Flash, pumped into online text-mangling engines, spammed to thousands of e-mail addresses, and imported into a sound editing program and spit out as music. The possibilities are endless.

In 1990 the Whitney Museum mounted a show called *Image World,* which speculated that as a result of television's complete rule and saturation words would disappear from media, replaced by images. It seemed plausible at the time, with the rise of cable and satellite concurrent with the demise of print. The catalog decried the ubiquity and subsequent victory of images:

> Every day . . . the average person is exposed to 1,600 ads. . . . the atmosphere is thick with messages. Every hour, every day, news, weather, traffic, business, consumer, cultural, and religious programming is broadcast on more than 1,200 network, cable, and public-access television channels. Television shows (*60 Minutes*) are constructed by like magazines, and newspapers (*USA Today*) emulate the structure of television. Successful magazine articles provide the plots for movies that manufacture related merchandise and then spin-off television series which, in turn, are novelized.[10]

Similarly, in 1998 Mitchell Stephens published a book called *The Rise of the Image, the Fall of the Word,* which charts the demise of the printed word, beginning with Plato's distrust of writing. Stephens, a great lover of print, saw the future as video: "Moving images use our senses more effectively than do black lines of types stacked on white pages."[11] Stephens is right, but what he couldn't see was that in the future video would be comprised entirely of black lines of type.

The curators of *Image World* and Mitchell Stephens were blindsided by the Web, a then-emerging text-based technology that would soon grow to challenge—and overwhelm—their claims of imagistic dominance. Even as the digital revolution grows more imagistic and motion-based (propelled by language), there's been a huge increase in text-based forms, from typing e-mails to writing blog posts, text messaging, social networking status updates, and Twitter blasts: we're deeper in words than we've ever been.

Even Marshall McLuhan, who was so right about so many things predicting our digital world, got this one wrong. He, too, saw the coming of *Image World* and railed against the linearity of Gutenberg, predicting that we were headed to a return of an orally based, sensual, tactile, multimedia world that would eradicate the narrow centuries of the textual prison. And, in that, he was right: as the Web grows, it becomes richer, more tactile, more intermediary. But McLuhan would still have to reckon with the fact that these riches are ultimately driven by language in neat rows, programmed by even stricter bonds than any rhetorical form that preceded it.

But, far from McLuhan's prison of words in straight lines, the flip side of digital language is its malleability, language as putty, language to wrap your hands around, to caress, mold, strangle. The result is that digital language foregrounds its material aspect in ways that were hidden before.

A Textual Ecosystem

If we think of words as both carriers of semantic meaning and as material objects, it becomes clear that we need a way to manage it all, an ecosystem that can encompass language in its myriad forms. I'd like to propose such a system, taking as inspiration James Joyce's famous meditation on the universal properties of water in the Ithaca episode of *Ulysses*.

When Joyce writes about the different forms that water can take, it reminds me of different forms that digital language can take. Speaking of the way water puddles and collects in "its variety of forms in loughs and bays and gulfs," I am reminded of the process whereby data rains down from the network in small pieces when I use a Bit-Torrent client, pooling in my download folder. When my download is complete, the data finds its "solidity in glaciers, icebergs, icefloes" as a movie or music file. When Joyce speaks of water's mutability from its liquid state into "vapour, mist, cloud, rain, sleet, snow, hail," I am reminded of what happens when I join a network of torrents and I begin "seeding" and uploading to the data cloud, the file simultaneously constructing and deconstructing itself at the same time. The utopian rhetoric surrounding data flows—"information wants to be free," for example—is echoed by Joyce when he notes water's democratic properties, how it is always "seeking its own level." He acknowledges water's double economic status in both "its climatic and commercial significance," just as we know that data is bought and sold as well as given away. When Joyce speaks of water's "weight and volume and density," I'm thrown back to the way in which words are used as quantifiers of information and activity, entities to be weighed and sorted. When he writes about the potential for water's drama and catastrophe "its violence in seaquakes, waterspouts, artesian wells, eruptions, torrents, eddies, freshets, spates, groundswells, watersheds, waterpartings, geysers, cataracts, whirlpools, maelstroms, inundations, deluges, cloudbursts," I think of electrical spikes that wipe out hard drives, wildly spreading viruses, or what happens to my data when I bring a strong magnet too close to my laptop, disastrously scrambling my data in every direction. Joyce speaks of water the way data flows through our networks with "its vehicular ramifications in continental lakecontained streams and confluent ocean-flowing rivers with their tributaries and transoceanic currents: gulfstream, north and south equatorial courses," while speaking of its upsides, "its properties for cleansing, quenching thirst and fire, nourishing vegetation: its infallibility as paradigm and paragon."[12]

While writers have traditionally taken great pains to ensure that their texts "flow," in the context of our Joyce-inspired language/data ecosystem, this takes on a whole new meaning, as writers are the custodians of this ecology. Having moved from the traditional position of being solely generative entities to information managers with organizational capacities, writers are potentially poised to assume the tasks once thought to belong only to programmers, database minders, and librarians, thus blurring the distinction between archivists, writers, producers, and consumers.

Using methods similar to Lethem, Joyce composed this passage by patchwriting an encyclopedia entry on water. By doing so, he actively demonstrates the fluidity of language, moving language from one place to another. Joyce presages uncreative writing by the act of sorting words, weighing which are "signal" and which are "noise," what's worth keeping and what's worth leaving. Identifying—weighing—language in its various states of "data" and "information" is crucial to the health of the ecosystem:

Data in the 21st century is largely ephemeral, because it is so easily produced: a machine creates it, uses it for a few seconds and over-writes it as new data arrives. Some data is never examined at all, such as scientific experiments that collect so much raw data that scientists never look at most of it. Only a fraction ever gets stored on a me-dium such as a hard drive, tape or sheet of paper, yet even ephemeral data often has "descendents"—new data based on the old. Think of data as oil and information as gasoline: a tanker of crude oil is not useful until it arrives, its cargo unladed and refined into gasoline that is distributed to service stations. Data is not information until it becomes available to potential consumers of that information. On the other hand, data, like crude oil, contains potential value.[13]

How can we discard something that might in another configura-tion be extremely valuable? As a result, we've become hoarders of data, hoping that at some point we'll have a "use" for it. Look at what's on your hard drive in reserve (pooled, as Joyce would say) as compared to what you actually use. On my laptop, I have hundreds of fully indexable PDFs of e-books. Do I use them? Not in any regular way. I store them for future use. Like those PDFs, all the data that's stored on my hard drive is part of my local textual ecosystem. My computer indexes what's on my hard drive and makes it easier for me to search what I need by keyword. The local ecosystem is pretty stable; when new textual material is generated, my computer indexes it as *data* as soon as it's created. On the other hand, my computer doesn't index *information*: if I'm looking for a specific scene in a movie on my drive, my computer will not be able to find that unless I have, say, a script of the film on my system. Even though digitized films are made of language, my computer's search function only, in Joycean terms, skims the surface of the water, recognizing only one state of language. What happens on my local ecosystem is prescribed, limited to its routine, striving to function harmoniously. I have software to protect against any viruses that might destabilize or contaminate it, allow-ing my computer to run as it's supposed to.

Things get more complicated when I connect my computer to a network, suddenly transforming my local ecosystem into a node on a global one. All I need to do is to send and receive an e-mail to show the linguistic effects of the networked ecosystem. If I take a plain text version of the nursery rhyme Edison used to test the phonograph with, "Mary Had a Little Lamb":

Mary had a little lamb,
little lamb, little lamb,
Mary had a little lamb,
whose fleece was white as snow.
And everywhere that Mary went,
Mary went, Mary went,
and everywhere that Mary went,
the lamb was sure to go.

and e-mail it to myself, it comes back:

Received: from [10.10.0.28] (unverified [212.17.152.146])
   by zarcrom.net (SurgeMail 4.0j) with ESMTP id
    58966155–1863875
   for <xxx@ubu.com>; Sun, 26 Apr 2009 18:17:50 -0500
Return-Path: <xxx@ubu.com>
Mime-Version: 1.0
Message-Id: <p06210214c61a9c1ef20d@[10.10.0.28]>
Date: Mon, 27 Apr 2009 01:17:55 +0200
To: xxx@ubu.com
From: Kenneth Goldsmith <xxx@ubu.com>
Subject: Mary Had A Little Lamb
Content-Type: multipart/alternative; boundary="============
   _-971334617==_ma============"
X-Authenticated-User: xxx@ubu.com
X-Rcpt-To: <xxx@ubu.com>
X-IP-stats: Incoming Last 0, First 3, in=57, out=0, spam=0
   ip=212.17.152.146
Status: RO
X-UIDL: 1685
<x-html><!x-stuff-for-pete base="" src="" id="0" charset="">
  <!doctype html public "-//W3C//DTD W3 HTML//EN">

```
<html><head><style type="text/css"><!—
blockquote, dl, ul, ol, li { padding-top: 0 ; padding-bottom: 0 }
—></style><title>Mary Had A Little Lamb</title></head><body>
<div><font size="+1" color="#000000">Mary had a little lamb,<br>
little lamb, little lamb,<br>
Mary had a little lamb,<br>
whose fleece was white as snow.<br>
And everywhere that Mary went,<br>
Mary went, Mary went,<br>
and everywhere that Mary went,<br>
the lamb was sure to go.</font></div>
</body>
</html>
</x-html>
```

While I haven't written a word, my simple e-mail comes back to me a much more complex document than I sent out. The nursery rhyme, front and center when it left me, returns buried among reams of language, to the point where I almost can't find it, padded out by many varieties of language. A remarkable amount of it is normal English words: Status, style, head, boundary; there's also odd, poetic compounding of words: X-Authenticated-User, padding-bottom, SurgeMail; then there's html tags: <br>, </font>, </div>; and strange stringings together of equal signs: ============; and finally, there's lots of long numbers 58966155–1863875; and hybrid compounds: <po6210214c61a9c1ef20d@[10.10.0.28]>. What we're seeing are the linguistic marks left by the network ecology on my text, all of which is a result of the journey the rhyme made by leaving my machine to interact with other machines. A paratextual reading of my e-mail would claim all the new texts as being of equal importance to the nursery rhyme. Identifying the sources of those texts and noting their subsequent impact is part of the reading and writing experience. The new text is a demonstration of local and networked ecologies acting together to create a new piece of writing.

We can create or enter into textual microclimates on a large scale—such as chat rooms or tweets—or more intimately with one-on-one instant messaging. Swarms of users on social networking sites around a keyword/trending topic can also create intensely focused microclimates of textuality.

I can take the transcript of an IM session, and, after stripping it of its networked context, it's immediately indexed by my machine and entered back into the safe stasis of my local ecology. Now, let's say I take that same transcript and upload a copy of it to a publicly accessible server where it can be downloaded, while keeping a copy on my PC. I have the identical text in two places, operating in two distinct ecosystems, like twins, one who spends his life close to home and the other who adventures out into the world: each textual life is marked accordingly. The text document on my PC sits untouched in a folder, remaining unchanged, while the text in play on the network is subject to untold changes: it can be cracked, password protected, stripped of its textual character, converted into plain text, remixed, written into, translated, deleted, eradicated, converted to sound, image, or video, and so forth. If a version of that text were somehow to find its way back to me, it might very well be more unrecognizable than my altered nursery rhyme.

The editing process that occurs between two people via e-mail of a word processing document is an example of a microclimate where the variables are extremely limited and controlled. The tracked editorial changes are extralinguistic and purposeful. Opening up the variables a little more, think of what happens when an MP3 is passed around from one user to another, each slightly remixing it, defying any definitive version. In these ecologies, final versions do not exist. Unlike the result of a printed book or pressed LP, there is no endgame, rather flux is inherent to the digital.

The text cycle is primarily additive, spawning new texts continuously. If a hosting directory is made public, language is siphoned off like water from a well, replicating it infinitely. There is no need to assume that—notwithstanding any of the aforementioned catastrophes—that a textual drought will occur. The morass of language does not deplete, rather it creates a wider, rhizomatic ecology, leading to a continuous and infinite variety of textual occurrences and interactions across both the network and the local environment.[14]

The uncreative writer constantly cruises the Web for new language, the cursor sucking up words from untold pages like a stealth encounter. Those words, sticky with residual junky code and formatting, are transferred back into the local environment and scrubbed with TextSoap, which restores them to their virginal states by removing extra spaces, repairing broken paragraphs, deleting e-mail forwarding marks, straightening curly quotation marks, even extracting text from the morass of HTML. With one click of a button, these soiled texts are cleaned and ready to be redeployed for future use.

2 LANGUAGE AS MATERIAL

There's been a lot of talk the past few years about net neutrality, a concept that argues either for or against assigning different values to the various types of data that flow through our networks. Net neutrality advocates claim that all data on the network be treated as equal, whether it be a piece of spam or a Nobel laureate's speech. Their advocacy reminds me of the post office, which charges by the pound, not by what's inside the package: you can't charge more to send a couture dress than you can for a book of poetry just because it's more valuable.

Uncreative writing mirrors the ethos of net neutral advocates, claiming that one way of treating language is materially, focusing on formal qualities as well as communicative ones, viewing it as a substance that moves and morphs through its various states and digital and textual ecosystems. Yet, like data, language works on several levels, endlessly flipping back and forth between the meaningful and the material: we can choose to weigh it *and* we can choose to read it. There's nothing stable about it: even in their most abstracted form, letters are embedded with semantic, semiotic, historical, cultural, and associative meanings. Think of the letter *a*, and it's anything but neutral. Associations for me include *The Scarlet Letter,* a top grade, the title of Louis Zukofsky's life poem, Andy Warhol's novel, and so forth. When nonobjectivist painters tried to rid painting of illusion and metaphor, you can see why they chose geometric forms, not letters, to do so.

Right now I am writing transparently: how I'm using words is supposed to be invisible to you so that you can follow what I'm saying. If, instead, I WAS TO WRITE IN ALL CAPS, I move into the material or oblique. You'd first notice the way it looked, then— noting that CAPS generally connote SHOUTING—its tone, and last, its message. In day-to-day life we rarely notice the material properties of language except for when, say, we encounter a stutterer or a person with a heavy accent, we first notice *how* they say, second we decode *what* they are saying.[1] When we listen to an opera sung in a language we don't understand, we push language's formal properties to the front—its cadences and rhythms—choosing sound over sense. If we further choose to invert the transparency of words, we can hear them as sound or see them as shapes. One of modernism's great aspirations was to skew language in this way, but the backlash it produced was equally strong: emphasizing its materiality disrupts normative flows of communication. Human beings have enough trouble understanding each other, critics complained. Why would we purposely want to make it more difficult?

In most literature, writers strive to strike a balance between these two states. A way to think of this is similar to the way the transparency slider bar in Photoshop functions: slide the bar far to the right and your image is 100 percent opaque; all the way to the left renders it barely visible, a ghost of its former self. In literature, if the slider is skewed toward complete transparency, language becomes functional discourse, the sort of language used to write a newspaper editorial or caption a photograph. Slide it back a little bit and it becomes prose: *Lo-lee-ta: the tip of the tongue taking a trip of three steps down the palate to tap, at three, on the teeth. Lo. Lee. Ta.* Nabokov's opening hits a perfect note between sound and sense, signal and noise, poetry and narrative. After this dynamic opener, Nabokov moves the slider back toward sense, swapping it for a more transparent style in order to tell a story.

Two movements in the middle of the twentieth century, concrete poetry and situationism, experimented with sliding the slider all the way up at 100 percent opacity. In uncreative writing, new meaning is created by repurposing preexisting texts. In order to work with text this way, words must first be rendered opaque and material. Both movements viewed materiality as primary goals, the situationists through *détournement* and the concretists by literally treating letters as building blocks. The situationists worked in a variety of mediums, realizing their vision of the city as canvas whereas the concretists took a more traditional tact, mostly publishing books. By envisioning the page as a screen, the concretists anticipated the way we would work with language in the digital world half a century later.

The Situationists: Out in the Streets

In the mid 1950s, a group of artists and philosophers who called themselves the Situationist International proposed three concepts designed to infuse magic and excitement into the dull routine of everyday life: the *dérive*, *détournement*, and *psychogeography*. Their idea, not unlike that of uncreative writing, was not to reinvent life but to reframe it, reclaiming dead zones as alive. A slight shift of perspective could lead to fresh takes on tired subject matter: renaming a symphony without altering the music, drifting through a city with no goal in mind, or putting new subtitles on an old movie. By creating new *situations*, such interventions were intended to be a catalyst for social change filtered through a reorientation of normal life.

If we were to map out our daily movements, we'd find that we tend to stick to what we know with little deviation. We move from our house to our job to the gym to the supermarket, back to the house, and get up the next day and do it all again. Guy Debord, one of the key figures in situationism, proposed taking a holiday from those routines in the form of the *dérive* or *drift*, which was meant to renew the urban experience by intentionally moving through our urban spaces *without* intention, opening ourselves up to the spectacle and theater that is the city. Debord claimed that our urban spaces are rich places—full of untold encounters, wondrous architecture, complex human interaction—that we've grown too numb to experience. His remedy was to take a day or two out and *disorient* ourselves (often with the aid of drugs or alcohol) by stumbling about our city, tempering the grid of urbanity with the organic quality of *not knowing*, being pulled by intuition and desire, not by obligation and necessity. We might want to spend a night in a house that's in the process of being torn down or hitchhike without a destination through Paris during a transportation strike—just to add more confusion—or break into graveyards and catacombs, wandering aimlessly through the bones.

By taking our city's physical geography and overlaying it with *psychogeography*—a technique of mapping the psychic and emotional flows of a city instead of its rational street grids—we become more sensitive to our surroundings: "The sudden change of ambiance in a street within the space of a few meters; the evident division of a city into zones of distinct psychic atmospheres; the path of least resistance that is automatically followed in aimless strolls (and which has no relation to the physical contour of the terrain); the appealing or repelling character of certain places."[2] Geography, then—that most concrete of propositions to which we are bound—is reconfigurable and customizable through the imagination. Psychogeography can take many forms: One could create an alternate map of a city according to specific emotions, for example, mapping Paris not by arrondissement but by every place you've shed a tear. Or you could create a psychogeographic map of a city's language by a making a *dérive* from point A to point B, writing down every word your eyes encounter on buildings, signage, parking meters, flyers and so forth. You'd end up with a trove of rich language, myriad in its tones and directives, comprised of peripheral words you'd most likely never paid attention to, such as the fine print on a parking meter.

Guy Debord tells of a friend who wandered "through the Harz region of Germany while blindly following the directions of a map of London,"[3] *détourning* that map by assigning it a purpose for which it was not intended; it still functioned as a map, but yielded unpredictable results. Taking his inspiration from Debord, Vito Acconci created a work in 1969 he called *Following Piece,* whereby he simply followed the first person he saw, walking a few paces behind him, until he disappeared into a private space. As soon as one person did, he would begin to follow the first person he saw until she went into a private space and so on.[4] By mapping the city according to voyeurism, Acconci was enacting a Debordian *dérive*, a psychogeographical cartography, a human chain of hypertext.

Détournement is a way of taking existing objects, words, ideas, artworks, media, etc., and using them differently so that they become entirely new experiences. For example, Debord proposed that we take Beethoven's Eroica Symphony and simply rename it Lenin Symphony. After having dedicated his symphony to Napoleon when he was first consul, Beethoven reneged on his dedication when Bonaparte proclaimed himself emperor. From that time on, the symphony had no dedication, and Beethoven changed the title to the generic "Heroic Symphony, Composed to Celebrate the Memory of a Great Man." Debord, sensing that this was a free space, ripe for *détournement*, decided to fill the vacancy with his great man: Lenin.

There's a series of wonderful films by René Viénet that takes B-grade foreign exploitation flicks and resubtitles them with political rhetoric: a sexist Japanese porn film is *détourned* into a protest statement about the oppression of women and the exploitation of workers. Similarly, a cheap kung fu flick, in which the master teaches disciples the secrets of martial arts, is subtitled so that the master schools the students in the finer points of Marxism and retitled *Can Dialectics Break Bricks?* "Anyway, most films only merit being cut up to compose other works," Debord says.[5]

Neither are the plastic arts immune to *détournement*. The Danish situationist painter Asger Jorn took old thrift shop paintings and painted new images over them. In an essay entitled "*Détourned* Painting," he wrote:

Be modern,
collectors, museums.
If you have old paintings,
do not despair.
Retain your memories
but *détourn* them
so that they correspond with your era.
Why reject the old
if one can modernize it
with a few strokes of the brush?
This casts a bit of contemporaneity
on your old culture.

Be up to date,
and distinguished
at the same time.
Painting is over.
You might as well finish it off.
Detourn.
Long live painting.[6]

Titles of books too could be *détourned*. Guy Debord and Gil Wolman stated that "we believe it would be possible to produce an instructive psychogeographical *détournement* of George Sand's *Consuelo*, which thus decked out could be relaunched on the literary market disguised under some innocuous title like *Life in the Suburbs*, or even under a title itself *détourned*, such as *The Lost Patrol*."[7]

Low culture was also subject to *détournement*. In 1951 the situationists envisioned "a pinball machine arranged in such a way that the play of the lights and the more or less predictable trajectories of the balls would form a metagraphic-spatial composition entitled *Thermal Sensations and Desires of People Passing by the Gates of the Cluny Museum Around an Hour after Sunset in November*."[8] Comic strip speech bubbles were replaced with new texts to create the most politically charged funnies ever written.

Debord saw these cultural efforts as first steps toward an ultimate goal of the complete transformation of daily life: "Finally, when we have got to the stage of constructing situations—the ultimate goal of all our activity—everyone will be free to *détourn* entire situations by deliberately changing this or that determinant condition of them."[9] Such situations were regularly enacted in the happenings of the early sixties and found their fullest flowering on the streets of Paris in May '68, when the walls of the city were sprayed with situationist slogans. Punk rock, too, claims situationism as its roots: On numerous occasions, Malcolm MacLaren has said that the Sex Pistols grew directly out of situationist theories.

For Debord, the city is an ecology, a series of networks, each replete with its own potential for meaningful exchanges and encounters: "The ecological analysis of the absolute or relative character of fissures in the urban network, of the role of microclimates; of distinct

A

B

C

neighborhoods with no relation to administrative boundaries, and above all of the dominating action of centers of attraction, must be utilized and completed by psychogeographical methods. The objective passional terrain of the *dérive* must be defined in accordance both with its own logic and with its relations with social morphology."[10]

Our digital ecology is a virtual corollary to Debord's urbanism, and many of the same gestures he proposed in meatspace can be enacted on the screen. As familiar as our urban movements are, our cyber-ramblings tend to be equally prescribed: we visit the same Web pages, blogs, and social networking sites again and again. We could break out by randomly clicking from one link to another, viewing a Web surfing session as *dérive*. Or we could take the source code and graphics from a major news site and populate it with text of our choosing, like the poet Brian Kim Stefans did by repopulating the contents of the *New York Times* Web site with the situationist writings of Raoul Vaneigem.[11]

When peer-to-peer file sharing began, widespread *détournement* of MP3s took a form referred to as a "dinosaur egg," wrongly titling a song for the purposes of promotion. A young unknown band would take a song of theirs, retitle it "Like a Virgin," and throw it out onto the networks with the hopes that the zillions of Madonna fans would download it and hear their music. The "dinosaur egg" is a cultural artifact that flows without direction, its author not knowing who would be receiving it or what the response would be.

Variants of situationist *détournement* can be found in the visual arts involving the eradication of texts. In 1978 the conceptual artist Sara Charlesworth took the front pages from forty-five newspapers from around the world and, with the exception of the newspaper's title header, erased all the text, leaving only the photographs in place. The day's paper she worked with featured a photograph of the Italian prime minister, Aldo Moro, who was held in captivity by the Red Brigade. The terrorist group released the photo to prove that, contrary to reports of his death a day earlier, he was still alive.

Figure 2.1A. Sarah Charlesworth, detail 1 of forty-five images from *April 21, 1978* (1978).
Figure 2.1B. Sarah Charlesworth, detail 2 of forty-five images from *April 21, 1978* (1978).
Figure 2.1C. Sarah Charlesworth, detail 3 of forty-five images from *April 21, 1978* (1978).

Why is Moro's image the only photograph on the front page of *Il Messaggero* and yet only one of three in the *New York Times*? What does this tell us about local versus international news? About the editorial decisions that were made? About the politics of the newspaper? A simple gesture of removal reveals a lot about the visual thinking, politics, and editorial decisions behind what is presented as stable and objective information, elegantly revealing the structures of power and subjectivity behind the news. In these pieces, language is displaced in the cloak of erasure, leaving behind only structure and image.

The anticorporate film *Food, Inc.* begins: "When you go through the supermarket, there is an illusion of diversity. So much of our industrial food turns out to be rearrangements of corn."[12] A similar sentiment could be made about the types of public language surrounding us. When we look closely at what types of words splatter across our environment, we'll find they are mostly prescriptive and directive: either the language of authority (parking signs, license plates) or the language of consumerism (advertising, product, display). While we have the illusion of abundance and variety, in our language-steeped cities the varieties are shockingly small. The photographer Matt Siber demonstrates this by shooting mundane scenes of streetscapes and interiors—parking lots, drug stores, subway stations, freeways—then systematically eradicating every trace of language in them. He lifts all the removed text intact from the photograph and drops it in situ—fonts and all—onto a blank white panel next to the photograph. The two are presented as one piece: a world devoid of language and a map of the removal.

By removing the language, we become aware of its layout as well as its prevalence and ubiquity, a fact we are blind to in our daily lives. We see how language in the city is ruled as much by the grid of architecture as the streets are: when the words are displaced on to a blank sheet of paper, the ghosts of architecture remain visible, enforcing its structure onto the words. Architecture, generally front and center, is demoted to a secondary role as a page for words; the buildings feel empty and forlorn without them. If we examine the types of language on the white panels, we become aware of its varieties, tonalities, and clusterings. We also see how bland and banal most of the public language is surrounding us. One could easily imagine laying Siber's maps of words over any number of gridded buildings in any number of cities with the same effect. Surely every city has a building that is inscribed with the words "SELL BUY / LOANS CASH / SELL LOANS."

In *Untitled #21* we're presented with language as branding. From the text adorning the car, to the dealership, to the logos on the sneakers of the figure, it's all commercial, a veritable landscape of consumerism. The ghost panel is a visual poem, a linguistic schema of logos describing forms: a ghost car, with the forms of its wheels described by logos. Looking at the text panel, the imperatives in advertising are absurd when decontextualized: who in America hasn't seen a Ford lately? Why would anyone want to look again? In fact, this photograph is nothing but Ford.

In the denser urban environment of *Untitled #13,* the ad language and branding is just as present, yet less homogeneous. The text panel looks like it could be a minimalist spread from a fashion magazine, with its elegant fonts strewn across the page in a dashing manner. But on closer examination, there's an intersection of tonalities and brands that would never be found on the pages of *Vogue.* Through the uncanny placement of the delivery van, the cosmetic brand Bliss dialogues with Lay's potato chips. Siber's accomplishment is remarkable since, had we been walking down the street and seen the van parked in front of the billboard, it is unlikely that we would have seen the intersection of chips and makeup the same way. Similarly, the Dior billboard text is neatly bisected by a line of words taken from the bar of the cherry picker. And the Bliss text, beginning with "wise" (a serendipitous coincidence with the Lay's below it) is itself truncated by the fold in the billboard being installed. Two hours later, with the delivery truck gone and the billboard installation finished, Siber would have mapped a very different landscape. Words are temporary, movable, and changeable in the city's commercial microclimates.

Moved indoors, branding has its own psychogeograpic topography. *Untitled #3* shows a drug store display, scrubbed of its texts. Here

Figure 2.2. Matt Siber, *Untitled #26, 2004.*

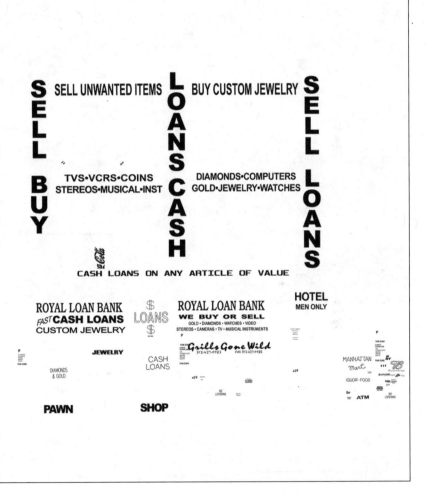

Figure 2.3. Matt Siber, *Untitled #21, 2003.*

packaging, with a slant toward natural beauty, sets the structure and tone of the work. It's no coincidence that the textual placement mirrors the forms of stems and flowers upon which they're placed. And when removed to the blank page, in fact, the words form a garden of language that could easily be titled, "The Healing Garden"—not unlike Mary Ellen Solt's word-flower concrete poems of the 1960s (figure 2.6).

Siber's words are derived from consumer notions of "organics": even the roots of the flowers are price tags. In 1985 Andy Warhol said, "When you think about it, department stores are kind of like museums."[13] While we may question the sincerity of this statement,

IF YOU HAVEN'T LOOKED AT FORD LATELY...
LOOK AGAIN

...is borne out by the generational difference in approaches from the unironic sweetness of Solt's word gardens to the nefarious consumer-driven language hothouse presented by Siber. Siber's drugstore brings to mind photographer Andreas Gursky's monumental consumerist landscapes, particularly his well-known *99 Cent,* an endlessly mirrored discount store showing us an infinite landscape of consumption, a modern-day bumper crop, a bounty of abundance that, upon closer inspection, reveals the same few brands and items Photoshopped over and over again.

The audio equivalent to Siber's and Charlesworth's practices is a shadowy group of anonymous artists who call themselves Language

Figure 2.4. Matt Siber, *Untitled #13, 2003.*

Removal Services. Their name literally describes what they do: they remove all language from celebrities' recorded speech. Legend has it that they began as Hollywood sound editors, whose job it was to clean up the stars' speech, removing all their ums, ahs, and stutters from the day's rushes. After work, they'd surreptitiously scoop up all the bits of tape left on the cutting room floor and reassemble them into nonverbal portraits of famous actors as artworks. What began as a joke became serious as their practice extended to all forms of pre-recorded speech. Before long they were making portrait of politicians, sports stars, and poets, leaving only the extralinguistic traces: stumbles, ums, ughs, sighs, sneezes, coughs, breaths, swallows. Whether it's Marilyn Monroe, Malcolm X, or Noam Chomsky, the intonation

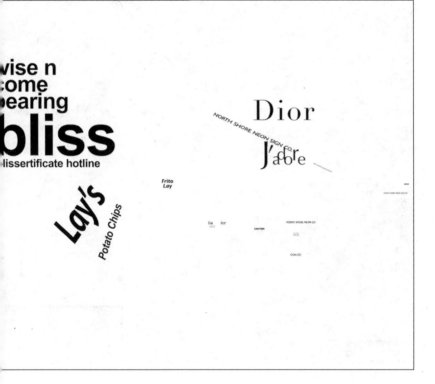

and rhythms distinctly belong to the speaker. William S. Burroughs's breathing and stutters contain his unmistakable nasal quality; even his grunts sound famously Burroughsian.[14]

By drawing our attention not to what they are saying but how they are saying it, Language Removal Services inverts our normative relationship to language, prioritizing materiality and opacity over transparency and communication. In the same way, by scrubbing out words where we usually find them, Matt Siber both concretizes and defamiliarizes marginally visible language. Both artists' practices—one using sound and the other using imagery—provide inspiration for how writers might be able to reframe, rethink, and invert standard uses of language for their own work. I attempted to do something similar when I wrote *Soliloquy,* a six-hundred-page unedited record

Figure 2.5. Matt Siber, *Untitled #3, 2002.*

of every word I spoke for a week, from the moment I woke up on Monday morning until the moment I went to bed the following Sunday. It was an investigation into how much one average person spoke over the course of a normal week. And this was the book's postscript: "If every word spoken in New York City daily were somehow to materialize as a snowflake, each day there would be a blizzard." There was a great snowstorm that year, and, as the trucks and backhoes moved up and down Broadway, I imagined this mass as language. Daily, such collections would happen, backhoes shoveling language into the back of trucks, which, in turn, like the snow, would be dumped in the Hudson River and floated out to sea. I was reminded of Rabelais, who tells of a winter battle when it was so cold that the sounds created during the battle instantly froze upon hitting the air,

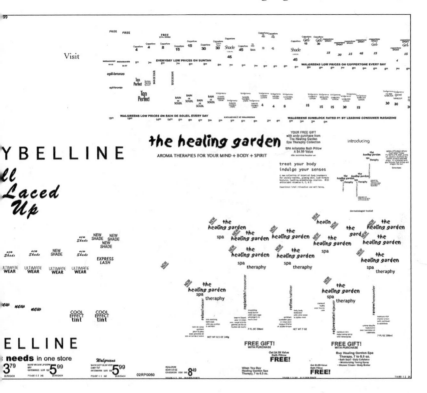

falling to the ground, never reaching the ears of the combatants. When springtime arrived, these long inaudible sounds began to melt randomly, creating a racket by skewing their original temporal sequences of action. It was suggested that some of the frozen sounds be preserved for later use by packing them in oil and straw.[15]

The mathematician Charles Babbage was correct when he speculated that the air had great capacities for carrying information. In 1837 he predicted our impossibly packed but invisible airwaves: "The air itself is one vast library, on whose pages are for ever written all that man has ever said or woman whispered. There, in their mutable but unerring characters, mixed with the earliest, as well as with the latest sighs of mortality, stand for ever recorded, vows unredeemed, promises unfulfilled, perpetuating in the united movements of each particle, the testimony of man's changeful will."[16]

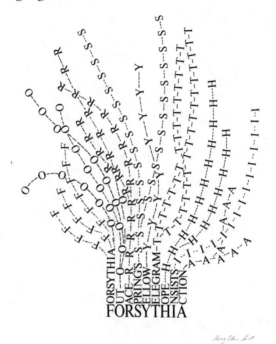

Figure 2.6. Mary Ellen Solt, "Forsythia" (1965).

The thought of all that invisible language racing through the very air we breathe is overwhelming: television, terrestrial radio, shortwave, satellite radio, citizen band, text messages, wireless data, satellite television, and cell phone signals, to name but a few. Our air is now chokingly thick with language posing as silence. Nowhere is it as thick as in New York City, with its density of population and architecture: language is both silent and screamingly loud. The New York City street is a place of public language. From signage to chatter, traces of language are inscribed on nearly every surface: T-shirts, sides of trucks, manhole covers, watch faces, baseball caps, license plates, food packages, parking meters, newspapers, candy wrappers, mailboxes, buses, posters, billboards, and bicycles. It's the density of population in New York that gives the illusion of anonymity, the sense that there are so many people around me that no one can possibly be listening to what I'm saying. In much of the world, talk goes on behind closed doors or sealed in climate-controlled cars, but on the streets of New York words are out there for all to hear. One of my favorite things to do is to walk a few steps behind two people engaged in conversation for several blocks, listening to their conversation progress, punctuated by red lights, giving the speech a certain pace and rhythm. John Cage said that music is all around us if only we had ears to hear it. I would extend that to say that, particularly in New York, poetry is all around us, if only we had the eyes to see it and the ears to hear it.

The modern city has added the complication of the mobile phone, yet another layer of language. A *dérive*—the desire to get lost—is hard when everyone either has a GPS embedded in their device or is broadcasting their coordinates to the public at large: "I'm walking north on Sixth Avenue, just past 23rd Street." The mobile phone has collapsed the space between private and public language. All language is public now. It's as if the illusion of public anonymity of the private conversation has been amped up. Everyone is intensely aware of the phenomenon of public cell phone use, most viewing it as inconsiderate, a nuisance. But I like to think of it as a release, a new level of textual richness, a reimagining of public discourse, half conversations resulting in a breakdown of narrative, a city full of mad people spewing remarkable soliloquies. It used to be this type of talk was limited to the insane and the drunken; today everyone shadowboxes language.

Public language on the streets used to include graffiti tagging, but, due to the cat-and-mouse game played by taggers and the authorities, it was a physical model of textual instability. Subway cars tagged in the morning would be scrubbed clean later that night. Documentation was a must: the constant movement of the cars demanded specific times and locations for viewing the surviving works. Language traveled at high speeds, coming and going very quickly. When the city rid the subways of graffiti, there were changes in textual tactics. Exterior spray paint application was replaced by interior glass etching and plastic scratching, leaving ghostlike traces of the full-blown markings that once covered the cars. Today train exteriors are covered once again in another sort of temporary language, this time official language: paid advertising. The MTA learned from graffiti culture and *détourned* its tactics and methodology into a revenue-producing stream by covering the subway cars with paid advertising. The language itself is computer generated, output as giant removable car-sized stickers; next week another series of advertisements will be stuck on the exterior of trains.

Impermanent language, moveable type, fluid language, language that refuses to be stuck in one form, sentiments expressed in language that can be swapped on a whim, a change of mind, a change of heart surround both our physical and digital environments. While deconstructionist theory questioned the stability of language's meaning, current conditions both online and in meatspace amp it up a notch, forcing us to view words as physically destabilized entities, which can't help but inform—and transform—the way that we, as writers, organize and construct words on the page.

Concrete Poetry and the Future of the Screen

Concrete poetry, a little, somewhat forgotten movement in the middle of the last century, produced poems that didn't look like poems: nothing was versified or lineated, there was no meter and very little metric rhythm. They often looked more like corporate logos than they did poems: clusters of letters atop one another, sitting in the middle of a page. These were poems that bore more relation to the visual arts or to graphic design, which, in fact, they were often mistaken for. Yet, sometimes a form is so ahead of its time—so predictive—that it takes many years to catch up to it. That's what happened in the case of concrete poetry.

Concrete poetry was an international movement that began in the early 1950s and faded from view by the end of the sixties. It had a utopian agenda of creating a transnational, panlinguistic way of writing that anyone—regardless of where they lived or what their mother tongue was—could understand. Think of it as a graphic Esperanto, taking language and rendering it as symbols and icons. Like most utopias, it never really got off the ground, yet scattered about in the ashes of its manifestos are several kernels anticipating how we would think about language in the future. Like many other efforts in the twentieth century, the thrust of the movement was to force poetry

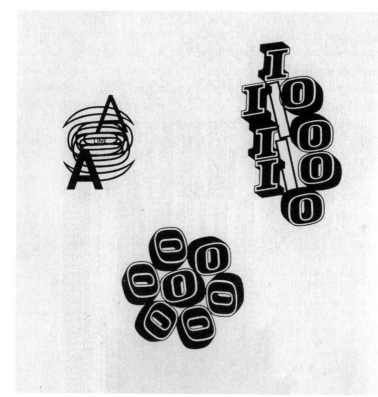

Figure 2.7. bpNichol, eyes (1966–67).

into the modern age, away from the long-winded prosaic sentences of, say, Henry James, toward the headline-inspired compactness of Ernest Hemingway. Concrete poetry's twist was to align the history of literature with the history of design and technology. By applying a Bauhaus sensibility to language, concrete poets invented new forms of poetry. Readability was the key: like a logo, a poem should be instantly recognizable. Interestingly, the ambitions of concrete poetry mirrored changes happening in computing, which was moving from the command line to the graphic icon. Indeed, the ideas that animated concrete poetry resonate with the use of language in our present-day digital environment.

The poems themselves sometimes looked like gaggles of letters coming together to form a constellation. Sometimes they would deconstruct and look like leaves blown across a page willy-nilly. Other times, letters would form images—a trophy or a face—taking their cue from George Herbert's 1633 poem "Easter Wings," in which a prayer is constructed visually, with lines getting successively longer and shorter, finally forming the images of a pair of wings.

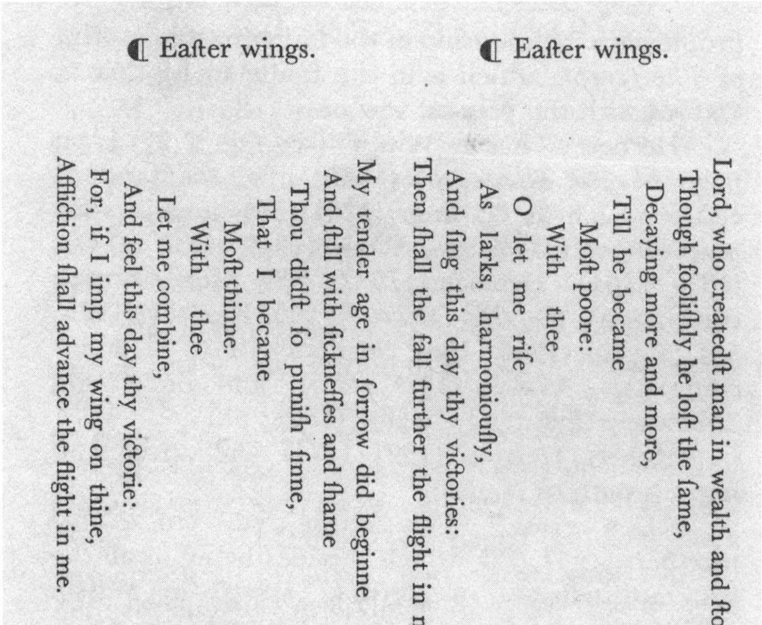

¶ Eafter wings.   ¶ Eafter wings.

Lord, who createdft man in wealth and ftore,
Though foolifhly he loft the fame,
Decaying more and more,
Till he became
Moft poore:
With thee
O let me rife
As larks, harmonioufly,
And fing this day thy victories:
Then fhall the fall further the flight in me.

My tender age in forrow did beginne
And ftill with ficknefles and fhame
Thou didft fo punifh finne,
That I became
Moft thinne.
With thee
Let me combine,
And feel this day thy victorie:
For, if I imp my wing on thine,
Affliction fhall advance the flight in me.

Figure 2.8. George Herbert, "Easter Wings" (1633).

The content of Herbert's poem—humankind's expanding and contracting fortunes—is embodied in the image of the words. One glance at the poem and you get its message. "Easter Wings" is an icon, boiling down complex ideas into a single, easily digested image. One of the aims of concrete poetry is to render all language into poetic icons, similar to the way that everyone can understand the meaning of the folder icon on the computer screen.

Concrete poetry's visual simplicity belies the informed sense of history and intellectual weight behind it. Anchored in the tradition of medieval illuminated manuscripts and religious tracts, concrete poetry's modernist roots date back to Stéphane Mallarmé's *Un coup de dés* where words were splayed across the page in defiance of traditional notions of versification, opening up the page as a *material* space, proposing it as a canvas for letters. Equally important was Guillaume Apollinaire's *Calligrammes* (1912–18) in which letters were used visually to reinforce a poem's content: The letters of the poem "Il Pleut" pour down the page in lines, looking like streams of rain. Later, extending the practice of both Mallarmé and Apollinaire, E. E. Cummings's stacks of atomized words proposed the page as a space where reading and seeing were mutually entangled. Ezra Pound's use of Chinese ideograms and Joyce's compound neologisms, wrought from many languages, gave concrete poetry ideas on how to carry out a transnational agenda.

Music played a part as well. The concrete poets borrowed Webern's notion of *Klangfarbenmelodie*—a musical technique that involves distributing a musical line or melody to several instruments rather than assigning it to just one instrument, thereby adding color (timbre) and texture to the melodic line.[17] A poem could enact a multidimensional space, being visual, musical, and verbal at once: they called it *verbivocovisual*.

But, for all its smarts, concrete poetry was often dismissed as being little more than commercial one-liners—akin to Robert Indiana's concrete poetry-inspired LOVE logo—easily usurped by commercial culture into blacklight posters, T-shirts, or baubles. Even as conceptual artists began to use language as their primary material, the art world distanced itself. In 1969 Joseph Kosuth wrote, "concrete poetry was a formalization of the poet's material. And when the poets become materialistic, the state is in trouble."[18] These sorts of dismissals resonate today. In a recent book about language and visual art from a top-notch academic press, an art historian writes:

Understood in its most general sense, as "language art," poetry is a form that explores the aesthetics, structures, and operations of language as much as any specific content. In the postwar era, various types of concrete and visual poetry, in particular, promised to probe the space of the typographic page and link contemporary literature with the visual arts. Yet a reliance on rather quaint illustrational or pictorial modes—as in poems that take on the shape of their subjects—left much concrete poetry out of touch with changing paradigms in the visual arts and the wider conditions of language in modernity.[19]

However, by focusing on concrete poetry's relationship to the art world, she misses the point: it turns out that the link was not so much with the visual arts but with the multimedia space of the screen. Had she gone back and read a 1963 tract written by the Swiss concretist Eugen Gomringer, she would have found much more than merely "quaint illustrational or pictorial modes": "Our languages are on the road to formal simplification, abbreviated, restricted forms of language are emerging. The content of a sentence is often conveyed in a single word. Moreover, there is a tendency among languages for the many to be replaced by a few which are generally valid. So the new poem is simple and can be perceived visually as a whole as well as in its parts . . . its concern is with brevity and conciseness."[20]

A few years later, the concrete poet and theorist Mary Ellen Solt critiqued poetry's inability to keep up with the rest of culture, which she saw racing by: "Uses of language in poetry of the traditional type are not keeping pace with live processes of language and rapid methods of communication at work in our contemporary world. Contemporary languages exhibit the following tendencies: . . . abbreviated statement on all levels of communication from the headline, the advertising slogan, to the scientific formula—the quick, concentrated visual message."[21]

The rise of global computer networks in the 1960s and their intensive use of language, both natural and computative, fueled these statements, which remain as relevant today as when they were written even as the phenomena of globalized computing has infinitely multiplied. As computing progressed from command line to icon, concrete poetry's parallel claim was that poetry, in order to remain relevant, needed to move from the verse and stanza to the condensed forms of the constellation, cluster, ideogram, and icon.

In 1958 a group of Brazilian concrete poets calling themselves the Noigandres group (after a word from Pound's *Cantos*) made a laundry list of physical attributes they wanted their poetry to embody. When we read it, we see the graphical Web described nearly four decades ahead of its time: "space ("blancs") and typographical devices as substantive elements of composition . . . organic interpenetration of time and space . . . atomization of words, physiognomical typography; expressionistic emphasis on space . . . the vision, rather than the praxis . . . direct speech, economy and functional architecture."[22]

All graphical user interfaces gives us "typographical devices as substantive elements of composition" in a dynamic setting of "time and space." Click on a word and watch it "atomize" in a "physiognomical" way. Without "functional architecture"—the coding beneath the graphics and sounds—the Web would cease to work.

As modernists, the concrete poets adored clean lines, sans serif fonts, and good design. Pulling theory from the plastic arts, they adhered closely to Greenbergian modernist tenets such as nonillusionistic space and autonomy of the artwork. Looking at early concrete poems, you can almost hear Clement Greenberg saying "look how these 'shapes flatten and spread in the dense, two-dimensional atmosphere.'"[23] In spite of ongoing attempts to prove otherwise, the screen and interface are, in essence, flat mediums. They generally employ sans serif fonts such as Helvetica for their classic design tropes. It's the same reason that Arial and Verdana have become the standard screen fonts: cleanness, readability, and clarity.[24]

The emotional temperature of their concrete poems is intentionally kept process-oriented, controlled, and rational: "Concrete poetry: total responsibility before language. Through realism. Against a poetry of expression, subjective and hedonistic. To create precise problems and to solve them in terms of sensible language. A general art of the word. The poem-product: useful object."[25]

Against expression: such statements, with their need to create "precise problems" and to solve them with "sensible language," emerging with "a poem-product," and a "useful object" read more like a scientific journal than a literary manifesto. And it's that sort of mathematical level-headedness which makes their poetry so relevant to today's computing. Cool words for a cool environment.

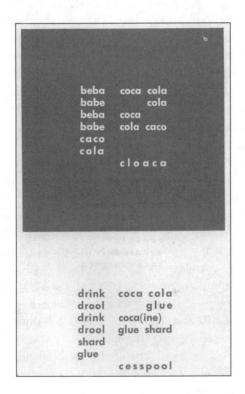

Figure 2.9. Decio Pignitari, "Beba Coca Cola" (1962).

Informed by Pop Art, the concretists engaged in the dialectics of language and advertising. As early as 1962, Decio Pignitari's poem "Beba Coca Cola" fused the red and white colors of Coke with clean design to make an alliterative visual pun on the hazards of junk food and globalism. Over the course of a mere seven lines, using only six words, the slogan "Drink Coca Cola" is transformed into "drool," "glue, "coca(ine)," "shard," and finally into "cloaca / cesspool," a sewer or the intestinal digestive cavity where bodily waste is produced. Pignitari's poem is a testament to the powers of the icon, yet also works as a social, economic, and political critique.

The international orientation of concrete poetry could be as celebratory as it could be critical. In 1965, poet Max Bense declared, "concrete poetry does not separate languages; it unites them; it combines them. It is this part of its linguistic intention that makes concrete poetry the first international poetical movement."[26] Bense's insistence on a combinatory universally readable language predicts the types of distributive systems enabled by the Web. It's a poetics of paninternationality, finding its ultimate expression in the decentered, constellation-oriented global networks where no one geographic entity has sole possession of content.

By 1968 the idea of reader as passive receiver was called into question. The reader must distance herself from poetry's long yoke and simply perceive the poem's reality as structure and material:

> The old grammatical-syntactical structures are no longer adequate to advanced processes of thought and communication in our time. In other words the concrete poet seeks to relieve the poem of its centuries-old burden of ideas, symbolic reference, allusion, and repetitious emotional content; of its servitude to disciplines outside itself as an object in its own right for its own sake. This, of course, asks a great deal of what used to be called the reader. He must now perceive the poem as object and participate in the poet's act of creating it, for the concrete poem communicates first and foremost its structure.[27]

But it works both ways. Concrete poetry has framed the discourse of the Web, but the Web has, in effect, given a second life to concrete poetry. Backlit by the screen, dusty, half-century-old concrete poems look amazingly bright, fresh, and contemporary. We're reminded of concrete poems when we see words skitter across screens as splash pages for Web sites, in car ads on television where the movement of words connotes automotive speed, or in the opening credits of films where restless words explode and dissolve. Like de Kooning's famous statement, "History doesn't influence me. I influence it,"[28] it's taken the Web to make us see just how prescient concrete poetics was in predicting its own lively reception half a century later. What had been missing from concrete poetry was an appropriate environment in which it could flourish. For many years, concrete poetry has been in limbo, a displaced genre in search of a new medium. And now it's found one.

3 ANTICIPATING INSTABILITY

Blurred: Parsing *Thinking* and *Seeing*

In 1970 the conceptual artist Peter Hutchinson proposed a work he called *Dissolving Clouds* which consisted of two parts, a written proposition and photographic documentation. The proposition states: "Using Hatha yoga techniques of intense concentration and pranic energy it is claimed that clouds can be dissolved. I tried it on the cloud (in square) in photographs. This is what happened. This piece happens almost entirely in the mind."[1] The work is a humorous send-up of new age practices—all clouds dissolve on their own without any help from us. It's also a piece that anyone can do: As I type this, I'm dissolving clouds in my mind.

Hutchinson's piece demonstrates one of the fundamental tenets of conceptual art: the difference between seeing and thinking.

Ludwig Wittgenstein used the optical illusion of the duck-rabbit to demonstrate the concept of visual instability. Like all optional illusions, it keeps flipping back and forth between being a duck and a rabbit. The way to stabilize it, at least momentarily, is to name what you see: "If you are looking at the object, you need not think of it; but if you are having the visual experience by the exclamation [I exclaim "A rabbit!"], you are also *thinking* of what you see."[2] In

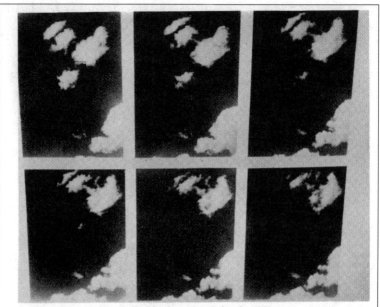

Peter Hutchinson. *Dissolving Clouds.* Aspen, Colorado. 1970.
Using Hatha yoga technique of intense concentration and pranic energy it is claimed that clouds can be dissolved. I tried it on cloud (in square) in photographs. This is what happened. "This piece happens almost entirely in the mind."

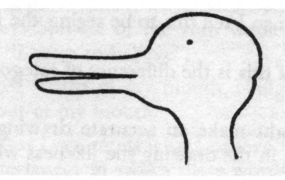

Figure 3.1. Peter Hutchinson, "Dissolving Clouds" (1970).
Figure 3.2. Wittgenstein's Duck-Rabbit.

Hutchinson's documentation, we are looking; in his linguistic proposition, we must *think* of what we see.

In 1960s and seventies conceptual art, the tension between materiality and proposition were continually tested to varying effects: how visual should an artwork be? In 1968 Lawrence Weiner began an ongoing series that he called *Statements,* which permitted the works to take on any number of manifestations:

1. The artist may construct the piece.
2. The piece may be fabricated.
3. The piece need not be built.

A piece could remain as a statement or it could be realized. Taking a classic work of Weiner's from this period, it's curious what happens when it's enacted. The proposition reads:

Two minutes of spray paint directly upon the floor from a standard aerosol spray can.[3]

This statement left propositional form—as language—open-ended. If two of us conceive of a mental image of *Two minutes of spray paint directly upon the floor from a standard aerosol spray can,* we're sure to have different ideas of what that might look like. You might think it was fire-engine red paint on a wooden floor; I might think it was Kelly green on a concrete floor. And we'd both be right.

The realization of the piece most frequently reproduced is the image from the catalogue *January 5–31, 1969,* which is very much a fixed image visually, historically, and circumstantially. It's got a great bloodline, hailing from the collection of famed conceptual artist Sol LeWitt, lending this particular realization a lineage of provenance and authenticity.

That authenticity is reinforced by the black and white photo—something that hardly exists any more—endowing it with historicity. Further credibility is bestowed by the material fact that there is an actual photographic print in existence, a negative from which copies were made. Yet, for the better part of the twentieth century, the photograph was suspect as not being capable of authenticity. Walter

Figure 3.3. Lawrence Weiner, photo documentation of *Two minutes of spray paint directly upon the floor from a standard aerosol spray can.* (1968).

Benjamin, writing in 1935, states, "From a photographic negative, for example, one can make any number of prints; to ask for the 'authentic' print makes no sense."[4] With the explosion of digital photography, Benjamin's proposition is exploded billions of times over.[5] Suddenly we find analog photos—particularly black and white reproductions—recast as being unique and authentic.

In the photograph the floor itself is not a neutral space, but an indicator of time and place: an old, rough, original industrial floor that was common in artists' lofts in lower Manhattan during this period. The realization as documented (figure 3.3) was from Weiner's own loft on Bleecker Street. After decades of gentrification, such floors have been routinely ripped out and replaced as real estate values have climbed. In fact, after Weiner was displaced from that loft due to rising real estate prices, the purchaser of the loft, in the midst of ripping out the old floorboards and replacing them with new wooden floors, had Weiner's piece cut out intact and sent to him as a gift. The piece resides in Weiner's storage vault to this day.[6] What this photograph is, then, is not simply a realization of a proposition, but a coded, historic period piece, which evokes nostalgia for a Manhattan that has long ceased to exist in a form signifying authenticity. We could refer to this documentation as the "classic" version of the work. In any case, it's a far cry from the neutral proposition *Two minutes of spray paint directly upon the floor from a standard aerosol spray can.* Although specific and pinned to a certain place and time, Weiner's work shows how much more limiting the realization of a work is as opposed to the simple proposition of it.

Is it possible to make a proposition and have it realized in a stable and neutral environment? Let's make a proposition: "A red circle with a two-inch diameter, drawn on the computer."

Yet, from the outset, we're plagued by language. This is what my computer calls "red," but the name *red* on the computer is merely shorthand for more language. "Red" is more accurately code: a hexadecimal code: "#FF0000"; or an RGB code: "R: 255, G:0, B:0"; or an HSB code: "H: 0, S: 0, B: 100". Even if you realize the identical proposition on your computer, because of your monitor's settings, age, manufacturer, and so forth, you're bound to come up with a different color than what's displayed on my monitor. What, then, is red? We're thrown into a digital version of a Wittgensteinian loop: "Does it make sense to say that people generally agree in their judgments of colour? What would it be like for them not to?—One man would say a flower was red which another called blue, and so on.—But what right should we have to call these people's words "red" and "blue" *our* colour-words?"[7]

Then there is the problem of scale and realization: while it might be created on the computer, should it be printed out? By a two-inch diameter, do we mean a two-inch diameter when it is printed or when it is on the screen? According to the directions, "drawn on the computer," I'll take that to mean it should be viewed on the computer. But that's problematic because I didn't specify a screen resolution. I could take a digital ruler and measure a 2-inch-diameter circle in 640 x 480 resolution but if I change it to 1024 x 768 resolution, although it still says two inches, it's considerably smaller on my screen.

If I e-mail you my red circle and you view it on your computer at an identical resolution, the circle will still be a different size, due to wide variances in monitors and their resolutions. When displayed on the Web, the variables are compounded: not only do we have screen resolution and monitor difference to reconcile, but there's the question of browsers and the way they each display information differently. My browser, for example, often scales images to fit on what it calls a "page." Only when you click on the image does it expand to its "actual" size in pixels. While the printed version will be able to stabilize the scale problem, we're left with the variables of printer output: contingent upon your ink and paper stock, what your printer outputs as "red" will certainly be a different shade and tone than mine.

Moving beyond the formal problems of instability, then, there's the slippage of meaning. When I look at my red circle and think of what it could mean, my associations include a stop light, a ball, the Japanese flag, the planet Mars, or the sun setting. In art I am reminded of the geometries found in Russian constructivism. Sitting on my screen, shimmering against the white of my "page," its primarily retinal quality reminds me of an Adolph Gottlieb abstract expressionist painting minus the expression, now a red circle reduced to a geometric icon.

Turning away from the bright red spot on my screen, I see that the image has been burned into my retina, so much so that when I gaze at the white wall over my desk I see a an afterimage, but it's not red at all: it's green, the opposite and complimentary color of red. And if I try to really examine it, it disappears, leaving a hovering ghost of its former self. What our eyes see is as restless and as unstable as trying to nail exactly what a digital red circle is.

Thinking makes it no better. If I turn away from the computer and think of the words *red circle,* I conjure a very different sort of red circle in my mind. The image I'm thinking of is a round shape with a red outline; the interior is white. Now, if I think of a filled red circle, the hues vary. Concentrating, I see the red as a fire-engine red. Now it's changing to a maroon. To my mind the image is restless, morphing and changing its properties. Just like the duck-rabbit optical illusion, I can't seem to make it sit still. Size, too, in my mind, is variable from cosmically huge (Mars) to a microscopic (a red blood cell).

When I type the words, I get all of these associations and more:

red circle

I see that these two words consist of ten elements: nine letters and a space. There are two *r*s and two *e*s, one in each word. The *d* of red is echoed in the *cl* of circle. There are also several instances of visual echoing in the letter forms: two repeated instances of *c* and *e*. The *cl* appears to be a split variation of the letter *d,* as the *i* could be read as the *l* with the top severed and floated above its stem.

The words *red circle* have three syllables. I can pronounce the words with the stress on both the first or second words with a significant change in meaning: *red* circle brings forth the color; red *circle* emphasizes the shape over the color. If I say the words *red circle* aloud, I can alter my intonation up and down in a singsongy way or speak them flat, in a monotone. The way I choose to speak them makes for an entirely different reception. In speaking the words, I also invoke the semiotic and emblematic properties of the Japanese flag or Mars.

Taking it one step further, if I perform an Internet search on the phrase *red circle,* it takes me places far outside what I, as an individual, can conjure. There are several businesses named Red Circle: a lounge called Red Circle in San Diego, an advertising agency in Minneapolis, a project that provides resources about HIV and AIDS for Native American gay men, and a company that runs tea tours in San Francisco. There are two films called *Red Circle*, one directed by Jean-Pierre Melville from 1970 and a 2011 film starring Liam Neeson and Orlando Bloom. There is an imprint of Archie comics starring non-Archie characters called Red Circle. In literature there is "The Adventure of the Red Circle," a Sherlock Holmes story, where the mark of a red circle means certain death. And that's just the first page of results.

When dropped into a semantically driven image search, the words *red circle* throw us back to the visual, but it's far from my initial simple red circle. Instead I find wide varieties of red circles. The first image is of the universal symbol for *not permitted*, an outlined red circle with a diagonal slash through it. The next is a sloppy spray-painted red circle outline on a concrete wall, which looks like it could be a variation of the Weiner proposition. Following that is what looks to be a Photoshopped outline of a red circle floating in a blue sky intersecting a cloud. Next is a veritable blizzard of red circles: painterly red circles, expressive Kandinsky-like red circles, a Swatch watch with a red circle around its face, a three-dimensional red circular piece of foam that holds test tubes and an image of a bonsai tree encapsulated within a red circle.

In fact, the results do not return a filled solid red circle until several pages deep, where we arrive at a thumbnail image that looks very much like my red circle. Yet when viewed full size, to my surprise, it's not a red circle at all, but an image of red shag rug, textured and modeled. And it's not really perfectly round: its perimeter is broken on the right side by some stray shag pieces. The color is different as well. This circle is, overall, more purplish than my red circle. And it's got a great deal of variety in its shading, getting darker in the bottom left quadrant and growing lighter toward the top. Clearly this is a very complex and unstable "red circle."

But we can complicate it further: When I download the shag rug to my computer and change its file extension from .jpg to .txt, and open it in a text-editor, I get a text (figure 3.4).

Clearly, this looks nothing like a red circle. In fact, neither the word *red* nor the word *circle,* nor even the image of a red circle, is anywhere to be found. We're thrown back into semantic language, but an entirely different one from the search term that lead me to this carpet or the hexadecimal color schemes. Where do we go from here? We could take this text and attempt to find patterns that would aid an investigation into the plasticity and mutability of language posing as image. Or we could do a close reading on this text alone, commenting, for example, how curious the row of fifty-one 7s is in the third line or on the random but somewhat even spatial distribution of graphical apples on the page. Metaphorically, we could even say that those

```
● ○ ○                          Untitled 2
¨ÿ˜+JFIF˜ЄC
 "" $(4,$&1'-=-157:::#+?D?8C49:7˜ЄC
 7%%7777777777777777777777777777777777777777777777¨¿cÇ"˜ƒ˜ƒ:Q!12Aqë
 ºaÅ#±BRr—"$3bÇ¿¡"·˜ƒ˜ƒ-1Aq!"±i—2Që·ÒaÅ♣˜/²ªò÷·Îì·nC≤7ÑtSÕ[êÏò[êÏ÷Òn…Ön VèjtëM
 §=Ú'Êâ˜ðÏ8]t6Ws>ÉΠXm#}jΣŸJ9fÒÒnÀÒ♣a,∫n *Øn≠QŒ÷T/ÒÒ+Úċ˜Ön+]ãÒ^_Ó{é˜8fiJãõ
 <•Ÿ/ç§"Ė≥ÌtÍ)âXΔÊQ⁺º‰◊≥anC≤Å≠Ċó◊¶Zj>)¿»'Êa¥na~&IºxXfiJ8g%èO∫˜ùÖn…
 Ön Ø≥öVs`Z   pÅˆ|LΠ7ƒœÅ≤≤Å&•Áe
 ºÄ Fdh1Ïà«^SM3âue^',¨q¸Ú2·nC≤anC≤ûh≤yH¬‹ád¬‹áe‹ëÊs[àÏÚE/¸=Qôº#¢˜sPfi—
 Jöp7¢Øtµi]NêmM¯f&/LgµêΣ]¸ĊG@sXoÙZЄŒÉ™«fΩ§+{º-.ã≤IΣð¸vã|¿?wÍ—WàãSy/ˆ÷
 ¥I©™t◊‰""iÊàÄ-Ç»/nÍ38ò≤èwŒñqÿÔQìΩ{≠}◊Vî*i¬k)ù5H©  '‰ œHƒ÷@ã/
 ò<ià^≈Ghæ"∫èYÍÑ√˜aùpiºÏás]ÔΠ ºdØ∫/(ºÍ6N"ðŒOÀ‰òã'ÀÙøàıDÍàÌ·ÙPfi—JHínöÊÎQUujø;>
 I¸ãÍÒ‰øï±£∞
 ºµ≥&NÄU#¥‹Ê ƒ¬r%§%sz◊6Z;;ExÍæûØ—""ÅgàÄ""àã]bÍ¶µf§gb:¯ŒáÇ)¸6ú$º›∫ÁEpÊVhæã?
 *ÓÓ¶Ċ«⁺sG`©Câⱴ◊Ê@Є)ÛãÙÓˆ¸^HàðîⱴŒ_#'¸G™ 3ΣÑtRºº#¢îø§ÿ/∞nÒˆˆA?Eœ+¶Í"b
 ºKúí&ÒàÄ˜WÅâ§îÄœcò˜1⁺µÓ7yÆ|Kggfù)√ÊÛ˜˜ÎDP¸aD@VæÑD
 ªœ   | =É˜0'™ÔwhÇD ŸSÒOqôéÉÉ♣ãö<¥©Gâ«◊&£f"Ê"ıÙ7ÑD[JAÁwÍà¸#'Є¬:)Ê°º#
 ¢î5DiBàÍM•ãã∫Zz¯-œ Ôã;Ìɝ⁺Øu♣ÍçùÉí(—$fiC#¥¸Å¨áã¨¸˜â≤ééóy♣Σ
 R¨_s˜¸éuEûzNbü7Rrº GÇ¸◊±ЄìX¢`ök("ªÄ""'LèèS®K» ΣhÔo•¸œ⁺flÍ∫Ñô%
 õÕñíó*6√m¸¿^¥MŸS⁺¬õ®√√5Σ@Ü-ð3è>R¨E≤3[ΩUí™p~˜éHà¶pœ;¯èTGÒ®ÄŒfi—
 JÜ♣éãPD@j˜™ΔI/h¿D
 Ñ6›8CÓΠsGÉIW(uŸñ©:K:ð-~ˆºf"ΠÆïX'dÄßÄ>/;/<odFá›E«'^√W
 ´jðK≈.û«0"n™`*§Õ8æõ1E«ÌòíĬM¸Vµ1çjÀ~vF+ybsÿ{a?U
 ¨≤R÷¸Í/öÿ+‰([Î=W<^bûïôã¸Ùj˜tÒ¿kÉ™i8è8r♣√ΠflÙX/…T'¨⁺≥ø=;ÆZ^4'v@ñÑ¯
 ±ûnd8m.sè⁺
 ÿ∞/8óáQ¥
 k„ðÄßîfi⁺fl»üM>yn'[?Jºⱴ¸¶IĊÇHn—7Ω>ⱴvØ@¶ºé'º`\ùd·Em„^Åàäg'™Œ_¸#'¸G'™
 àĬ≠o¸îÏùÑDXÏ¸&±Ÿ¯D@5éœ¬küÑDXÏ¸&±Ÿ¯D@5éœ¬küÑDXÏ¸&±Ÿ¯D@5éœ¬küÑDXÏ¸&
 ±Ÿ¯D@`s›àÍÁí" ?˜Ÿ
```

Figure 3.4. Image of a red circle saved as .txt and opened in a text-editor

black and white apples are pictographic metaphors for the abstraction we find ourselves in now—after all, apples should be red. If we were visual or concrete poets, we could scoop up all this language into a text-editing program, shade the letters "red" and line them up to create an ascii image of a red apple or a red circle. But, once we get into a digital image of an apple, it's no longer an *apple,* it's an Apple. Enough.

All this is to point out how slippery and complex the play between materiality and concept, word and image, proposition and realization, thinking and seeing has become. What used to be a binary play between Weiner's proposition, "the artist may [or may not] construct the piece," has now become an example of how language is suspect to so many variables: linguistic, imagistic, digital, and contextual. Words seem to have become possessed by some spirit, an ever-changing cipher, sometimes manifesting itself as image, then changing into words, sounds, or video. Writing must take into account the multiple, these fluid and ever-shifting states, from the very conceptual to the very material. And writing that can mimic, reflect, and morph itself in similar ways seems to be pointed in the right direction.

Nude Media: Tony Curtis Defrocked

These sorts of slippages take place across all forms of media and can be best described by a phenomenon I call *nude media*. Once a digital file is downloaded from the context of a site, it's free or naked, stripped bare of the normative external signifiers that tend to give as much meaning to an artwork as the contents of the artwork itself. Unadorned with branding or scholarly liner notes, emanating from no authoritative source, these objects are nude, not clothed. Thrown into open peer-to-peer distribution systems, nude media files often lose even their historic significance and blur into free-floating works, traveling in circles they would normally not reach if clad in their conventional clothing. Branding, logos, layout, and context all create meaning, but, when thrown into the digital environment, such attributes are destabilized, stripping a fully clothed document into nakedness as more variables are thrown into the mix.

All forms of traditional media that are morphed onto the Web are in some way defrocked. An article about Tony Curtis, for example, that appeared in the Sunday Arts and Leisure section of the *New York Times* is fully clothed in the authoritative conventions of the *Times*. Everything from the typeface to the pull quote to the photo layout bespeaks the authority of the paper of record. There's something comforting about reading the Arts and Leisure section on Sunday produced and reinforced by the visual presentation of the paper. The *New York Times* represents stability in every way.

If we look at that same article on the *New York Times* Web site, however, we find that much of what gave the piece its rock steadiness in the traditional print version is gone. For starters, there's a big sans serif *W* for Washington instead of the classic black serifed *T* for Tony. Thus, the message is that the place in which the interview happened has greater significance than the subject of the article. Other things have changed as well, most notably the size and character of the typeface. The default typeface on any browser is Times

THEATER

At 77, Tony Curtis Still Likes It Hot

By MATTHEW GUREWITSCH

WASHINGTON

TONY CURTIS'S weight-control strategy, which seems to be working for him, is to avoid cooked foods as much as possible.

In late August, for several days running, he was following a regimen of oysters for breakfast, oysters for lunch, oysters for dinner. One Sunday at the venerable Old Ebbitt Grill, across 15th Street from the White House, he was tucking into the evening ration of a half-dozen bluepoints (accompanied by a wedge of iceberg drizzled with balsamic vinegar), when a waiter danced up from another station and introduced himself as Kevin.

"I've always admired your work, Mr. Curtis," Kevin said. "Are you in town for a show?"

"Yeah," Mr. Curtis said almost bashfully, in the Bronx accent immortalized by lines like "Yonder is the valley of the sun and my father's castle." (Contrary to various inconsistent authorities, Mr. Curtis attributes it to "The Prince Who Was a Thief," 1951.)

At 77, after more than 100 starring film roles and half a century before the cameras, Mr. Curtis seemed to be basking in the gleam of imaginary klieg lights. The glossy black hair has gray in it now, but thanks to what Mr. Curtis calls "an unexaggerated hair piece," it has turned white for the new show. The big ice-blue eyes can still stop traffic though. Across the table was the former Jill Ann VandenBerg, 32, the statuesque equestrian and American history buff

The sole surviving star of a Billy Wilder film classic takes the stage in its theatrical adaptation.

who is his fifth wife and with whom he lives in Las Vegas. For the first time, Mr. Curtis, who has painted all his life, even has an art studio.

"Starting Tuesday, we're doing this musical of 'Some Like It Hot' out at Wolf Trap," Mr. Curtis continued, his baritone a smoky mix of silk and husk.

The show is his first stab at singing and dancing since the film "So This Is Paris" (1954), which led Gene Kelly to advise him, "Keep fencing." (That was in Mr. Curtis's swashbuckling days.)

The lone surviving star of the original "Some Like It Hot," Billy Wilder's Hollywood comedy of 1959, Mr. Curtis now has the marquee to himself. He has given up the role of the saxophone player Joe, perhaps the most popular of his career, for that of the eccentric millionaire Osgood Fielding III.

Wilder's masterpiece has acquired something more than mere classic status since its release; in 2000, the American Film Institute ranked it the funniest American movie ever made. You'll remember the premise: having witnessed the St. Valentine's Day massacre in Prohibition Chicago, two down-on-their-luck musicians (Mr. Curtis and Jack Lemmon), fearing for their lives, dress up as women and run off to Palm Beach with an all-girl band in which Marilyn Monroe plays the ukulele.

The new version has a book credited to Peter Stone (leaning heavily on the original screenplay, by Wilder and I. A. L. Diamond) and songs mostly by Jule Styne and Bob Merrill, some recycled from the Broadway adaptation, "Sugar" (1972). The show, directed and choreographed by Dan Siretta, opened in June, as the inaugural attraction at the Hobby Center for the Performing Arts in

Tony Curtis sketches with pastels outside his McLean, Va., hotel in August before performing in "Some Like It Hot" at Wolf Trap in Vienna, Va., left. The show had played there as part of its national tour.

Houston, the new $100 million home of Theater Under the Stars. By August, it had made its leisurely way to the capital's Virginia suburbs and Wolf Trap.

On Tuesday, the real push begins: four weeks at the Golden Gate Theater in San Francisco, followed by dates in 21 other cities coast to coast. The New Jersey Performing Arts Center in Newark has the

show from Feb. 4 through Feb. 9, and the Shubert Theater in New Haven from March 11 through March 16. (The tour schedule appears on the production's Web site, thehotmusical.info.)

Mr. Curtis's accumulated stage experience before the new "Some Like It Hot" adds up to less than

Continued on Page 22

Figure 3.5. *New York Times,* Sunday, October 6, 2003, Arts & Leisure, print edition.

Roman, but, if we look at the newspaper compared to the screen, we'll see that Times Roman is not New York Times Roman.

Figure 3.6. Screen shot from, Sunday, October 6, 2003, Arts & Leisure, nytimes.com.

The image of Mr. Curtis, too, is different. It's shoved over to the side and shrunken, reminding us of Sarah Charlesworth's newspaper *détournements*. The Starbucks banner—which appears nowhere in the print edition—almost functions as a caption. I could go on, but I think the point is obvious. The Web version of the article might be termed scantily clad, missing the authoritative indicators of the traditional print version.

In the upper right-hand corner of the Web page is an option to e-mail the article. When we do that, what arrives in our inbox is extremely stripped down compared to the Web page. It's just a text. The only indication that it comes from the *New York Times* is a line at the top that says "This article from NYTimes.com has been sent to you by . . . " The Times font has vanished, to be replaced—at least in my inbox—by Microsoft's proprietary sans serif screen font Verdana. There are no images, no pull quotes, and no typographical treatments, save the capitalization of the words *WASHINGTON* and *TONY CURTIS'S*. How easy it would be to strip out the words *NYTimes.com*. If we do that, this file becomes detached from any authority, completely naked. In fact, it is entirely indistinguishable from any number of text-based attachments that arrive in my inbox daily.

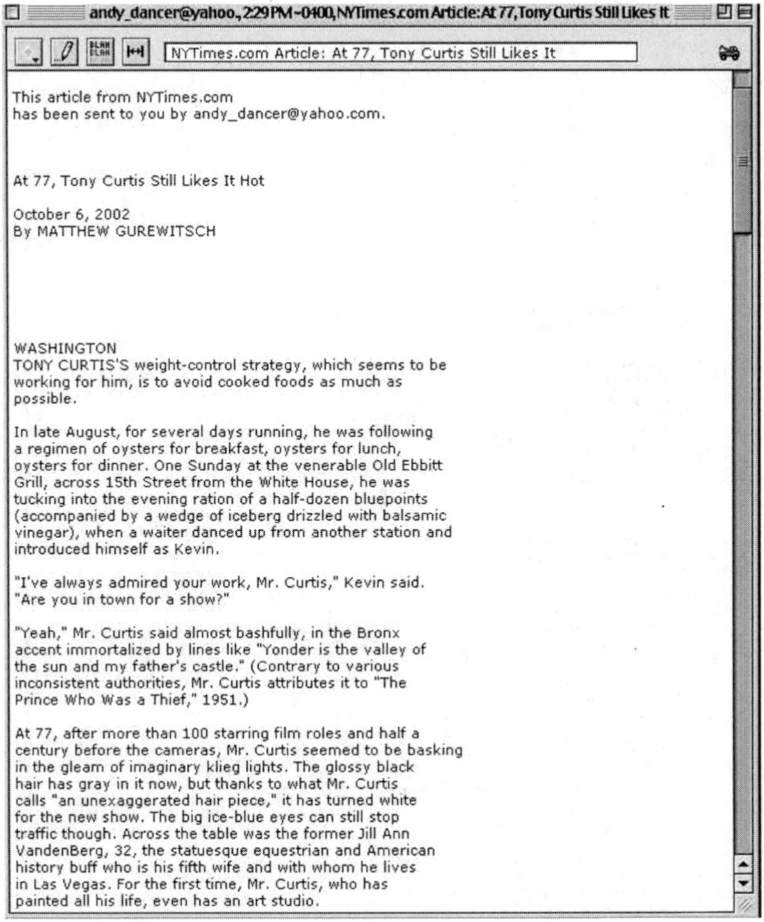

---

andy_dancer@yahoo., 2:29 PM -0400, NYTimes.com Article: At 77, Tony Curtis Still Likes It

NYTimes.com Article: At 77, Tony Curtis Still Likes It

This article from NYTimes.com
has been sent to you by andy_dancer@yahoo.com.

At 77, Tony Curtis Still Likes It Hot

October 6, 2002
By MATTHEW GUREWITSCH

WASHINGTON
TONY CURTIS'S weight-control strategy, which seems to be
working for him, is to avoid cooked foods as much as
possible.

In late August, for several days running, he was following
a regimen of oysters for breakfast, oysters for lunch,
oysters for dinner. One Sunday at the venerable Old Ebbitt
Grill, across 15th Street from the White House, he was
tucking into the evening ration of a half-dozen bluepoints
(accompanied by a wedge of iceberg drizzled with balsamic
vinegar), when a waiter danced up from another station and
introduced himself as Kevin.

"I've always admired your work, Mr. Curtis," Kevin said.
"Are you in town for a show?"

"Yeah," Mr. Curtis said almost bashfully, in the Bronx
accent immortalized by lines like "Yonder is the valley of
the sun and my father's castle." (Contrary to various
inconsistent authorities, Mr. Curtis attributes it to "The
Prince Who Was a Thief," 1951.)

At 77, after more than 100 starring film roles and half a
century before the cameras, Mr. Curtis seemed to be basking
in the gleam of imaginary klieg lights. The glossy black
hair has gray in it now, but thanks to what Mr. Curtis
calls "an unexaggerated hair piece," it has turned white
for the new show. The big ice-blue eyes can still stop
traffic though. Across the table was the former Jill Ann
VandenBerg, 32, the statuesque equestrian and American
history buff who is his fifth wife and with whom he lives
in Las Vegas. For the first time, Mr. Curtis, who has
painted all his life, even has an art studio.

Figure 3.7. Article e-mailed to myself.

To go one step further, if we cut and paste the *text*—and it is a text and no longer an "article"—into Microsoft Word and run a primitive altering function on it, for example, the auto summarize feature, we end up with something bearing minimal resemblance to the original article as printed in the paper or on the Web. Now the lead line is "SUMMARY OF ARTICLE," followed by its provenance and then the headline. Curiously, the word *Washington,* which figured so prominently in prior versions, is nowhere to be found. The body text, too, now becomes radically unhinged and stripped down.

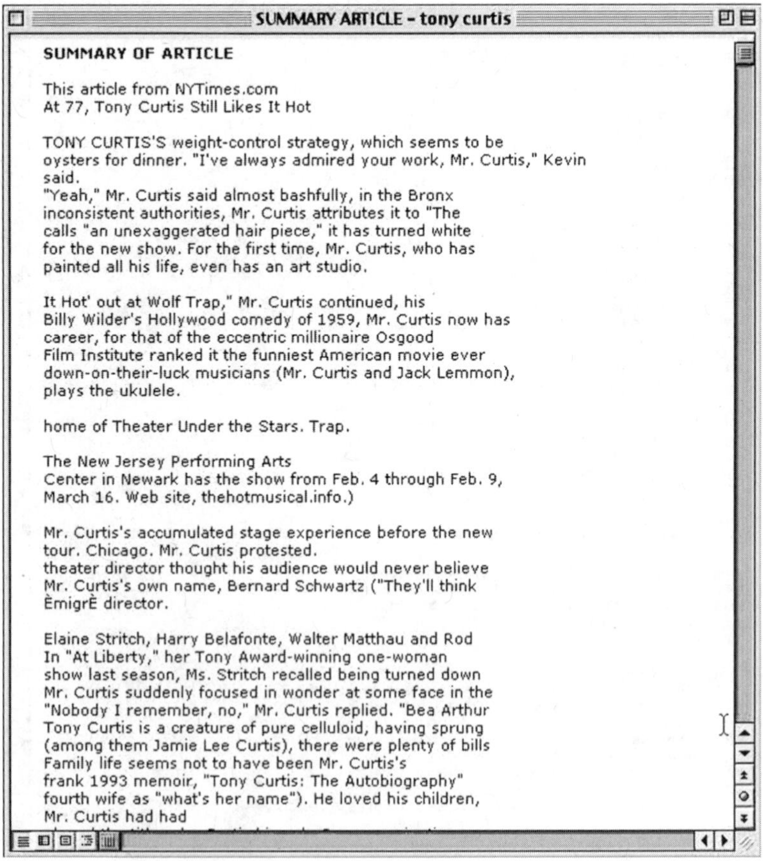
SUMMARY ARTICLE - tony curtis

SUMMARY OF ARTICLE

This article from NYTimes.com
At 77, Tony Curtis Still Likes It Hot

TONY CURTIS'S weight-control strategy, which seems to be
oysters for dinner. "I've always admired your work, Mr. Curtis," Kevin
said.
"Yeah," Mr. Curtis said almost bashfully, in the Bronx
inconsistent authorities, Mr. Curtis attributes it to "The
calls "an unexaggerated hair piece," it has turned white
for the new show. For the first time, Mr. Curtis, who has
painted all his life, even has an art studio.

It Hot' out at Wolf Trap," Mr. Curtis continued, his
Billy Wilder's Hollywood comedy of 1959, Mr. Curtis now has
career, for that of the eccentric millionaire Osgood
Film Institute ranked it the funniest American movie ever
down-on-their-luck musicians (Mr. Curtis and Jack Lemmon),
plays the ukulele.

home of Theater Under the Stars. Trap.

The New Jersey Performing Arts
Center in Newark has the show from Feb. 4 through Feb. 9,
March 16. Web site, thehotmusical.info.)

Mr. Curtis's accumulated stage experience before the new
tour. Chicago. Mr. Curtis protested.
theater director thought his audience would never believe
Mr. Curtis's own name, Bernard Schwartz ("They'll think
ÈmigrÈ director.

Elaine Stritch, Harry Belafonte, Walter Matthau and Rod
In "At Liberty," her Tony Award-winning one-woman
show last season, Ms. Stritch recalled being turned down
Mr. Curtis suddenly focused in wonder at some face in the
"Nobody I remember, no," Mr. Curtis replied. "Bea Arthur
Tony Curtis is a creature of pure celluloid, having sprung
(among them Jamie Lee Curtis), there were plenty of bills
Family life seems not to have been Mr. Curtis's
frank 1993 memoir, "Tony Curtis: The Autobiography"
fourth wife as "what's her name"). He loved his children,
Mr. Curtis had had

Figure 3.8. Summary of article.

If I were to take this text and either e-mail it to a number of people or enter it into an online text-mangling machine, the nude media game could continue ad infinitum. Think of it as an ever-evolving game of telephone. Free-floating media files around the net are subject to continuous morphing and manipulation as they become further removed from their sources.

When destabilized texts are recontextualized and reclothed back into "authoritative" structures, the results can be jarring. Examples of this include the now-defunct Pornolizer (pornolize.com) machine, which turned all Web pages into smutty, potty-mouthed documents while retaining their authoritative clothing, sporting the architecture of the *New York Times* site.

Figure 3.9. Pornolizer (pornolize.com).

Sound also goes through various states of instability, with increasing variables once digital. Over the course of the last half-century, Henri Chopin's sound poem "Rouge" has been subjected to various mutations, both clothed and unclothed. Chopin began his tape recorder experiments in the mid-fifties, and "Rouge," recorded in 1956, was one of his first pieces.[8] It's a literal sound painting, with the word *red* repeated with different emphases, almost like varying brush-strokes. Manipulated audio techniques and track layering build up an increasingly dense surface. The piece reflects its time: think of it as an abstract expressionist canvas:

rouge rouge rouge
rouge rouge rouge
rouge rouge rouge

rouge rouge rouge
rouge rouge rouge
rouge rouge rouge

choc choc choc
dur & rouge dur & rouge
rouge rouge rouge

bruit bruit bruit
rouge rouge rouge
choc choc choc

rouge rouge rouge
rouge rouge rouge
rouge rouge rouge

nu nu nu
nu nu nu
rouge rouge rouge
rouge nu nu nu nu

il n'est que veine il n'est que veine
il n'est que sang il n'est que sang
il n'est que chair

rouge rouge rouge
rouge rouge rouge
rouge rouge rouge

rouge rouge rouge
rouge rouge rouge
rouge rouge rouge

rouge rouge rouge rouge rouge
rouge rouge rouge rouge rouge
rouge rouge rouge rouge rouge
rouge rouge rouge rouge rouge

il n'est que veine il n'est que veine
il n'est que sang il n'est que sang
il n'est que chair

rouGE rouGE rouGE rouGE rouGE rouGE rouGE rouGE rouGE
rouGE rouGE rouGE rouGE rouGE rouGE rouGE rouGE
rouGE rouGE rouGE rouGE

choc choc choc

ROUge ROUge ROUge ROUge ROUge ROUge ROUge ROUge
ROUge ROUge ROUge ROUge ROUge ROUge ROUge ROUge
ROUge[9]

The piece describes the intersection between the body and the voice, a main concern for Chopin, who later became well-known for his audio pieces that were derived entirely from the sounds of his body. Chopin would amplify the sound of his blood circulation system, heartbeat, digestive tract, and so forth, which would form the basis for his works. This early work still uses language to describe the body instead of using the body itself.

In its day, "Rouge" never made it to LP as an "official" release by a record label. It was born naked and remained that way, unreleased and without a publisher until twenty-four years later when it was put out by a German gallery.[10] Thanks to Chopin's highly visible work as a promoter and publisher of sound poetry, however, tapes of his work were making the rounds in advanced musical circles of the day.[11]

A decade after "Rouge's" recording, it curiously appears in the first "Region" of Karlehinz Stockhausen's 1966 composition *Hymnen*, an electronic mélange of national anthems from around the globe. Although truncated, "Rouge" forms the basis for a short spoken-word section based around varieties of the color red. Chopin's voice alternates with German-inflected voices reading a portion of a list of Windsor Newton paints. To listen to this excerpt alone and decontextualized, it sounds like an extension of Chopin's sound painting. But, squeezed between magnetic tape deconstructions of "L'Internationale" and "La Marseillaise," its meaning becomes very different. The nude poem is now clothed in the garments of leftist politics.

Twenty-one years later, in 1997, the sample-based group called Stock, Hausen & Walkman (note the group's name) brought "Rouge" back into its original context when it was sampled into an ironic pop track, "Flagging" (*flagging* means dwindling, weak, fatigued, or drooping; a condition that occurs with the loss of blood). Amidst the cheesy vocals, snappy drumbeats, and appropriated mathematical recitations from children's records, Chopin's piece is snatched away from Karlheinz Stockhausen's political agenda and returned closer to its bodily origins. But it's an emptying gesture: finally "Rouge" is just one sample of many, part of a noisy landscape, in which sounds are easily obtained and just as easily manipulated. In such a landscape, no sound appears to have more meaning than any other. The corporeal and brutal image of Chopin's *red* is now clothed in kitsch, more akin to Betty Page than to Antonin Artaud.

Stock, Hausen & Walkman are known for their graphic sense. They understand how to create a package that visually approximates their musical practice. Packaging—or, in other words, *dressing*—creates a context of value. Stock, Hausen & Walkman's redressing of "Rouge" places Chopin's poem back into circulation fully clothed.

In the clothed realm, popular culture's fetishization of the historical avant-garde reached a plateau when the enormously successful rock band Sonic Youth released a CD called *Goodbye 20th Century* (1999). On it the rockers rattled their way through cover versions of some of the more difficult works by John Cage and George Maciunas, among others. Through a curious confluence of Downtown sensibility and mass marketing, thousands of rock-loving, Lollapalooza-attending Sonic Youth fans bought the disc and were exposed to what until very recently has resided on the fringes of the historical avant-garde.

Through gestures like these, the avant-garde becomes well marketed and, in some cases, commodified. Stroll through any good record store or museum gift shop and you'll notice hundreds of artifacts of the historical avant-garde gorgeously repackaged to be snapped up by consumers, whether it be reissues of avant-garde music or sleek, handsomely produced monographs of once marginal artists or movements like Fluxus. As soon as these items are purchased, however, they can be recruited as nude media via peer-to-peer file sharing. In the case of some of this material, what was originally created as an antiauthoritarian gesture has, thanks to the Internet, been restored to its original radical intention. Due to the manipulative properties of digital media, such artworks are susceptible to remixing and mangling on a mass scale, hence never having *the* one authoritative version bestowed upon these objects in traditional media. They are ever-changing works in progress operating in the most widespread gift economy yet known.

Such circumstances raise many questions: How does having a variety of contexts influence the cultural reception of such objects? Who or what determines an artifact's value, both commercially and intellectually? How does this, in turn, impact the artist's reputation, both commercially and intellectually? If artifacts are always in flux, when is a historical work determined to be "finished"?

It's a little too early to answer such questions. Brought up on books and records—media in a clothed and stable form—it's hard for us to accept cultural artifacts in constant flux as "genuine." Once *Ulysses* arrived on our shelves, the only new versions of the book that came along were typesetters' corrections and annotated editions, which only reified our sense that Joyce was a singular genius. With the exception of Xeroxing and collaging, remixing texts on the scale of

Ulysses was difficult. When it comes to text, we haven't seen anything nearly like the bootlegging phenomenon, but sites freely circulating unauthorized books with copyable and searchable text—in particular, academic and theory texts—are burgeoning. And as e-readers capable of reading open-source files emerge, we'll begin to see more textual remixes. While nude Microsoft Word documents or .rtfs of texts have been floating around the Web forever, the lack of provenance and branding has, curiously, discouraged these sorts of gestures. Now, with fully clothed and gorgeously formatted PDFs, emanating from university presses in illicitly distributed circulation, the texts themselves are being more carefully catalogued and archived as potentially useful objects on one's local computer. Although they're free, an authoritative version of a text signifies that it's ripe for deconstruction.[12] As early as 1983, John Cage predicted and embraced the idea of unstable electronic texts as potential source texts for remixing:

> Technology essentially is a way of getting more done with less effort. And it's a good thing rather than a bad thing. . . . The publishers, my music publisher, my book publisher—they know that Xerox is a real threat to their continuing; however, they continue. What must be done eventually is the elimination not only of the publication but of the need for Xeroxing, and to connect it with the telephone so that anyone can have anything he wishes at any time. And erase it—so that your copy of Homer, I mean, can become a copy of Shakespeare, mmm? By quick erasure and quick printing, mmm? . . . Because that's the—electronic immediacy is what we're moving toward.

4 TOWARD A POETICS OF HYPERREALISM

The rise of identity politics of the past have given voice to many that have been denied. And there is still so much work to be done: many voices are still marginalized and ignored. Every effort must be made to be made to ensure that those who have something to say have a place to say it and an audience to hear it. The importance of this work cannot be underestimated.

Still, identity is a slippery issue, and no single approach can nail it. For instance, I don't think that there's a stable or essential "me." I am an amalgamation of many things: books I've read, movies I've seen, televisions shows I've watched, conversations I've had, songs I've sung, lovers I've loved. In fact, I'm a creation of so many people and so many ideas, to the point where I feel I've actually had few original thoughts and ideas; to think that what I consider to be "mine" was "original" would be blindingly egotistical. Sometimes, I'll think that I've had an original thought or feeling and then, at 2 A.M., while watching an old movie on TV that I hadn't seen in many years, the protagonist will spout something that I had previously claimed as my own. In other words, I took his words (which, of course, weren't really "his words" at all), internalized them, and made them my own. This happens all the time.

Often—mostly unconsciously—I'll model my identity of myself on some image that I've been pitched to by an advertisement. When I'm trying on clothes in a store, I will bring forth that image that I've seen in an ad and mentally insert myself and my image into it. It's all fantasy. I would say that an enormous part of my identity has been adopted from advertising. I very much live in this culture; how could I possibly ignore such powerful forces? Is it ideal? Probably not. Would I like not to be so swayed by the forces of advertising and consumerism? Of course, but I would be kidding myself if I didn't admit that this was a huge part of who I am as a member of this culture.

Transgendered persons are trying to become the people who they are, not the ones they were born as. Transsexual persons too are in a constant state of remaking themselves, laboring courageously their whole lives to adopt new and fluid identities. I feel inspired by such fluid and changeable notions of identity.

On the Internet, these tendencies move in different directions, with identity running the gamut from authenticity to total fabrication. With much less commitment than it takes in meatspace, we project various personae with mere stokes of a keyboard. Online, I tend to morph in different directions: in this chat room I'm a woman; on this blog I'm a political conservative; in this forum I'm a middle-aged golfer. And I never get called out for not being authentic or real. On the contrary, I am addressed as "madam" or "you right-wing asshole." As such, I've come to expect that the person I think I'm addressing on the Internet isn't really "that person."

If my identity is really up for grabs and changeable by the minute—as I believe it is—it's important that my writing reflect this state of ever-shifting identity and subjectivity. That can mean adopting voices that aren't "mine," subjectivities that aren't "mine," political positions that aren't "mine," opinions that aren't "mine," words that aren't "mine" because, in the end, I don't think that I can possibly define what's mine and what isn't.

Sometimes, by the noninterventionist reproduction of texts, we can shed light on political issues in a more profound and illuminating way than we can by conventional critique. If we wished to critique globalism, for example, uncreative writing's response would be to replicate and reframe the transcript from a G8 summit meeting where they refused to ratify climate control threats as is, revealing much more than one ever could by editorializing. Let the text speak for itself: in the case of the G8, they'll hang themselves through their own stupidity. I call this poetry.

No matter what we do with language, it will be expressive. How could it be otherwise? In fact, I feel it is impossible, working with language, not to express oneself. If we back off and let the material do its work, we might even in the end be able to surprise and delight ourselves with the results.

Uncreative writing is a postidentity literature. With digital fragmentation, any sense of unified authenticity and coherence has long been shelved. Walter Ong claims that writing is a technology and is therefore an artificial act: "Technologies are not mere exterior aids but also interior transformations of consciousness, and never more than when they affect the word . . . Technologies are artificial, but—paradox again—artificiality is natural to the human being. Technology, properly interiorized, does not degrade human life but on the contrary enhances it."[1] Robert Fitterman, whose works embrace our shifting identities shaped by the forces of consumerism, posits:

> Can we express subjectivity, even personal experience, without necessarily using our own personal experience? . . . There has clearly been a desire to engage or re-claim the personal. I am interested in the inclusion of subjectivity and personal experience; I just prefer if it isn't my own. Today I have access to an unlimited number of personal utterances and expressions from the gut, or the heart. Why listen to my gut when I could listen to thousands of guts? . . . For writers coming of age in the 70s and 80s, the notion of multiple identities and appropriated identities is a sort of native language, a natural outgrowth of the multiple personas that have been engineered and then targeted by market strategists.[2]

Fitterman cites the visual artist Mike Kelley, who also frames the identity discourse in terms of consumerism: "Glam rock was a music that fully understood the commercial music world and accepted its arena of façade and emptiness, using the image of the drag queen as a sign of its status. . . . David Bowie adopts personas, throws them away at whim, and constantly reinvents himself for the market. He mirrors our culture of planned obsolescence. For consumer culture, it has been suggested, the constantly changing, chameleon persona *represents* empowerment."[3] Writing needs to move in this direction.

And yet, who isn't moved by an authentic story? Surely one of the most inspiring identity-based narratives in recent history is that of Barack Obama. In a speech he gave at his family's ancestral village in Kenya on the occasion of a school named in his honor, he spoke of pride from whence he came as well as of how Kenya imbued his grandfather with the values that would propel the Obama family to stupendous achievements in the United States: "He grew up around here. He was taking care of goats for my grandfather, and, maybe, sometimes, he would go to a school not so different from the Senator Barack Obama School. Except, maybe, it was smaller, and had even less in terms of equipment and books, the teachers were paid even less, and, sometimes, there wasn't enough money to go to school full time. Yet, despite all that, the community lifted him up, and gave him the opportunity to go to secondary school, then go to university in America, then get a Ph.D. in Harvard."[4]

America is full of such incredible stories. Another comes from the Armenian American writer Ara Shirinyan. He was born in the Armenian Socialist Republic in the USSR into a family that was dispersed all over the Middle East in the wake of the Armenian genocide. In 1987 his family moved to the United States with $1,500 and a few suitcases. His father went to work the second day after they arrived as a jeweler. His mother did the same as an antique rug restorer. They worked seven days a week and bought a house a year after they arrived. His father's business grew when he began manufacturing jewelry, selling tons of kilos of it. By the time he retired, his business occupied an entire floor of a large building in downtown LA. Ara, a product of public and state schools, now has an international reputation and thriving career as a writer. He is very much involved with the close-knit community of Armenian Americans.

It's moving story. Why, then, would he choose to *not* to write about it when he penned an award-winning book about nationalities? In his book *Your Country Is Great*, he's taken the names of every country in the world, organized them A to Z, and Googled the phrase "[*country name*] is great"—coming up with mostly user-reviewed travel sites—selecting and sorting the results by nation. He then lineated the comments, with each stanza representing another opinion. The result is a multinational Baedeker of user-driven content and opinion. Unsourced and unsigned, the piece is by turns ugly and gorgeous, helpful and harmful, truthful and misleading, vital and completely irrelevant. By bringing a cool and rational methodology to these inherently passionate identity-based discussions, Shirinyan lets the words speak for themselves, permitting the reader to process the opinions expressed.

In his book, his home country Armenia is treated no differently than Aruba, the next country that appears alphabetically:

ARMENIA IS GREAT

armenia is great country
famous for its christianity!

Armenia is great, and Yerevan is a city
where people live their lifes to the maximum
I love you Yerevan,
I love your streets,
your sidewalks,

Armenia is great
everyone should go back
at least once

the new information on Armenia is great—
lots of good information—
I'll have to remember not to give
anyone 2 flowers!

I also do not speak our language
Armenia is great though.
I have been there

and made good friends,
even though I could not
speak a word to them.

Tour to Armenia is a great success!
To Understand Our
Past,
Is To Understand
Ourselves.

renovated sidewalks, roads, and
unprecedented High Rise buildings
going up
the future of Armenia is great.

With such warm summers
and very cold winters
you will learn a great deal
about the history of Yerevan

Armenia is great
I love it, but I dont think
it is for me.[5]

ARUBA IS GREAT

aruba is great
its beaches are beautiful
and the people are great

Aruba is great for diving
and seeing marine life
with visibility up to 90 ft.
You will see sponge tubes,
gliding manta rays, sea turtles, lobsters,
The taxi service on Aruba is great,
but we like to pick up and go wherever

and whenever we want,
so the rental is great for us.

Aruba is great for sightseeing, shopping,
and a variety of water sports.
You should plan on renting a car
to explore the island.

Aruba is great,
not a drop of rain,
barely a cloud and yet
never felt too hot

Aruba is great,
that is where i went
on my honeymoon last year.
I love it!
There are many places to stay.
The Marriott is nice,
the Wyndham is nice.

Aruba is great for singles,
couples and families. Probably
the best miniature golf courses
in the world are in Aruba

Aruba is great for a honeymoon
for the following reasons:
1. No hurricanes
2. Predictable weather
3. Tons to do

Aruba is great.
If you bust out early,
be sure to go snorkelling.
They have a party bus
for bar hopping[6]

What does this tell us about Armenia or Aruba? Not much. Shirinyan foregoes a personal narrative to demonstrate a larger point: the deadening effects of globalization on language. Collapsing the space between the "real world" and the World Wide Web, his book calls into question: What is local? What is national? What is multicultural? Instead of accepting current notions of language as a medium of differentiation, Shirinyan persuasively demonstrates its leveling quality, demolishing meaning into a puddle of platitudes in a time when everything is great, yet nothing is great. It's great if I've been there: global tourism as authority.

Shirinyan's careful selection and juxtaposition of phrases makes this work a textbook example of how a writer might go about carving a technology-fueled postidentity writing practice, one that makes the reader wonder whether the author's identity actually had anything to do with the person who wrote it. Yet it doesn't shy away from employing the first person, using it strategically and liberally, but nonspecifically, producing a work that is at once fiercely nationalistic and, at the same time, surprisingly bland.

The French artist Claude Closky, in his book *Mon Catalog*, takes a different but equally dispassionate tact by listing every possession he owns accompanied by the actual catalog or ad copy which advertised that possession. For the piece, he simply , substituted the directive "you" or "yours" for a subjective "I" or "mine."

An excerpt reads:

MY REFRIGERATOR

The usable volume of my refrigerator is far superior to conventional capacities, and allows me to store my fresh and frozen products. The meat compartment with adjustable temperature and the crisper with humidity control assure me a perfect preservation of my food. Furthermore, the fan-cooling makes and dispenses my ice to me as well as fresh water. Moreover, my refrigerator is equipped with an anti-bacterial coating that helps me maintain it.

My Cleansing Gel

To gradually mattify the shiny appearance of my skin, tighten my dilated pores and clean my blackheads, I have a solution: clean my face every night with my purifying gel with zinc—known to be an active controller of sebum that eliminates, without chafing, the impurities accumulated during the day. My skin is no longer shiny. The soothing power of zinc, reinforced by a moisturizing agent, softens and relaxes the dry areas of my face. My skin no longer pulls.

My one-piece glasses

I tame the sun's rays with my one-piece glasses. True shields against harmful UV radiation and too-bright light, I can also appreciate them as glasses, as they surround my face perfectly. I benefit from the panoramic vision of the enveloping impact-resistant Lexan glass. Filtering ultraviolet rays on all sides, they protect my eyes not only from the sun, but also wind, sand, and dust. The ultimate refinement: a small foam band contours perfectly to my face, assuring comfort and a perfect fit. Extremely lightweight, I enjoy wearing them in all circumstances. With their removable cord, I also appreciate them while playing my favorite sports.[7]

Closky creates a consumer-frenzied overload of language, a contemporary form of self-portraiture, voluntarily defining oneself not only by what one owns, but professing to let oneself be completely possessed by one's possessions. Refusing to moralize, editorialize, or emote in any way, he's propping himself up as the ultimate consumer, an *uber*-consumer. He doesn't need to be won over, he's already sold. If I tell you that I will not only buy everything you're trying to sell me, but that I will embrace your products to the point of strangulation, what good are your pitches? Closky is one step ahead of the marketers and, by so doing, offers a linguistically based antidote to consumer-oriented capitalism.

In *S/Z* Roland Barthes performs an exhaustive structuralist deconstruction of Honoré de Balzac's short story "Sarrasine." In it he reveals how signifiers of class are expressed in seemingly innocuous statements about parties, furnishings, or gardens. His book gives you the tools to tease out these codes from any work of art. But what uncreative writing potentially allows is an inversion of Barthes's project, a situation in which those normally hidden codes are brought front and center, comprising the entire artwork. Like so much advertising, music, film, and visual art, the literary discourse has been moved to the next level.

What do we do with a work like Alexandra Nemerov's "First My Motorola," which is a list of every brand she touched over the course of a day in chronological order, from the moment she woke up until the moment she went to sleep? The piece begins:

First, my Motorola
Then my Frette
Then my Sonia Rykiel
Then my Bvulgari
Then my Asprey
Then my Cartier
Then my Kohler
Then my Brightsmile
Then my Cetaphil
Then my Braun
Then my Brightsmile
Then my Kohler
Then my Cetaphil
Then my Bliss
Then my Apple
Then my Kashi
Then my Maytag
Then my Silk
Then my Pom

and ends:

Then my Ralph Lauren
Then my La Perla
Then my H&M

Then my Anthropology
Then my Motorola
Then my Bvulgari
Then my Asprey
Then my Cartier
Then my Frette
Then my Sonia Rykiel
And finally, my Motorola[8]

Nemerov doesn't situate these brands in terms of likes and dislikes as opposed to Closky who "cheerfully" professes to "like" his humidity controlled refrigerator. There's nothing here but brands. Nemerov is a cipher, a shell, a pure robotic consumer. Enacting Barbara Kruger's famous slogan, "I shop therefore I am," she boldly creates a new type of self-portraiture: a complicit demographic, a marketer's dream.

In 2007 *Time Magazine* questioned whether the $200 million gift that pharmaceutical heiress Ruth Lilly gave to the Poetry Foundation could really change the way people feel about poetry: "The $200 million won't change that; nothing, not even money, can get people to enjoy something against their will. What poetry really needs is a writer who can do for it what Andy Warhol did for avant-garde visual art: make it sexy and cool and accessible without making it stupid or patronizing. When that writer arrives, cultural change will come swiftly, and relatively effortlessly."[9] While there are a number of problems with this statement—by choosing Warhol, he's hoping for a return to a specific cultural moment, which permitted Warhol to become Warhol: the sixties, a time that isn't coming back anytime soon—his challenge does however make me wonder why there hasn't been an Andy Warhol for poetry.

You might think that during the boom years of the George W. Bush administration, pro-consumerist poets would have come out of the woodwork. But no. Instead Bush's poet laureates, such as Billy Collins, who wrote about fishing on the Susquehanna in July (though the poem is really about him *not* fishing there), or Ted Kooser, with his pastoral descriptions of porch swings in September, or Donald

Hall and his nostalgic rural ox cart men, were hopelessly out of touch with what was obsessing most Americans (and most of the world): buying things. Ultimately, it's not surprising that a Bush poet laureate hearkens back to a form of nostalgic poetry, unaware that they were performing a simulacra for a time when poets genuinely wrote about "true" American values.

The poetry world has yet to experience its version of Pop Art—and Pop Art happened over fifty years ago In spite of the many proposed alternative uses of language (concrete poetry, language poetry, FC2-style innovative fiction, etc.), writing in the popular imagination has by and large stuck to traditional, narrative, and transparent uses, which have prevented it from experiencing a kind of Pop Art–like watershed. While, for example, the New York school fondled consumerism sweetly, using pop as a portal to subjectivity—(O'Hara: "Having a Coke with you /is even more fun than going to San Sebastian, Irú, Hendaye, Biarritz, Bayonne")[10]—it never came close to the cold objectivity, the naked, prophetic words of Warhol: "A Coke is a Coke and no amount of money can get you a better Coke than the one the bum on the corner is drinking. All the Cokes are the same and all the Cokes are good. Liz Taylor knows it, the president knows it, the bum knows it and you know it."[11]

The July/August 2009 issue of *Poetry* magazine, published by the Poetry Foundation, kicks off with a short poem by Tony Hoagland called "At the Galleria Shopping Mall," warning us of the pitfalls of consumerism:

> Just past the bin of pastel baby socks and underwear,
> there are some 49-dollar Chinese-made TVs;
>
> one of them singing news about a far-off war,
> one comparing the breast size from Hollywood
>
> to the breast size of an actress from Bollywoood.
> And here is my niece Lucinda,
>
> who is nine and a true daughter of Texas,
> who has developed the flounce of a pedigreed blonde

And declares that her favorite sport is shopping.
Today is the day she embarks upon her journey,

swinging a credit card like a scythe
through the meadows of golden merchandise.

Today is the day she stops looking at faces,
and starts assessing the labels of purses;

So let it begin. Let her be dipped in the dazzling bounty
and raised and wrung out again and again.

And let us watch.
As the gods in olden stories

turned mortals into laurel trees and crows
to teach them some kind of lesson,

so we were turned into Americans
to learn something about loneliness.[12]

Poor Lucinda is taken in by the oldest adage in the book—all
that glitters is not gold—losing her humanity in the process: "Today
is the day she stops looking at faces / and starts assessing the labels
of purses." The only way this young girl can learn her lesson is the
way we elders/gods have learned ours: only after succumbing to the
temptations, did we come to realize the folly of our pursuits. Ah,
youth! The telescopic nature of the piece in the last stanza widens
to give us—as a culture, as a nation—pause to think how alienated,
lonely and how disconnected from humanity such encounters have
made us. It's a poem that has something specific to teach us; one
that imparts true and wise values, wagging its knowing finger at
the folly of youth.

By giving us snapshots of specific moments—pastel baby socks,
underwear, Chinese-made TVs—Hoagland attempts to express in
shorthand what Rem Koolhaas calls "Junkspace": a type of provisional architecture that has given us malls, casinos, airports, and so

forth. But trying to specify or stabilize anything in Junkspace works against the nature of Junkspace: "Because it cannot be grasped, Junkspace cannot be remembered. It is flamboyant yet unmemorable, like a screensaver; its refusal to freeze insures instant amnesia. Junkspace does not pretend to create perfection, only interest. . . . Brands in Junkspace perform the same role as black holes in the universe: essences through which meaning disappears."[13] Like an easel painter setting up outside the mezzanine-level entrance of J. C. Penny and trying to render the mall experience in oils, Hoagland chooses the wrong approach using the wrong materials: deep image doesn't fly in this weightless space.

In the same issue of *Poetry* is a poem by Robert Fitterman called "Directory," which is simply a directory from an unnamed mall, looped with poetic concerns for form, meter, and sound. Koolhaas tells us that Junkspace is a labyrinth of reflection: "It promotes disorientation by any means (mirror, polish, echo)."[14] Fitterman's listing of a mall directory purports to be as numbing, dead, and dull as the mall experience itself, purposely encouraging linguistic disorientation by *reflecting* rather than *expressing*:

Macy's
Circuit City
Payless Shoes
Sears
Kay Jewelers
GNC
LensCrafters
Coach
H & M
RadioShack
Gymboree

The Body Shop
Eddie Bauer
Crabtree & Evelyn
Gymboree
Foot Locker

Land's End
GNC
LensCrafters
Coach
Famous Footwear
H & M

LensCrafters
Foot Locker
GNC
Macy's
Crabtree & Evelyn
H & M
Cinnabon
Kay Jewelers
Land's End

Hickory Farms
GNC
The Body Shop
Eddie Bauer
Payless Shoes
Circuit City
Kay Jewelers
Gymboree

The Body Shop
Hickory Farms
Coach
Macy's
GNC
Circuit City
Sears

H & M
Kay Jewelers
Land's End

LensCrafters
Eddie Bauer
Cinnabon

RadioShack
GNC
Sears
Crabtree & Evelyn[15]

Fitterman's list is reminiscent of Koolhaas, speaking about the Junkspace of the Dallas/Fort Worth airport (DFW): "DFW is composed of three elements only, repeated ad infinitum, nothing else: one kind of beam, one kind of brick, one kind of tile, all coated in the same color—is it teal? rust? tabacco? . . . Its drop-off is the seemingly harmless beginning of a journey to the heart of unmitigated nothingness, beyond animation by Pizza Hut, Dairy Queen . . ."[16] Fitterman's repeated nonspecificity mirrors the nature of global capitalism by giving us instantly recognizable name brands in a numbing stream. It's as if RadioShack is interchangeable with Circuit City—and aren't they, really? The effect of Fitterman's poem is like the looping background of *The Flintstones*, where the same tree and mountain keep scrolling by again and again: H&M, Kay's Jewelers, and The Body Shop keep repeating. And, as alienated or invigorated as Hoagland's niece is purported to feel, running our eyes down Fitterman's list of deadening stores gives us, the reader—first hand—the feeling of being in a mall. By doing very little, Fitterman has actually given us a more realistic experience than Hoagland, without having to resort to sermonizing to convince us of his point. The lesson of the poem is the experience of the poem.

The former United States poet laureate Donald Hall, in his poem "Ox Cart Man," writes of a different kind of market experience:

In October of the year,
he counts potatoes dug from the brown field,
counting the seed, counting
the cellar's portion out,
and bags the rest on the cart's floor.

He packs wool sheared in April, honey
in combs, linen, leather
tanned from deerhide,
and vinegar in a barrel
hoped by hand at the forge's fire.

He walks by his ox's head, ten days
to Portsmouth Market, and sells potatoes,
and the bag that carried potatoes,
flaxseed, birch brooms, maple sugar, goose
feathers, yarn.

When the cart is empty he sells the cart.
When the cart is sold he sells the ox,
harness and yoke, and walks
home, his pockets heavy
with the year's coin for salt and taxes,

and at home by fire's light in November cold
stitches new harness
for next year's ox in the barn,
and carves the yoke, and saws planks
building the cart again.[17]

Unlike Hoagland's niece, who produces nothing and is, at this stage of her life, only capable of blind consumption, or Fitterman's objectified view of consumerism, Hall presents us with an idealized, nostalgic picture that feels like something out of a Currier and Ives lithograph. This was a time when *men* were honest and did honest work; when a man not only grew, harvested, packed, transported nature's bounty but also sold them. From October to November he worked hard, at once depleting and replenishing for the next season, in touch with nature's cycle.

In a review of Hall's *Selected Poems*, Billy Collins wrote, in the *Washington Post*: "Hall has long been placed in the Frostian tradition of the plainspoken rural poet. His reliance on simple, concrete diction and the no-nonsense sequence of the declarative sentence gives his poems steadiness and imbues them with a tone of sincere authority. It is a kind of simplicity that succeeds in engaging the reader in the first few lines." [18] I'd argue that the "simplicity" of Fitterman expresses truths much closer to the everyday experience of most people than the morality-fueled sentiments of Hoagland or the nostalgic rustic rural vignettes of Donald Hall. And, in that, I think these are truly *populist* expressions: what could be easier to understand than a list of mall stores, reflecting most Americans' daily commutes past and common interactions with our endless malls?

A common accusation hurled at the avant-garde is that it is elitist and out of touch, toiling away in its ivory tower, appealing to the few who are in the know. And I'd agree that a lot of "difficult" work has been made under the mantle of populism only to be rejected by its intended audience as indecipherable or, worse, irrelevant. But uncreative writing is truly populist. Because Fitterman's uncreative writing makes its intentions clear from the outset, telling you exactly what it is before you read it, there's no way you *can't* understand it. But then the real question emerges: *why*? And with that question, we move into conceptual territory that takes us away from the object into the realm of speculation. At that point, we could easily throw the book away and carry on with a discussion, a move uncreative writing applauds: the book as a platform to leap off into thought. We move from assuming a readership to embracing a *thinkership*. By relinquishing the burden of reading—and thereby a readership—we can begin to think of uncreative writing as having the potential to be a body of literature able to be understood by anyone. If you get the concept (and the concepts are simple)—regardless of your geographic location, income level, education, or social status—you can engage with this writing. It's open to all.

This mode of uncreative writing offers a poetics of *realism*, reminiscent of the documentary impulse behind Zola's Les Rougon-Macquart series where, in the guise of dime store potboilers, he took on the massive project of how best describe in full French life during the second French Empire. From farmer to priest to food markets to department store, Zola claimed that his work transcended mere fiction; his intention was "strictly naturalist, strictly physiologist,"[19] a claim closer to de Certeau than to Balzac. Inspired by Zola, the new writing is a realism beyond realism: it's hyperrealist—a literary photorealism.

It's commonly said that you can only teach the avant-garde in advanced courses, but Craig Dworkin, a professor at the University of Utah, feels differently. He thinks that a text like Gertrude Stein's *Tender Buttons* works well at any level because you don't need to know any Greek myths, literary allusions, old British royal history, literary tropes, or even have a good vocabulary. You know all the words, and there they are.[20] Christian Bök, a poet and professor, describes his students as objecting to works like *Tender Buttons* at first because they dislike familiar language being rendered unfamiliar and feel that the whole point of their education is to make unfamiliar things readily understandable (not the other way around). He spends much of his time in class trying to show the students the wonders of the strange enigma that is Stein. He showcases, for example, that when Stein takes a familiar object, such as a pinbox, and describes it as "full of points," all of which we find "disappointing," she is in fact making a very simple, but subtle, point about the thorniness of something so "pointless" as poetry itself.[21]

In its self-reflexive use of appropriated language, uncreative writing embraces the inherent and inherited politics of the borrowed words: far be it for conceptual writers to dictate the moral or political meanings of words that aren't theirs. However, the method or machine that makes the poem sets the political agenda in motion or brings issues of morality or politics into question. Vanessa Place is a writer who re-presents ethically challenging and unsavory legal documents as literature. She doesn't alter them one bit, instead she simply transfers them from the legal framework to the literary, leaving it to the reader to pass moral judgment.

There's a touch of Melville's Bartleby in the work of Vanessa Place. As a beacon of stillness and silence in a frenzied workplace, Bartleby's composure and strict sense of self-imposed ethics exposed the hollowness and habitualness of the busy routine that surrounded him. Like a black hole, he sucked everyone into him, finally causing a total implosion. Place is a lawyer and, like Bartleby, much of her work involves scribing appellate briefs, that task of copying and editing, rendering complex lives and dirty deeds into "neutral" language to be presented before a court. That is her day job. Her poetry is an appropriation of the documents she writes during her day job, flipping her briefs after hours into literature. And, like most literature, they're chock-full of high drama, pathos, horror, and humanity. But, unlike most literature, she hasn't written a word of it. Or has she? Here's where it gets interesting. She both has written them and, at the same time, she's wholly appropriated them—rescuing them from the dreary world of court filings and bureaucracy—and, by mere reframing, turned them into compelling literature.

Place represents indigent sex offenders on appeal, no easy job. As she puts it: "All my clients have been convicted of a felony sex offense and are in state prison at the time I am appointed to their case. Because of my experience/expertise, many of my clients have been convicted of multiple offenses, and sentenced to hundreds of years and numerous life terms. I primarily represent rapists and child molesters, though I have also represented a few pimps and sexually violent predators (those who, after having served their sentences, have been involuntarily committed to state hospitals: I appeal their commitments)."[22]

After having published two fine successive experimental novels— one is a 130-page single sentence—her literary production these days consists of republishing statements of facts from her courtroom cases. An appellate brief is composed of three parts: a statement of the case, which sets forth the procedural history of the case; a statement of facts, which sets forth, in narrative form, the evidence of the crime as presented at trial; and an argument, which are the claims of error and (for the defense) the arguments for reversing the judgment. For her literary production, she only uses the statement of facts—the most objective and most narrative part of the brief.

Place does not alter the original document in any way other than to remove specific witness/victim information as necessary to protect those people's identities. By re-presenting the statements as literature, she does not violate any formal ethical standards or professional codes of conduct: all her briefs are matters of public record and could be found or read by anyone. But it seems like she is violating some sort of unwritten rules of her profession in order to critique and expose the language in Bartleby-like ways. Place claims, "All of my clients are legally guilty. Most are morally guilty. As their advocate, I may be morally guilty, though I am not legally guilty."[23] By shifting the context from law to art, and by stripping the language of any legal purpose, we suddenly see these documents in ways impossible to see them before. The type of questions that this gesture provokes is at the heart of Place's practice.

Language is never neutral, never stable, and can never be truly objective, thus the statement of facts is an argument in the guise of factual documentation. Even the basic rules for writing a statement of facts acknowledge this bias: "In the Statement of Facts . . . we are not allowed to argue explicitly. So what do we do? We argue implicitly. What is an implicit argument? Just as an explicit argument is one that explicitly states the because, an implicit argument is one that does not explicitly state a because in answer to the question "Why?" Rather, an implicit argument arranges and emphasizes the facts to lead the recipient of the argument to the desired conclusion."[24] For her day job, Place is intentionally writing an implicit argument; for her art, she is exposing that fallacy.

A published section of her four-hundred-page *Statement of Facts*—comprised of the documents from twenty-five cases—tells the lurid tale of Chavelo, a child-molesting uncle, and Sara, his niece. It wends its way for ten pages with graphic descriptions of sex interspersed with psychological impasses and heart-rending struggles to cope. In spite of the clerk's transcript notes—the log of matters heard in court in the form of summary notations that continually interrupt the textual flow—a clear narrative written emerges, written in plain English. An excerpt reads:

> Once, Sara's mother noticed Sara's underwear was wet and smelled of semen. She asked Sara about it, but Sara said she didn't know how it got there, and walked away. So her mother put Sara's underwear in the wash and told herself not to think about "this evil of what's happening."
>
> The last time appellant touched Sara was at her house. (RT 1303) Sara's private hurt when appellant touched her: it felt like "poking." It also hurt later when she went to the bathroom. (RT 1302) Sara

went to the doctor because her private was bothering her, "Like, when you put alcohol on your cut, but kind of worse than that." (3) Sara's mother saw blisters "like blisters that you get when you get on the monkey bars." The blisters itched. The doctor asked Sara what happened, but Sara didn't want to say. The doctor gave Sara pills to take every day for a month, and the blisters went away. They returned; Sara had to take the medicine again. The blisters again went away, and again returned. Sara went back to the doctor, and saw Dr. Kaufman. (RT 1306–1309, 1311–1313, 1318, 2197)

---

(3) Sara complained to her mother about pain during urination; her mother gave her medicinal tea for three days. When the pain didn't abate, her mother checked her vagina, saw a blister, and took Sara to the doctor. (RT 2196–2197, 2218–2221) Sara had never had blisters on her vagina before. (RT 2199)[25]

In reframing the work as literature, the first thing Place does is to remove the serif font required by the profession ("those little epaulets of authority," as she calls them), thus casting the document as something other than that which belongs in a courtroom. But, outside of that, the statement is identical to the original, with everything from footnotes to the Clerk's notations left intact. Wearing her double hat as both a lawyer and an uncreative writer, Place says "My job is information 'processing.' That is the job of all rhetoric, all language."

Yet Place plays both angles—this is both real life *and* art—clouding my rosy picture of art and ethics. While *Statement of Facts* might strike many as merely lurid and sensational, to linger on the content is to miss the concept: it's the matrix of apparatuses surrounding it— social, moral, political, ethical—that give the work its real meaning. And when you hear Place read these words, you realize that the vile content of the work is just the tip of the iceberg. What happens to you, the listener, during the reading is what makes what she's doing so important.

Not surprisingly, it's hard to listen to her read. I recently sat through a reading of *Statement of Facts* that lasted forty-five minutes. Onstage, Place dons the same outfit she does when appearing before a judge and reads in a low monotone, tamping down the wildly heated subject matter with a cool and mechanical delivery. Upon hearing the work, the first reaction is of shock and horror. How can people be so terrible? But you keep listening. It's hard to stop. The narrative draws you in, and you find yourself listening to the small incidents pile up: doctor's examination of the victim, the victim's slow and painful admission that a criminal act has been perpetrated upon her, leading to the climax, where the appellant is finally arrested and it appears that justice, after all, will be served. After some time, this begins to feel like a Hollywood movie, replete with tragedy and redemption.

Andy Warhol said that "when you see a gruesome picture over and over again, it doesn't really have any effect,"[26] and the longer Place read for, the more immune I became to the horrors of what she was saying. Like a detective, I began to divorce my emotional response from the facts, scratching my chin, logically trying to poke holes in her argument, passing judgments on each incident. Like Bartleby's workmates, I found myself shifting my position to accommodate Place's narrative. Unconsciously, I had been transformed from passive listener to active juror. She actually transformed my position as receiver of the work, spinning me around in ways that were very much against my will. I didn't want to objectify my experience, but I did. Place used passive coercion, a sort of courtroom logic, to enact a change in me, the reader/listener, as she does to jurors every day. What I was experiencing was the legal system; to my horror, I was caught up in its machinations. As I listened to the litany of crimes, I found my circuits overloaded. As Place puts it: "I am considering information—even of a most disturbing variety—as linguistic compost. There is too much to consider, too many words, of both thin and thick content. It is too much to bear, and so we don't. And still, I am asking the reader to bear witness, or to choose not to. Either way, they become complicit. There's no such thing as an unbiased witness. There's no such thing as an innocent bystander. Not after they've listened for a while. Never after they've stopped listening."[27]

In the 1930s the objectivist poet Charles Reznikoff began an epic called *Testimony: The United States (1885–1915) Recitative*. It consists of hundreds of courtroom witness statements, which have then been lineated and versified.[28] They're short pieces, each one telling a story:

> Amelia was just fourteen and out of the orphan asylum; at her first
>   job—in the bindery, and yes sir, yes ma'am, oh, so anxious to
>   please.
> She stood at the table, her blonde hair hanging about her shoulders,
>   "knocking up" for Mary and Sadie, the stitchers
> ("knocking up" is counting books and stacking them in piles to be
>   taken away).
> There were twenty wire-stitching machines on the floor, worked by
>   a shaft that ran under the table;
> as each stitcher put her work through the machine,
> she threw it on the table. The books were piling up fast
> and some slid to the floor
> (the forelady had said, Keep the work off the floor!);
> and Amelia stooped to pick up the books—
> three or four had fallen under the table
> between the boards nailed against the legs.
> She felt her hair caught gently;
> put her and up and felt the shaft going round and round
> and her hair caught on it, wound and winding around it,
> until the scalp was jerked from her head,
> and the blood was coming down all over her face and waist.[29]

Reznikoff's tale feels like a folk song, a blues recitation, or a Dickensian tale, metaphorically intoning a timeless rite of passage. The short passage is ripe with sexual metaphor: the pubescent girl with long "blond hair hanging around her shoulders," "oh, so anxious to please," whose job is "knocking up." The inevitable denouement happens when she feels the "shaft going round and round," its symbolic deflowering, replete with the flow of blood "coming down all over her face and waist." It's a complex play of eros and thanatos, poetic and nuanced, expressed in surgically selected lineation and enjambment. It's remarkably economical, painting a picture of an entire world in just a few lines, packing a wallop of an emotional punch.

Place, conversely, doesn't deal in metaphor. There's nothing subtle about what she does, adhering to Beckett's motto, "no symbols where none intended." We are horrified by Reznikoff's tales, but they're only a stanza or two, and we quickly move on to the next encapsulated tragedy. Unlike Place's durational onslaught, Reznikoff permits us to keep our objectivity intact: we're still readers—safe and distanced—witnessing tragedy. But we're never forced to alter our position as readers or listeners in the way that Place compels us to do. Reznikoff's work reeks of a world passed, and it is often easy to separate from the content, as opposed to Place, whose lurid tales continue to happen every day. In fact, Reznikoff's poem lives up to its moniker as *objectivist*, keeping reader and author outside in ways that Place refuses. Hers is a poetics of realism: one so real that's it's almost too much to bear.

Place's works have a lot on their plate and recall a legend of the Warhol years. When Warhol first showed his Brillo boxes in New York, to great controversy, at the Stable Gallery in 1964, an intoxicated, angry man at the opening approached Warhol and expressed his disgust for what he felt to be a one-trick, cheap shot gesture. He accused Andy of ripping off somebody else's hard work. As it turns out, this man, James Harvey, was a failed yet earnest second-generation abstract expressionist painter whose day job was as a graphic designer for Brillo: he designed the prototype of the box in 1961. He was doubly felled by Warhol, once on account of his day job and in a larger sense on account of Warhol's Pop Art rendering his abstract expressionist "fine art" obsolete. Place complicates the already-complicated Warhol tale by playing both the victim and the victor, outsmarting herself by taking her alienated labor and *détourning* it into a satisfying and challenging practice.

I recall a holiday dinner with my curious and bright, but very bored, cousin who is a lawyer. He was complaining about the drudgery of his job, having to write endlessly dull legal briefs day in and day out. Prodding him, I would say, why don't you think of what you do all day as art? If you reframe those documents, they don't look too far from many conceptual art documents I've seen. In fact, part of the practice of certain artists such as Christo is to include all the legal briefs that he had to file in order to, say, run a fence across miles of

California wilderness. There's a certain fascination with documentation and the dry authoritativeness of legalese that runs through much conceptual art and writing. "You could be a part of that tradition," I suggested. I could have told him about the work of Vanessa Place. My cousin, although intrigued, demurred and continued being bored for many years henceforth.

5 WHY APPROPRIATION?

The greatest book of uncreative writing has already been written. From 1927 to 1940, Walter Benjamin synthesized many ideas he'd been working with throughout his career into a singular work that came to be called *The Arcades Project*. Many have argued that it's nothing more than hundreds of pages of notes for an unrealized work of coherent thought, merely a pile of shards and sketches. But others have claimed it to be a groundbreaking one-thousand-page work of appropriation and citation, so radical in its undigested form that it's impossible to think of another work in the history of literature that takes such an approach. It's a massive effort: most of what is in the book was not written by Benjamin, rather he simply copied texts written by others from a stack of library books, with some passages spanning several pages. Yet conventions remain: each entry is properly cited, and Benjamin's own "voice" inserts itself with brilliant gloss and commentary on what's being copied.

With all of the twentieth century's twisting and pulverizing of language and the hundreds of new forms proposed for fiction and poetry, it never occurred to anybody to grab somebody else's words and present them as their own. Borges proposed it in the form of

Pierre Menard, but even Menard didn't copy—he just happened to write the same book that Cervantes did without any prior knowledge of it. It was sheer coincidence, a fantastic stroke of genius combined with a tragically bad sense of timing.

Benjamin's gesture raises many questions about the nature of authorship and ways of constructing literature: isn't all cultural material shared, with new works built upon preexisting ones, whether acknowledged or not? Haven't writers been appropriating from time eternal? What about those well-digested strategies of collage and pastiche? Hasn't it all been done before? And, if so, is it necessary to do it again? What is the difference between appropriation and collage?

A good place to start looking for answers is in the visual arts, where appropriative practices have been tested and digested for the past century, particularly in the approaches of Duchamp and Picasso, both of whom were reacting to the previous century's shifts in industrial production and its subsequent technologies, particularly the camera. A useful analogy is Picasso as a candle and Duchamp as a mirror. The light of the candle draws us to its warm glow, holding us spellbound by its beauty. The cool reflectivity of the mirror pushes us away from the object, throwing us back on ourselves.

Picasso's *Still Life with Chair Caning* (1911–12) incorporates an industrially produced piece of oilcloth printed with an image of chair caning into its composition, and an actual rope is wrapped around the painting, framing the picture. Other elements include the letters *J, O, U*, presumably referencing the word *journal*. These elements intermingle with various painted human and still life forms in the painting, all done in the typical browns, grays, and whites of the cubist style. Picasso's painting is an example of what a painter generally does: like a bird constructing a nest, discreet elements are gathered and stitched together to create a harmonious whole. The fact that the collaged elements are not rendered by hand does not serve to disrupt the composition in any way; rather they reinforce the strength of it. Picasso struts his mastery over several mediums and methods, and we are justifiably impressed by his skill. Like a candle, *Still Life with Chair Caning* is a picture that draws you into its composition; clearly, you could spend a lot of time absorbed in this picture and basking in its warm glow.

Figure 5.1. Pablo Picasso, *Still Life with Chair Caning* (1911–12).

Conversely, Duchamp's *Fountain*, from just a few years later, 1917, is a urinal turned on its side, signed and put on a pedestal. Here, as opposed to Picasso, Duchamp appropriated an entire object, thus defamiliarizing and rendering this industrially produced fountain functionless. Unlike Picasso's constructive method, Duchamp didn't use collage to create a harmonious, compelling composition, rather he eschewed the retinal qualities to create an object that doesn't require a *viewership* as much as it does a *thinkership*; no one has ever stood wide-eyed before Duchamp's urinal admiring the quality and application of the glaze. Instead, Duchamp invokes the mirror, creating a repellent and reflective object, one that forces us to turn away in other directions. Where it sends us has been exhaustively documented. Broadly speaking, we could say that Duchamp's action is generative—spawning worlds of ideas—while Picasso's is absorptive, holding us close to the object and close to our own thoughts.

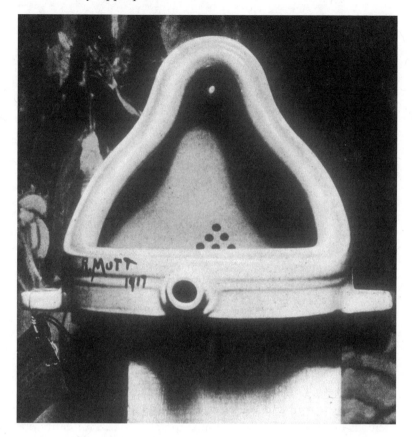

Figure 5.2. Marcel Duchamp, *Fountain* (1917).

In literature, a similar comparison can be made in the constructive methodology of Ezra Pound's *Cantos* and the scrivenerlike process of Walter Benjamin's *The Arcades Projects*. The assemblage and collage quality of *The Cantos* stitches together thousands of lines, drawn from a number other sources, literary and nonliterary, all held in place with the glue of Pound's own language to create a unified whole. Like a gleaner of history, he collects heaps of ephemera from the ages and sorts through it looking for the gems out of which he will construct his epic; sound, sight, and meaning coalesce, frozen in shimmering verse. Everything seems to have come from somewhere else, but it has been chosen with distinctive and carefully cultivated taste; his genius is in synthesizing found material into a cohesive whole. The flotsam includes offhanded notes, price lists, shards of language, erratic typography and odd spacing, chunks of correspondence, arcane legalese, slabs of dialogue, a dozen languages, and numerous unreferenced footnotes, to name a few, all bound together in a life's work. Written according to neither system or constraint, this rambling mess is remarkably sensuous. The result is an exquisitely built construction cobbled together by a master craftsman. We could say that, like Picasso, Pound's practice is synthetic, one that draws us in to tease out its puzzles and bask in the light of its sheer beauty. Pound does have clear ambitions and ideas—social and political, not to mention aesthetic—yet all these are so finely distilled and synthesized through his own filters that they become inseparable from his exquisite creation.

Benjamin, on the other hand, taking his cues from cinema, creates a work of literary montage, a disjunctive, rapid-fire juxtaposition of "small fleeting pictures."[1] With some 850 sources crashed up against each other, Benjamin makes no attempt at unification, other than loosely organizing his citations by category. The scholar Richard Sieburth tells us that "of a quarter of a million words that comprise [this] edition, at least 75 percent are direct transcriptions of texts."[2] As opposed to Pound, there is no attempt to blend the shards into a whole; instead there is an accumulation of language, most of it not belonging to Benjamin. Instead of admiring the author's synthetic skills, we are made to think about the exquisite quality of Benjamin's choices, his taste. It's what he selects to copy that makes this work successful. Benjamin's insistent use of fragmentary wholes does not make the text the final destination, rather, like Duchamp, we are thrown away from the object by the power of the mirror.

Both Pound's and Benjamin's writing methods are largely based on appropriating shards of language that they themselves didn't generate, yet they demonstrate two different approaches to constructing an appropriated text. Pound's is a more intuitive and improvisatory method of weaving textual fragments into a unified whole. Oftentimes it takes a great deal of Pound's intervening—finessing, massaging, and editing those found words—to make them all fit together just so. Benjamin's approach is more preordained: the machine that makes the work is set up in advance, and it's just a matter of filling up those categories with the right words, in the order in which they're found, for the work to be successful. While it's impossible to determine Benjamin's exact methodology, the general consensus among scholars is that *Arcades* was sheaves of notes for a great, unrealized project that he planned to call *Paris, Capital of the Nineteenth Century*. And, although there are chapters and sketches for such a book, which boil the notes down into a well-argued, logical essay, such a reading of the final work denies that possibility. As Benjamin scholar Susan Buck-Morss says: "Every attempt to capture the *Passagen-Werk* within one narrative frame must lead to failure. The fragments plunge the interpreter into an abyss of meanings, threatening her or him with an epistemological despair that rivals the melancholy of the Baroque allegoricists. . . . To say that the *Passagen-Werk* has no necessary narrative structure so that the fragments can be grouped freely, is not at all to suggest that it has no conceptual structure, as if the meaning of the book were itself totally up to the capriciousness of the reader. As Benjamin said, a presentation of confusion need not be the same as a confused presentation."[3] The book can be read (or misread, depending upon how you wish to frame it) as a stand-alone work. It is a book made up of refuse and detritus, writing history by paying attention to the margins and the peripheries rather than the center: bits of newspaper articles, arcane passages of forgotten histories, ephemeral sensations, weather conditions, political tracts, advertisements, literary quips, stray verse, accounts of dreams, descriptions of architecture, arcane theories of knowledge, and hundreds of other offbeat topics.

The book was constructed by reading through the corpus of literature about Paris in the nineteenth century. Benjamin simply copied down the passages that caught his attention on cards, which were then organized into general categories. Anticipating the instability of language in the later part of the twentieth century, the book had no fixed form. Benjamin would endlessly shuffle his note cards, transferring them from one folder to another. In the end, realizing that no passage could live forever in one category, he cross-referenced many entries, and those notations have traveled with the printed edition, making *The Arcades Project* an enormous proto-hypertextual work. With the inevitable printing of the book, the words were forced to settle down, as an editor pinned them to fixed entities on the page forever. What Benjamin intended as a final version was never made clear; instead, posterity has nailed his words down for him in the form of a one-thousand-page tome. Yet it's that mystery—was this the form he intended for his life's work?—that gives the book so much energy, so much life and play, some sixty years after it was written. In the ensuing half-century, all sorts of experiments in unfixed pages have occurred. Today, in places like Printed Matter and book arts exhibitions, it's not uncommon to find books comprised entirely of unbound sheets that purchasers may arrange according to their will. The catalogue to John Cage's retrospective *Rolywholyover* was one such book, with nearly fifty pieces of printed ephemera laid in, with no hierarchical order. The book embodies Cage's chance operations, a book without fixity or finality, a work in progress.

Even in its final form, *The Arcades Project* is a great book to bounce around in, flitting from page to page, like window-shopping, pausing briefly to admire a display that catches your eye without feeling the need to go into the store.

In *Convolute G: Exhibitions, Advertising, Grandville*, for example, opening the chapter at random, you stumble upon a quote from Marx about price tags and commodities, then, a few pages later, there's a description of a hashish vision in a casino; jump two pages ahead and you're confronted with Blanqui's quote, "A rich death is a closed abyss." Quickly you move on to the next window. Because the book is ostensibly about the Parisian arcades—an early incarnation of the shopping mall—Benjamin encourages the reader to be a consumer of language the way we would allow ourselves to be seduced by any other commodity. It's the sense of sheer bulk and abundance that makes it impossible to ever finish; it's so rich and so dense that trying to read it induces amnesia—you're not sure whether you've already read this or that passage. It's really a text without end. What holds the work together—while at the same time ensuring that you remain lost—is the fact that many entries are cross-referenced, but often lead to dead ends. For example, a citation about advertising and Jugendstil is appended with a cross-reference to "Dream Consciousness," a chapter that doesn't exist. Losing your way, or drifting, is part and parcel of the reading experience as it's come to us in its finalized form, regardless of whether or not Benjamin's book is "unfinished." Instead, if you wanted to follow Benjamin's "hyperlink," you would have to choose between two chapters with the word *dream* in them: *Convolute K—Dream City and Dream House, Dreams of the Future, Anthroplogical Nihilism, Jung* or *Convolute L—Dream House, Museum, Spa*. Once you flipped forward to either of those chapters, you'd be hard-pressed to find any direct reference to advertising and Jugendstil. Instead, you'd most likely find yourself lost like a flaneur, drifting through those seemingly endless fascinating and engrossing chapters.

In many ways, the way we read *The Arcades Project* points toward the way we have learned to use the Web: hypertexting from one place to another, navigating our way through the immensity of it; how we've become virtual flaneurs, casually surfing from one place to another; how we've learned to manage and harvest information, not feeling the need to read the Web linearly, and so forth.

By having *The Arcades* published in book form as opposed to sheaves of loose note cards, Benjamin's work is frozen in a way that permits us to study it, a condition he called a constellation: "It's not that what is past casts its light on what is present, or what is present casts its light on what is past; rather what has been comes together in a flash with the now to form a constellation." Following Benjamin's death in 1940, his friend Georges Bataille, who was an archivist and librarian at the Bibliothèque Nationale, stashed Benjamin's unpublished sheaves of note cards deep in an archive where they remained safely hidden until after the war. It wasn't until the 1980s that a manuscript was constructed, after years of piecing it together into a solid form or constellation. The Web can be seen as having a similar constellation-like construction. Let's say that you're reading a newspaper online. When you load the page, it's pulling from a myriad of servers across the Web to form the constellation of that page: ad servers, image servers, RSS feeds, databases, style sheets, templates, and so forth. All those component servers, too, are connected to a myriad of other servers across the Web, which feed them updated content. Chances are that the newspaper you're reading online has an AP news feed integrated into that page, which is dynamically updated by various servers to deliver you the breaking headlines. If one or more of those servers goes down, a chunk of the page you're trying to access won't load. It's a miracle that it works at all. Any given Web page is a constellation, coming together in a flash—and potentially disappearing as fast. Refresh the front page of, say, the *New York Times* site and it won't look the same as it did just seconds ago.

That Web page, in constellation-like form, is what Benjamin calls a "dialectical image," a place where past and present momentarily fuse together creating an image (in this case the image of the Web page). He also posits that "the place where one encounters [the dialectical image] is language." When we write a book, we construct it in dialectical manner, not too different from a Web page, by pulling together strands of knowledge (personal, historical, speculative, etc.) into a constellation that finds its fixed form as a book. And since the Web is comprised of alphanumeric code, we can posit the Web— with its digital text, image, video, and sound—as one massive Benjaminian dialectical image.

In Benjamin's *Arcades Project* we have a literary roadmap for appropriation, one that is picked up across the twentieth century by writers such as Brion Gysin, William Burroughs, and Kathy Acker, to name but a few, and one that points toward the more radically appropriative texts being produced today. Yet, contrary to Benjamin's groundbreaking forays into appropriation, the twentieth century embraced and ran with the fragmentary, not the whole, playing itself out into smaller and smaller bits of shattered language. *The Arcades* still deals in fragments—although often large ones—rather than in wholes: Benjamin never copied the entirety of someone else's book and claimed it as his own. And, for all his professed love of copying, there is still a great deal of authorial intervention and "original genius" in the book. It makes me wonder, then, if his book could really be termed appropriation, or if it wasn't just another variant on fragmented modernism.

Things get tricky when we try to nail down exactly what literary appropriation is. We could try to use my own appropriated work *Day* (2003) as a test case. I wanted to see if I could create a work of literature using the most minimal amount of intervention possible, by recasting the text from one entity into another (from a newspaper into a book). When reset as a book, would the newspaper have literary properties that we're not able to see during our daily reading of it?

The recipe for my appropriation seems direct and simple enough: "On Friday, September 1, 2000, I began retyping the day's *New York Times*, word for word, letter for letter, from the upper left hand corner to the lower right hand corner, page by page." My goal was to be as uncreative as possible, one of the hardest constraints an artist can muster, particularly on a project of this scale; with every keystroke comes the temptation to fudge, cut and paste, and skew the mundane language. But to do so would be to foil the exercise. Instead, I simply made my way through the entire newspaper, typing exactly what I saw. Every place where there was an alphanumeric word or letter, I retyped it: advertising, movie timetables, the numbers of a license plate on a car ad, the classifieds, and so forth. The stock quotes alone ran for more than two hundred pages.

Sounds simple, right? Yet, in order for me to simply "appropriate" the newspaper and turn it into a work of literature, it involved dozens of authorial decisions. First came lifting the text off the page of the newspaper and getting it into my computer. But what to do with the font, font sizes, and formatting? If I remove the images (while grabbing the texts embedded in the images, such as the numbers on the license plate in a car ad), I still must keep the captions. Where do the line breaks occur? Do I remain faithful to the slim columns or do I flow each article into one long paragraph? What about the pull quotes: where do those lines break? And how do I make my way around a page? I know I have a rough rule to move from the upper left corner to the lower right, but where do I go when I reach the end of a column and it says "continued on page 26"? Do I go to page 26 and finish the article or do I jump to the adjacent column and start another article? And, when I make those jumps, do I add another line break or do I flow the text continuously? How do I treat the advertisements, which often have playful text elements of varying fonts and styles? Where do line breaks occur in an ad where words float about a page? And what about the movie timetables, the sports statistics, the classified ads? In order to proceed, I have to build a machine. I have to answer each question and set up a number of rules that I must then strictly follow.

And once the text is entered into my computer, what font do I choose to reset the piece in, and what statement will that make about my book's relationship to the *New York Times*? The obvious decision would be to use the font called "Times New Roman"? But, by doing that, I might lend the original publication more credibility than I wish to give it, making my book appear more like a replica of the newspaper than a simulacrum. Perhaps it would be better if I skirted the issue entirely by using a sans serif font like Verdana. But, if I use Verdana, a font designed specifically for the screen and licensed by Microsoft, will that push my book too much toward a paper/screen battle? And why would I want to give Microsoft any more support than they already have? (I ended up giving it a serif font, Garamond, which alluded to the *Times*, but was not Times New Roman.)

Then there are dozens of paratextual decisions: what size is the book going to be and how will that impact the reception of the book? I know that I want it to be big, to reflect the massive size of the day's newspaper, but if I make it coffee table sized, I risk getting close to the paper's original format, which would run contrary to my wanting to represent the newspaper as a literary object. Conversely, if I made it too small, say, the size of Chairman Mao's *Little Red Book*, it would be cute and perhaps be seen as a novelty you might pick up next to the cash register at your local Barnes and Noble. (I ended up making it the exact size and bulk of the paperbound Harvard edition of *The Arcades Project*.)

What paper stock will the book be printed on? If I print it on too fine a stock, it runs the risk of being seen as a deluxe artist's book, something that only a few people can afford. And since the project was based on the reinterpretation and redistribution of a mass media product, I felt that as many people should have the book as wanted it for an affordable price. Yet, if I printed it on newsprint, it would allude too closely to the actual paper, thus running the risk of being a facsimile edition. (In the end, I just went with a generic plain white stock.)

What will the cover look like? Should I use an image from the day's paper? Or replicate the day's front page? No. That would be too literal and illustrative. I wanted something that would signify the paper, not replicate the paper. (I went with no image, just a dark blue cover with the word "Day" in a white sans serif font and my name below it in a serif font printed in sky blue.)

How much should the book sell for? Limited edition artist's books sell for thousands of dollars. I knew that I didn't want to go down that road. Ultimately, I decided that it should be published as an 836-page book in an edition of 750, selling for $20.[4]

Once those formal decisions are made, there are ethical issues to consider. If I truly "appropriate" this work, then I must faithfully copy/write every word of the newspaper. No matter how tempted I might be to alter the words of a disagreeable politician or film critic, I cannot do so without undermining the strict "wholes" that appropriation trucks in. So, for a simple appropriation, it's not so simple. There were as many decisions, moral quandaries, linguistic preferences, and philosophical dilemmas as there are in an original or collaged work.

And yet I still trumpet the work's "valuelessness," its "nutrition-lessness," its lack of creativity and originality when clearly the opposite is true. In truth, I'm not doing much more than trying to catch literature up with appropriative fads the art world moved past decades ago. There may, in fact, be a lot of truth when my detractors claim that I'm not that radical, that my name is still on these objects, and all those decisions are so much in the service of upholding notions of my own genius. For an egoless project, there sure is a lot of investment in me here. One prominent blogger acutely commented, "Kenny Goldsmith's actual art project is the projection of Kenny Goldsmith."[5]

But, during the twentieth century, the art world was full of such gestures, artists like Elaine Sturtevant, Louise Lawler, Mike Bidlo, or Richard Pettibon who, for the past several decades, have recreated the works of other artists, claiming them as their own, and they have long been absorbed into a legitimized practice. How can younger writers proceed in an entirely new way, using current technologies and modes of distribution? Perhaps a glimmer into the battlegrounds of the future was perceived when three anonymous writers edited the now infamous *Issue 1*, a 3,785-page unauthorized and unpermissioned anthology, "written" by 3,164 poets whose poems were actually authored not by the poets to whom they were attributed. Instead, the poems were generated by computer, which randomly synced each author with a poem. Stylistically, it made no sense: a traditional poet was paired with a radically disjunctive poem penned by a computer and vice versa. The intention of *Issue 1*'s creators was to provoke, along many fronts. Could the largest anthology of poetry ever written be pieced together without anyone's knowledge and distributed worldwide overnight? Could this gesture cause an instant literary scandal? Does it matter if poets write their own poems anymore or is it good enough for a computer to pen them for them? Why where those specific 3,164 poets chosen and not the thousands of other poets writing in the English language today? What did it mean to be included? What did it mean to be excluded? And who was behind this? Why were they doing it? With its conceptually based agenda and denial of the traditional methods of creation, distribution, and authorship, *Issue 1* shares many of the touchstones of uncreative writing.

Yet it wasn't so much the stylistics that raised eyebrows, it was the mechanics of it—the distribution and the notification—which riled the "contributors." The work was stitched into a massive PDF, which was placed on a media server late one evening. Many people found about their inclusion the first thing in the morning, when finding that the Google Alert they had set for their name had notified them that they were included in a major new anthology. Clicking on the link brought them to the anthology, whereupon, downloading it, they found their name attached to a poem they didn't write. Like wildfire, reaction spread through the community: Why was I in it? Why wasn't I in it? Why was my name matched with that poem? Who was responsible for this act? Half the "contributors" was delighted to be included and the other half was wildly angered. Several of the poets included said that they would include the poem ascribed to them in their next collection. Speaking on behalf of the disgruntled authors whose reputations for genius and authenticity were sullied was blogger and poet Ron Silliman, who said, "*Issue 1* is what I would call an act of anarcho-flarf vandalism. . . . Play with other people's reps at your own risk." He went on to cite a lawsuit in which he and a group of authors won a sum of money for copyright infringement back in the seventies, suggesting that such a gesture might be a good idea for those scammed by *Issue 1*. Addressing the creators of *Issue 1*, Silliman strikes an ominous tone, stating, "As I certainly did not write the text associated with my name on page 1849 . . . I don't think you wrote your work either."[6]

And yet, does Silliman really write his own work? Like many poets, the answer is both yes and no. Over the past forty years, one of the main goals in Silliman's practice has been to challenge the notion of a stable, authentic authorial voice. His poems are comprised of shards of language, stray sentences and observations that keep the reader guessing at their origins. Silliman often uses "I," but it's not clear that it's really him speaking. An early poem, "Berkeley," explicitly challenges authorial singularity. In a 1985 interview, he says: "In 'Berkeley,' where every line is a statement beginning with the word 'I,' something very similar occurs. Most of the lines are found materials, very few of which are from any one source, and they're ordered so as to avoid as much as possible any sense of narrative or normative exposition. Yet by sheer juxtaposition these reiterated 'I's form into a character, a felt presence which is really no more than an abstraction of a grammatical feature. . . . And this presence, in turn, impacts significantly on how a given line is read or understood, which can be vastly different from its meaning within its original context."[7] Bob Perlman, writing about "Berkeley," reiterates Silliman's claims, "An early poem such as 'Berkeley' . . . seems specifically to destroy any reading which would produce a unified subject. The poems consists of a hundred or so first-person sentences whose mechanical aspect— each starts with 'I'—makes them impossible to unite: 'I want to redeem myself / I can shoot you / I've no idea really / I should say it is not a mask / I must remember another time / I don't want to know you / I'm not dressed / I had to take the risk / I did look / I don't care what you make of it / I am outside the sun / I still had what was mine / I will stay here and die / I was reinforced in this opinion / I flushed it down the toilet / I collapsed in my chair / I forgot the place, sir.' "[8] For a poet who has spent much of his time dismantling a stable authorship, Sillman's response to *Issue 1* is indeed puzzling. Doesn't *Issue 1* extend Silliman's ethos to logical ends?

As there really wasn't much to discuss about the poems—in regard to everything else going on about this gesture, they seemed pretty irrelevant—we were forced to consider the conceptual apparatus that the anonymous authors had set into motion. With one gesture, they had swapped the focus *from content to context,* showing us what it might mean to be a poet in the digital age. Being a poet in any age—digital or analog—places one's practice outside normative economies, theoretically enabling the genre to take risks that more lucrative ventures wouldn't. Just as we've seen some of the most adventurous linguistic experimentation in the past century in poetry, it's now poised to do the same when it comes to notions of authorship, publishing, and distribution as proved by the *Issue 1*'s provocations.

At the center of it all is appropriation. The twentieth century's fuss over authorial authenticity seems tame compared to what is going on here. Not only are the texts themselves appropriated, but that is compounded by the appropriation of names and reputations, randomly synced with poems that were not written by the authors so linked. It's the largest anthology of poetry ever compiled and it was distributed to thousands one weekend from a blog and then commented upon endlessly on other blogs and subsequently in the comments streams of those blogs.

The candle has blown out, and we're left with a hall of mirrors. In fact, the Web has become a mirror for the ego of an absent but very present author. If Benjamin made writing safe for appropriation, and my own analog works have extended his project by borrowing in book-length form, then projects like *Issue 1* move the discourse into the digital age, greatly broadening appropriative possibilities in scale and scope, dealing a knockout blow to notions of traditional authorship. To dismiss this as simply an "act of anarcho-flarf vandalism" is to miss the wakeup call of this gesture, that the digital environment has completely changed the literary playing field, in terms of both content and authorship. In a time when the amount of language is rising exponentially, combined with greater access to the tools with which to manage, manipulate, and massage those words, appropriation is bound to become just another tool in the writers' toolbox, an acceptable—and accepted—way of constructing a work of literature, even for more traditionally oriented writers. When accused of "plagiarism" in his latest novel, which was called a "work of genius" by the newspaper *Libération*, the best-selling French author Michel Houellebecq claimed it as such: "If these people really think that [this is plagiarism], they haven't got the first notion of what literature is. . . . This is part of my method. . . . This approach, muddling real documents and fiction, has been used by many authors. I have been influenced especially by [Georges] Perec and [Jorge Luis] Borges. . . . I hope that this contributes to the beauty of my books, using this kind of material."[9]

6 INFALLIBLE PROCESSES
What Writing Can Learn from Visual Art

The visual arts have long embraced uncreativity as a creative practice. Beginning with Marcel Duchamp's readymades, the twentieth century was awash with artworks that challenged the primacy of the artist and questioned received notions of authorship. Particularly in the 1960s, with the advent of conceptual art, Duchampian tendencies were tested to the extreme, producing important bodies of often ephemeral and propositional work by towering artists such as Dan Flavin, Lawrence Weiner, Yoko Ono, and Joseph Kosuth. What they made was often secondary to the idea of how it was made.

There's a lot that writers can learn from these artists in how they went about eradicating traditional notions of genius, labor, and process. These ideas seem particularly relevant in today's digital climate, since the basis of much conceptual art was systematic, logical language. Like the concrete poets and situationists, there's a direct tie-in to the use of language materially. In fact, many conceptual artists used words as their primary medium in the form of proposition and/or as a gallery-based expression.

There's a lot, too, that a contemporary readership can learn from the precedent of conceptual art. While no one flinches today upon walking into a gallery and seeing a few lines drawn on a wall according to a recipe (Sol LeWitt) or entering a theater or gallery showing a film of a man sleeping for eight hours (Andy Warhol's *Sleep,* 1963), parallel acts bound between the pages of a book and published as writing still raise many red flags and cries: "That's not literature!" In the 1960s gallery viewers quickly learned—as in the case of Warhol's films—how *not* to watch them, but rather to think about them, write about them, and discuss them without being burdened by the need to watch in full. Similarly, many learned the futility of demanding an emotional kick from a LeWitt drawing, knowing there wouldn't be any. Instead, they learned to ask different questions, recognizing that mechanical expressions can be equally—but differently—beautiful and moving. For many, any resistance to such approaches in art quickly collapsed, and both Warhol and LeWitt have become canonized and even mainstream artists.

While the history of conceptual art is widely known, the overlaps and connections between it, contemporary writing, and digital culture are seldom made. What follows is an examination of Sol LeWitt and Andy Warhol's practices in ways that are applicable to uncreative writing. While both work on freeing the artist from the burden of "genius," each goes about it differently, LeWitt by mathematics and systems, Warhol by contraction, falsification, and ambiguity.

One of my favorite descriptions of procrastination is this portrait of John Ashbery written for the *New Yorker* in 2005:

> It's late already, five or five-thirty. John Ashbery is sitting at his type-writer but not typing. He picks up his cup of tea and takes two small sips because it's still quite hot. He puts it down. He's supposed to write some poetry today. He woke up pretty late this morning and has been futzing around ever since. He had some coffee. He read the newspaper. He dipped into a couple of books: a Proust biography that he bought five years ago but just started reading because it suddenly occurred to him to do so, a novel by Jean Rhys that he recently came across in a secondhand bookstore—he's not a systematic reader. He flipped on the television and watched half of something dumb. He didn't feel up to leaving the apartment—it was muggy and putrid out, even for New York in the summer. He was aware of a low-level but continuous feeling of anxiety connected with the fact

that he hadn't started writing yet and didn't have an idea. His mind flitted about. He thought about a Jean Helion painting that he'd seen recently at a show. He considered whether he should order in dinner again from a newish Indian restaurant on Ninth Avenue that he likes. (He won't go out. He's seventy-eight. He doesn't often go out these days.) On a trip to the bathroom he noticed that he needed a haircut. He talked on the phone to a poet friend who was sick. By five o'clock, though, there was no avoiding the fact that he had only an hour or so left before the working day would be over, so he put a CD in the stereo and sat down at his desk. He sees that there's a tiny spot on the wall that he's never noticed before. It's only going to take him half an hour or forty minutes to whip out something short once he gets going, but getting going, that's the hard part.[1]

No need to worry, Mr. Ashbery: there's plenty of people out there to help you. There are dozens of books offering up antidotes for people like you. For instance, you might want to change your clothes ("to get a truly fresh start, John"); or try stretching a bit; it's a good idea to get up and get a glass of water every twenty minutes; you really should try freewriting—just let your mind relax and let it flow, John; or you could try writing "badly"; it might be a "good idea to turn off the Internet"; and perhaps it would help if you got up from your writing desk and did just one chore. But there's one solution that each and every book on writer's block offers: *write five words. Any five words.* Follow this advice, Mr. Ashbery, and you'll never have writer's block again.

The irony is that that last suggestion was actually realized as an artwork twice in the past century: once by Gertrude Stein who, in 1930, wrote a one-sentence poem that simply went "Five words in a line" and by Joseph Kosuth who, in 1965, realized the Stein piece in red neon by writing in capital letters FIVE WORDS IN RED NEON, of course, in red neon. Stein and Kosuth make it seem so easy. With gestures like these, one wonders how anyone could still suffer writer's block.

And yet, the poet Kwame Dawes tells us that "on NPR a few years ago Derek Walcott confessed to feeling terror at the blank page— the terror of someone wondering whether he can do it again, whether he can make a successful poem again. The interviewer laughed with some disbelief remarking that even the great Nobel laureate could feel such terror. Walcott insisted, 'Anyone [meaning any poet] who tells you otherwise is lying.'"2

I'm not so sure about that. This sort of writer's block is something you don't hear too much about in the contemporary art world. While some might get stuck—those clinging to older ideas of "originality"—there's a well-honed tradition of adopting mechanical, process-based methods that help make the decisions. Beginning with Duchamp, who used the world as his art supply store: if you come up with a good recipe, add the right ingredients and follow the directions and you're bound to come up with a good artwork. Particularly in the 1960s, scores of artists swapped perspiration for procedure, thus expiating the struggle to create. I'm reminded of the sculptor Jonathan Borofsky running out of juice in graduate school in the mid-1960s. Sitting alone in his Yale studio, he simply began counting, and kept counting for weeks, until the numbers moved from his mind to his mouth to the page and from there into three dimensions, until insane figurative worlds grew out of this practice.

The implications for writing are profound: imagine writers adopting these ways of working so that they'd never have writer's block again. That's what Sol LeWitt did when he wrote "Paragraphs on Conceptual Art" (1967) and "Sentences on Conceptual Art" (1969), which are remarkable manifestos that spoke for a generation more interested in ideas than in objects. The ideas are so good that, once he embraced them, he never looked back; by virtue of a rigorous series of self-imposed constraints, his subsequent production blossomed in every fruitful direction for decades. Never again did LeWitt suffer any sort of blocks. If we look closely at his thinking and methodology, we'll find a model for uncreative writing all the way through, from its inception to execution, right up it to its distribution and reception. By swapping LeWitt's visual concerns for literary ones, we can adopt "Paragraphs" and "Sentences" as roadmaps and guidebooks for conceptual or uncreative writing.

In these documents LeWitt calls for a recipe-based art. Like shopping for ingredients and then cooking a meal, he says that all the decisions for making an artwork should be made beforehand and that the actual execution of the work is merely a matter of duty, an action that shouldn't require too much thought, improvisation, or even genuine feeling. He felt that art shouldn't be based on skill: anyone can realize the work. In fact, throughout his career, LeWitt never made his work himself; instead he hired teams of draftsmen and fabricators to execute his works, a gesture that goes back to the Renaissance painters' workshops and their schools of disciples. He got the idea while working in an architect's office, when it dawned on him that "an architect doesn't go off with a shovel and dig his foundation and lay every brick";[3] he conceived the idea and contracted it out to others to realize.

In this way he's close to Marcel Duchamp, who claimed to have given up making art to become a *respirator*. Duchamp said, "I like living, breathing, better than working . . . if you wish, my art would be that of living: each second, each breath is a work which is inscribed nowhere, which is neither visual nor cerebral. It's a sort of constant euphoria."[4] (But of course Duchamp never gave up making art; he just worked for decades in secrecy. And it's this sort of contradiction between what is claimed and what actually happens that really ties LeWitt to Duchamp, as we'll see later.) Imagine writers feigning silence or having others write their books for them the way Andy Warhol did.

I'm intrigued by the idea that writing need not be based on skill, understood in the conventional sense. John Cage, famous for his works based on chance via a throw of the dice, I Ching, or randomizing computer programs, was often asked why he did what he did. Couldn't anyone do the same? Cage's response was, "yes, but nobody did." What if we followed LeWitt's lead and devised the recipe as an open invitation for anyone to realize the work? I could take any one of my books—say, *Day*—and devise a recipe: "Retype a day's edition of the *New York Times* from beginning to end, working your way across the page, left to right. Retype every letter in the paper, making no distinction between editorial or advertising." Surely your choices—the way you make your way through the paper, how you choose to break your lines, etc.—will be different than mine, making for a completely different work.

LeWitt echoed Duchamp's claim that art need not be exclusively retinal and goes further by stating that a work of art should be made with the minimum of decisions, choices, and whimsy. It's better, LeWitt suggests, if the artist makes deliberately *uninteresting* choices so that a viewer won't lose sight of the concepts behind the work, a sentiment close to the ideas of uncreative writing. And, sometimes, the final product shouldn't be judged as the artwork; instead, all the background documentation of how the work was conceived and executed might prove to be more interesting than the art itself. Gather up that documentation and present it instead of what you thought was going to be the artwork. LeWitt begs the artist to stop worrying about trying to be original and clever all the time, saying that aesthetic decisions can be resolved mathematically and rationally. If you're in a bind, just space everything equidistant, which, like dance music, gives the work a predetermined, hypnotic beat. You can't lose. Finally, he warns us: don't get blinded by new materials and technology, for new materials do not necessarily make for new ideas, something that is still a pitfall for artists and writers in our technologically infatuated age.

Now, there are some problems with the stated intent of LeWitt and the gorgeous results that are the hallmark of his career. When I look at Lewitt's wall drawing, regardless of how conceptually based it might be, to me it's about the most eye-poppingly beautiful artwork ever made. How can such a sterile rhetoric and process produce such sensual and perfect results? When LeWitt claimed that the resultant work of art may be unappealing, he certainly couldn't have been referring to the fruits of his own practice. So something is happening here that makes me wonder if LeWitt is pulling our leg. As far as I can see, he's a singular genius with an exquisitely refined sense of the visual, a perfectionist who would stand for nothing less than finely honed, crafted products that give a maximal bang for the buck, intellectually, visually, and emotionally.

Perhaps we can find some clues to this discrepancy if we take a closer look at how these works were actually made. First off, all LeWitt's works are dictated by short single recipes.

Here's one from 1969:

On a wall, using a hard pencil, parallel lines about 1/8″ apart and 12″ long are drawn for one minute. Under this row of lines, another row of lines are drawn for ten minutes. Under this row of lines another row of lines are drawn for one hour.[5]

and another from 1970:

On a wall (smooth and white if possible) a draftsman draws 500 yellow, 500 gray, 500 red and 500 blue lines, within an area of 1 square meter. All lines must be between 10 cm. and 20 cm. long.[6]

Lewitt himself never executed these pieces; he conceived them and then had someone else realize them. Now, why would a conceptual artist need to realize anything, particularly one who had an aversion to the retinal? Isn't he contradicting himself when he states, "The conceptual artist would want to ameliorate this emphasis on materiality as much as possible or to use it in a paradoxical way (to convert it into an idea)"? [7] Why not just present them as ideas like Yoko Ono:

TIME PAINTING

Make a painting in which the color
comes out only under a certain light
at a certain time of the day.
Make it a very short time.

1961 summer[8]

We have no evidence that Ono's time painting was ever executed. And, if it was, the variables for success are elusive, nonspecific, and subjective. It's not entirely clear where this piece should be performed. One might assume that, since she's referring to a "certain time of day," then it's to be done outdoors. Assuming that's true, how are we to know which "certain light" she is referring, since light over the course of the day changes infinitely? How do we know what time is a "certain time?" And, furthermore, what does a "very short time" mean: one second? five minutes? short in relation to what? the course of day? a lifetime? Conversely, if we attempt to make the painting indoors, what type of light is the "certain light"? incandescent? fluorescent? candlelight? blacklight? And, finally, if we are somehow able to get all the coordinates right, how are we to know if we got the right color? There are mystical implications here as well: if we can somehow figure out how to line up all the coordinates— like Indiana Jones does in order to move a rock that's sealing a hidden cave—we, too, might be rewarded with a similarly cosmic vision.

LeWitt agrees with Ono. Art should exist exclusively in the mind. He states: "Ideas can be works of art; they are in a chain of development that may eventually find some form. All ideas need not be made physical."[9] Yet he insists that they may eventually be realized, a claim that Ono never makes, as she never specifies whether her work is literature, conceptual art, a recipe or visual art, or if it needs to be realized or remain as a concept. Conversely, over the course of his career, LeWitt becomes famous for enacting his own instructions, making them highly visible, explicitly stating that "the plan exists as an idea but needs to be put into its optimum form. Ideas of wall drawings alone are contradictions of the idea of wall drawings."[10] Contradiction is a state that LeWitt, for all his posturing and hyperbole, seems to embrace. His "Sentences on Conceptual Art" begins with the new age statement "Conceptual artists are mystics rather than rationalists. They leap to conclusions that logic cannot reach"[11] and makes Mad Hatter-like pronouncements, such as "Irrational thoughts should be followed absolutely and logically."

His instructions, too, could be just as vague and elusive as Ono's. Take, for example, this recipe for his 1971 wall drawing, which was executed at the Guggenheim Museum:

> Lines, not short, not straight, crossing and touching, drawn at random, using four colors (yellow, black, red and blue), uniformly dispersed with maximum density covering the entire surface of the wall.[12]

Someone had to interpret and execute this drawing, and I'm glad it wasn't me. What does "not short" and "not straight" mean? And what does "random" mean? A few summers ago, when I was redoing a bathroom, I told the contractor that I wanted the colors of the tiles to be random. I figured that he'd place them about, willy-nilly, making them appear random. Each night when I came home from work, I'd pop my head into the bathroom and wonder why the work was proceeding so slowly. The next day, when I stopped in during lunchtime to find out, I saw Joe sitting there, rolling a dye to ensure that, in fact, each tile was put in completely randomly.

Other questions: how is "maximum density" achieved? I might interpret that to mean that not one speck of the white wall should be seen by the time the piece is finished. This seems to me like an awful lot of work, and, combined with having to make it random, I could spend the rest of my life doing this.

And then, let's say I spent ten years doing it the way I thought it should be done, what if it wasn't "successful?" What if LeWitt wasn't pleased with my work? What if my "not short" lines were too long and my "not straight lines" were too wavy? In some Sisyphean nightmare, would he make me start all over again?

Fortunately we have documentation from a draftsman named David Schulman who took notes during the time he executed the aforementioned 1971 Guggenheim piece:

[Lines, not short, not straight, crossing and touching, drawn at random, using four colors (yellow, black, red and blue), uniformly dispersed with maximum density covering the entire surface of the wall.]

Started Jan. 26, having no idea how long it would take to reach a point of maximum density (a very ambiguous point at that). Being paid $3.00 per hour, trying to let my financial needs have little effect on the amount of time I worked. . . . I was exhausted after 3 days of working without the slightest intimation of density. Having only one mechanical pencil, even the energy expended changing leads had an accumulative tiring effect. . . . I pushed to get the lines down faster while keeping them as not short as not straight and as crossing, touching and random as possible. I decided to use one color at a time, and use that color until it reached a point I considered one quarter "Maximum Density." . . . Signals of discomfort became an unconscious time clock determining when I would stop and step back from the drawing. Walking up the ramp to look at the drawing from a distance provided momentary relief from the physical strain of the drawing. From a distance, each color had a swarming effect as it slowly worked its way across a portion of the wall. . . . The drawing in ways was paradoxical. The even density and disbursement of the lines took on a very systematic effect. Once the individual difficulties of each color were determined, any thought as to how the lines were going down in relation to lines previously drawn gradually diminished until there was no conscious thought given to the lines being drawn. Doing the drawing I realized that totally relaxing my body was only one way of reaching a deep level of concentration. Another was in the mindless activity of doing the drawing. Keeping my body totally active in an almost involuntary way—in a sense, totally relaxed my mind. When my mind became relaxed, thoughts would flow at a smoother and faster pace.[13]

While Schulman gives us some answers, his take is also foggy. He doesn't know what density means either and he's very vague about what "not short," "not straight" means or what exactly "random" is. And, by the end of it, he's no longer talking about making a work of art; he's rambling on about mind/body splits. The whole thing starts to feel oddly spiritual, more like yoga than conceptual art.

It's curious how the work begins to make itself, answering Schulman's questions, by following its own orders and rules. LeWitt had prescribed—almost predicted—this state when he said "The draftsman and the wall enter a dialogue. The draftsman becomes bored but later through this meaningless activity finds peace or misery."[14] How could he possibly know? At this point, he's getting very close to the mystical speculations of Ono.

John Cage, who took an explicitly mystical Zen Buddhist attitude toward his work, said something similar: "If something is boring after two minutes, try it for four. If still boring, then eight. Then sixteen. Then thirty-two. Eventually one discovers that it is not boring at all,"[15] which was something Cage said to soothe baffled musicians who were hired to play his music. In a way, a contract musician is similar to a fabricator like David Schulman, an anonymous crafts-man who is paid to execute works of art in the service of someone else's name. Unlike a novelist who, with the exception of an editor, labors in a state of solitary creation, music played by orchestras, bands, live performances, etc. and sometimes visual art—as in the case of LeWitt—is an enactment of a social contract. If the laborer feels he is being mistreated, he can subvert the success of the art, which is what frequently happened to Cage.

There are many stories of John Cage storming out of rehearsal sessions in anger after contract musicians of orchestras refused to take his music seriously. Cage, like LeWitt, gave musicians a lot of leeway with his scores, providing only vague instructions, but was often frus-trated with the results. In the middle of an abstract chance opera-tions piece, for instance, a trombonist would slip in a few notes from "Camptown Races," angering Cage no end. Speaking about an inci-dent in New York, he said, "Faced with music such as I had given them, they simply sabotaged it. The New York Philharmonic is a bad orchestra. They're like a group of gangsters. They have no shame—when I came off the stage after one of those performances, one of them who had played badly shook my hand and said, 'Come back in ten years; we'll treat you better.' They turn things away from music, and from any professional attitude toward music, to some kind of a social situation that is not very beautiful."[16]

For Cage, music was a place to practice a utopian politics: An orchestra—a social unit which he felt to be as regulated and con-trolled as the military—could each be given the freedom *not* to act as a unit, instead permitting each member to be an individual within a social body. By undermining the structure of the orchestra—one of the most established and codified institutions in Western culture—he felt that, in theory, the whole of Western culture could work within a system that he termed "cheerful anarchy." Cage said, "The reason we know we could have nonviolent social change is because we have nonviolent art change."[17]

LeWitt took pains to avoid the awkward situations Cage faced with established orchestras. (He was working with a smaller group of craftsmen as opposed to Cage, who was sometimes dealing with a 120-piece orchestra. Also, the draftsmen, some whom he trained, were generally sympathetic to the project and shared the expectation that they would train others, who would, in turn, train—Renaissance workshop style—still others, stretching on through generations.)[18] To this end, in 1971, the same year that Schulman worked on the Guggenheim piece, LeWitt wrote a detailed contract to clear up any ambiguity regarding the social and professional relationship between artist and draftsman, allowing the latter a great deal of freedom:

> The artist conceives and plans the wall drawing. It is realized by draftsmen. (The artist can act as his own draftsman.) The plan written, spoken or a drawing, is interpreted by the draftsman.
>
> There are decisions which the draftsman makes, within the plan, as part of the plan. Each individual, being unique, given the same instructions would carry them out differently. He would understand them differently.
>
> The artist must allow various interpretations of his plan. The draftsman perceives the artist's plan, the reorders it to his own experience and understanding.
>
> The draftsman's contributions are unforeseen by the artist, even if he, the artist, is the draftsman. Even if the same draftsman followed the same plan twice, there would be two different works of art. No one can do the same thing twice.
>
> The artist and the draftsman are collaborators in making the art.
>
> Each person draws a line differently and each person understands the words differently.
>
> Neither lines nor words are ideas. They are the means by which ideas are conveyed.
>
> The wall drawing is the artist's art, as long as the plan is not violated. If it is, then the draftsman becomes the artist and the drawing would be his work of art, but art that is a parody of the original concept.
>
> The draftsman may make errors in following the plan without compromising the plan. All wall drawings contain errors. They are part of the work.[19]

Yet although LeWitt claimed that the artist and draftsman are collaborators, all of his collaborators went—and continue to go—

unnamed, as compared with the very generous method of Scottish concrete poet and sculptor Ian Hamilton Finlay who never released a work of art without the fabricator's name given in the title of the work: *A Rock Rose (with Richard Demarco)* or *Kite Estuary Mode (with Ian Gardner)*.

LeWitt held a remarkably lax and forward-looking concept of copyright, permitting, up until the mid-eighties, anyone to freely copy his works as long as they strictly adhered to the recipe, something he viewed as a compliment. In this way, he presages the 2006 sentiments of the science fiction writer Cory Doctorow, who makes his books freely available on the Internet as well as in print. Doctorow says: "Being well-enough known to be pirated is a crowning achievement. I'd rather stake my future on a literature that people care about enough to steal than devote my life to a form that has no home in the dominant medium of the century."[20] Unlike digital material, which can be replicated infinitely without any quality loss, LeWitt eventually reneged on his stance due to the sheer number of *bad* copies that unskilled draftsmen made, in spite of his utopian notion that "anyone with a pencil, a hand, and clear verbal directions" could make copies of his drawings.[21] By doing this, LeWitt reminds us of just how difficult it is to make good conceptual art; for him, the solution was to strike a delicate balance between keen thought and precise execution. For other artists, the mix might be different.

He put his foot down and turned the tide: the later works became better. There is evidence that, as time has gone on, "the quality of the LeWitt drawings have improved as many of LeWitt's draftsmen have specialized in particular techniques, becoming 'samurai warriors' in their crafts. A LeWitt skillfully executed today dwarfs the quality of what the artist himself regularly produced."[22] In the early eighties LeWitt left New York and moved to Italy. While there, living among Italian Renaissance frescos, his work went through enormous changes: suddenly it became wildly sensual, organic, and playful. Gone were the austere lines and measurements and in its place came colorful and whimsical works that seemed to owe more to the 1970s pattern and decoration movement than it did to recipe-based procedural conceptual art. Yet these works were created through methods identical to the early works, it's just that he swapped out different ingredients. So while the early works might only permit the four primary colors, adhering to strict geometry, the new works could be psychedelic with day-glo apple greens alternating with fluorescent oranges in wavy patterns. Oftentimes, they were garish in taste, looking out of place in the white box of a museum. "When he was asked about the switch he made in the 1980's—adding ink washes, which permitted him new colors, along with curves and free forms— Mr. LeWitt responded, 'Why not?' "[23]

To the untrained eye, these works were a complete betrayal of everything he had stood for up until that point. They seemed whimsical and overtly retinal, lacking any kind of formal rigor. But, upon closer examination, they were as recipe based as ever. These pieces from 1998, have the instructions:

Wall Drawing 853: A wall bordered and divided vertically into two parts by a flat black band. Left party: a square is divided vertically by a curvy line. Left: glossy red; right: glossy green; Right part: a square is divided horizontally by a curvy line. Top: glossy blue; bottom: glossy orange.

Wall Drawing 852: A wall divided from the upper left to the lower right by a curvy line; left: glossy yellow; right: glossy purple.

But that, to me, is the beauty of it all. These are works that, no matter what you did to them, really could not fail. All done exactly to plan, they were executed perfectly and were therefore successful regardless of how un-LeWittian they may appear to the eye.

There's a lot to take away from LeWitt: the idea of authorless art, the socially enlightened dance between the author and the fabricator, the debunking of the romantic impulse, the usefulness of well-spun rhetoric and precise logic—not to mention the freedom that it brings, the elegance of primary form and structure, overcoming the fear of the white page, the triumph of good taste, the embrace of contradiction. But there's one thing above all the others that stands out. We're always bending over backward trying to express ourselves, yet LeWitt makes us realize how impossible it is *not* to express ourselves. Perhaps writers try too hard, hitting huge impasses by always trying to say something original, new, important, profound. LeWitt offers us ways out of our jams. By constructing the perfect machine and setting it in motion, the works creates itself. And the results will reflect the quality of the machine: build a poorly conceived and executed machine, you'll get poor results; build an airtight, well-crafted, deeply considered machine and the results can't help but be good. LeWitt wants us to invert our conventional idea of art, which is often focused exclusively on the end result; in so doing so he inverts conventional notions of genius as well, showing us the potential and power of "unoriginal genius."

Andy Warhol is perhaps the single most important figure for uncreative writing. Warhol's entire oeuvre was based on the idea of uncreativity: the seemingly effortless production of mechanical paintings and unwatchable films where literally nothing happens. In terms of literary output, too, Warhol pushed the envelope by having other people write his books for him, yet the covers bore his name as author. He invented new genres of literature: *a: a novel* was the mere transcription of dozens of cassette tapes, spelling errors, stumbles, and stutters left exactly as they were mistyped. His *Diaries*, an enormous tome, were spoken over the phone to an assistant and transcribed, charting the minute, yet mostly mundane, movements of one person's life. In Perloffian terms, Andy Warhol was an unoriginal genius, one who was able to create a profoundly original body of work by isolating, reframing, recycling, regurgitating, and endlessly reproducing ideas and images that weren't his, yet, by the time he was finished with them, they were completely Warholian. By mastering the manipulation of information (the media, his own image, or his superstar coterie, to name a few), Warhol understood that he could master culture. Warhol reminds us that to be the originator of something widely *memed* can match being the originator of the trigger event. These *regestures*—such as reblogging and retweeting—have become cultural rites of cachet in and of themselves. Sorting and filtering—moving information—has become a site of cultural capital. Filtering is taste. And good taste rules the day: Warhol's exquisite sensibility, combined with his finely tuned taste, challenged the locus of artistic production from creator to mediator.

In a 1966 television interview, Warhol reluctantly answered questions fired at him by an aggressive and skeptical offscreen interlocutor. In the interview, a tight-lipped Warhol sat on a stool in front of a silver Elvis painting. The camera frequently zoomed in on Warhol's face, framed by a broken pair of dark sunglasses; his fingers cover his lips, causing him to mumble hesitant and barely audible responses:

> WARHOL: I mean, you should just tell me the words and I can just repeat them because I can't, uh. . . . I can't . . . I'm so empty today. I can't think of anything. Why don't you just tell me the words and they'll just come out of my mouth.
>
> Q: No, don't worry about it because . . .
>
> WARHOL: . . . no, no . . . I think it would be so nice.
>
> Q: You'll loosen up after a while.
>
> WARHOL: Well, no. It's not that. It's just that I can't, ummm . . . I have a cold and I can't, uh, think of anything. It would be so nice if you told me a sentence and I just could repeat it.
>
> Q: Well, let me just ask you a question you could answer . . .
>
> WARHOL: No, no. But you repeat the answers too.[24]

A few years earlier, in a 1963 interview, Warhol asks, "But why should I be original? Why can't I be nonoriginal?" He sees no need to create anything new: "I just like to see things used and reused." Echoing then-current notions of eradicating the division between art and life, he says, "I just happen to like ordinary things. When I paint them, I don't try to make them extraordinary. I just try to paint them ordinary-ordinary. . . . That's why I've had to resort to silk screens, stencils and other kinds of automatic reproduction. And still the human element creeps in! . . . I'm antismudge. It's too human. I'm for mechanical art . . . If somebody faked my art, I couldn't identify it."

Warhol himself was a series of contradictions: he could barely speak, but what he did say became cultural truisms; he was low (the most commercial) and high (creating some of the most difficult and challenging art of the twentieth century), kind and cruel, profane yet religious (Warhol attended church every Sunday), a seemingly dull man who surrounded himself with exciting men and women. The list could go on forever.

His artwork embodies some of the same tensions as Vanessa Place's writing regarding ethics and morality: what happens when one's artistic practice is programmatically predicated upon deceit, dishonesty, lying, fraudulence, impersonation, identity theft, plagiarism, market manipulation, psychological warfare, and consensual abuse? When humanism is tossed out the window and the machine is prioritized over flesh and bone? When a practice adamantly denies emotion, promoting style over substance, vapidity over genius, mechanical process over touch, boredom over entertainment, surface over depth? When art is made with alienation as a goal, art that intentionally disconnects from what we normally ascribe to as having cultural and social value?

Warhol embraced a flexible morality, one that is almost impossible for most of us to conceive of in either theory or in practice. He spent his career testing these moral waters in his art and in his life where the consequences were often devastating. In Warhol's world there were no happy endings; the ride was fast and glamorous, but there was always doom ahead. With the notable exception of Lou Reed, few Factory denizens went on to a substantial life or career outside of the moment. For several the results were deadly. Wayne Koestenbaum, in his biography of Warhol, comments that "many of the people I've interviewed, who knew or worked with Warhol, seemed damaged or traumatized by the experience. Or so I surmise: they might have been damaged before Warhol got to them. But he had a way of casting light on the ruin—a way of making it spectacular, visible, audible. He didn't consciously harm people, but his presence became the proscenium for traumatic theater."[25] Warhol set the stage for people to systematically and publicly destroy themselves, convincing these somewhat lost young people that they were "superstars," making films of them being themselves (talking, taking drugs, having sex) and taking them to parties around town, when, at the end of the day, it was Warhol's name and career that benefited from their illusions. After Warhol was shot, the door to the once-open Factory was shut, and many former superstars were no longer part of clique. For his behavior, Warhol earned the moniker Drella—a mixture of Dracula and Cinderella—because of his powers to both give and take.

This is an often-told side of Warhol, the train wreck narrative with which we are all familiar. But there is another way to look at it. I'd like to propose that we use his example of ambiguity and contradiction as a utopian experiment in artistic practices as a way of testing the limits of morality and ethics in a positive sense. If we are able to separate the man from the work, we may see that in this series of negative dialectics Warhol was actually proposing a free space of play within the safe confines of art. Art as a free space to say "what if . . . ?" Art as one of the only spaces available in our culture that would allow such experiments.

We're back in contradictory territory again: how can we separate Warhol's life from his art or any artists' lives from their art for that matter? To answer that question, I think we need to invoke a bit of theory in order to connect the dots, using Roland Barthes's seminal essay, "The Death of the Author." In it he made a distinction between literature and autobiography, saying that, for instance, "if we were to discover, after admiring a series of books extolling courage and moral fidelity, that the man who wrote them was a coward and a lecher, this would not have the slightest effect on their literary quality. We might regret this insincerity, but we should not be able to withhold or admiration for his skill as writer."[26] Barthes referred to the idea of an authorless work as *text* rather than *literature*.

The Barthesian premise was demonstrated most powerfully in the vast body of literary works that Warhol produced. Take, for example, *The Andy Warhol Diaries,* which spent four months on the *New York Times* best-seller list. In some ways, it's hard to imagine a less engaging narrative: more than eight hundred pages of Andy's diary entries recording every cent spent on taxis and documenting each phone call he made. The idea of autobiography falsely permeates the book: on the book's front cover, the *Boston Globe* exclaims, "The ultimate self-portrait." The book's accumulation of minute and insignificant detail resembles Boswell's *Life of Johnson,* except for the fact that it's presented as an autobiography. Take the entry from Monday, August 2, 1982:

> Mark Ginsburg was bringing Indira Gandhi's daughter down and
> he was calling and Ina was calling and Bob was calling saying how

important this was, so I gave up my exercise class and it turned out just to be the daughter-in-law, who's Italian, she doesn't even look Indian.

Went to 25 East 39th Street to Michaele Vollbracht's (cab $4.50) Ran into Mary McFadden on the way in and I told her she looked beautiful with no makeup and she said she'd never worn more. I told her that in that case, as one made-up person to another, it looked like she didn't have any on. Giorgio Sant'Angelo was there. The food looked really chic but I didn't have any.

Went to Diane Von Furstenberg's party for the launching of her new cosmetics (cab $4). and all the boys at the party were the same ones who had been on Fire Island. It was fun seeing Diane, she was hustling perfume. Her clothes are so ugly though, they're like plastic or something. And she had all the high-fashion girls there wearing them. Barbara Allen was there and even she looked awful in the clothes. I did get an idea for decorating though—big boxes of color that you can put in a room and move around and change your decorating scheme.[27]

What a life! Warhol's workout is canceled so he can meet with influential public figures. Then it's off to meet Vollbracht—a designer for Geoffrey Beene—where he runs into a fashion editor and hangs out with yet another fashion designer. Next is a party for, yes, another fashion designer, this one replete with fabulous gay boys from Fire Island and beautiful models. He snubs rich people and gets inspired by interior design.

Is this really autobiography? No. It's a highly edited work of fantasy fiction based on Warhol's life. Where is the author? It was Warhol who dictated and shaped his unreal image; no trips to the grocery store or the dry cleaners, no traffic jams, no self-reflection, no doubt, no friction. Warhol, as he portrayed his life, was one whirl of glamour. But when everything is glamorous, nothing is. This is a specifically Warholian glamour: it's flat and featureless, with one person and experience interchangeable with another. The characters and settings are disposable: what's important is the wow factor. It's unabashedly autobiography as fiction, which, of course, all autobiographies are. Warhol meticulously reported the edited version of his life every morning for the last twelve years of his life, calling his secretary/ ghost writer Pat Hackett and telling her what happened the day before. The daily phone calls began innocently enough as a log of Andy's personal expenses for keeping the IRS at bay, but soon developed into a full-blown record of his life. Hackett acted as gatekeeper and editor for the book, becoming as much of an author and shaper of Warhol's life as Boswell was for Johnson. In fact, she boiled the book down from the original manuscript of twenty thousand pages, choosing what she felt to be "the best material and most representative of Andy."[28] Hackett ruthlessly edited the material: "On a day when Andy went to five parties, I may have included only a single one. I applied the same editing principle to names to give the diary a narrative flow and to keep it from reading like the social columns. . . . I've cut many names. If Andy mentioned, say, ten people, I may have chosen to include only the three he had conversations with or spoke of in the most detail. Such omissions are not noted in the text since the effect would serve only to distract, and slow the reader down."[29]

But isn't the reader slowed down enough? Hackett is mistaken to think that anybody would actually "read" the *Diaries* straight through. The way to ingest the work is to skim it, and even that, after a while, becomes exhausting because of the sheer amount of trivial data. In fact, to lift the onus of having to read the book at all, later editions included an index of names and places to make *ego surfing* easier for those in the club—and to make those with their noses pressed up against the window envious. It was a book not to *read* but to reference. Warhol would have been delighted by this. He claimed, "I don't read much about myself, anyway, I just look at the pictures in the articles, it doesn't matter what they say about me; I just read the textures of the words."[30]

Warhol, a man who claimed not to read, naturally published what is largely considered to be an unreadable book, *a: A Novel.* Yet, as a work of literature, it has all the marks of a Warhol: mechanical processes, off-register marks (spelling errors) and a good deal of modernist difficulty and attention to quotidian detail. If there is a story, it's so buried in literal transcription and typographical inconsistency that the signal-to-noise ratio makes a conventional reading nearly impossible, which, of course, was Warhol's intention. Warhol

conquered the experimental film world in the early sixties by a similar tactic. The prevalent trend was the quick edit and jump cut, but
Warhol did the opposite: he plunked the camera on a tripod and let
it run . . . and run. . . . and run . . . There were no edits, no pans.
When asked about the slowness of his films, he said that he was not
interested in moving forward but moving backward to the very beginning of filmmaking when the camera was fixed to a tripod, cap-
turing whatever happened to be in front of it. If you've seen his
3-minute screen tests, where the camera is fixed on a face, you can't
but be persuaded by Warhol's point of view: they're among the most
striking and gorgeous portraits ever made. *Sleep*, six hours of a man
sleeping and *Empire*, a still, eight-hour shot of the Empire State
Building, are incredible time-based portraits. Although Warhol's
early films often consisted of one durational image, and his novel
was more like a series of quick jump cuts, the effect on the viewer
and the reader was intentionally one and the same: boredom and
restlessness leading to distraction and introspection. The lack of narrative permits the mind to wander away from the artwork, which
was Warhol's way of moving the viewer away from art and into life.

a purported to be a twenty-four-hour tape-recorded portrait of
Factory superstar Ondine, but turned out to be a mix of over one
hundred characters recorded over a two-year period. Each section of
the book has a different typographical layout as a result of the idiosyncrasies of the various typists that worked on the tapes. Warhol
decided to leave these as they were given to him as well as maintaining all misspellings. What *a* ends up as is approaching the idea of a
literary *vérité* that is a multiauthored text, riddled with the formal
subjectivity of several transcribers, radically questioning the notions
of singular authorial genius. As in all of Warhol's production, his
role was that of conceptualist or, as he saw it, factory boss, making
sure that his legions executed his concepts with enough latitude to
make it feel like they had some stake in it, when in actuality they
had none.

His other books, *The Philosophy of Andy Warhol, POPism, America,* and *Exposures,* were written by his assistants, who channeled the
voice of Andy Warhol. Their voice became his public voice, wheras
Warhol largely remained silent. Those famous Warholian sound

bites you hear—famous for fifteen minutes, etc.—often weren't written by him.

While mid-century modernism dipped a toe into what William Carlos Williams called "the speech of Polish mothers," the actual speech of Polish mothers was too ugly, too unrefined for much of the poetry world. Frank O'Hara, father of the "talk" poem, approached in his late works what Marjorie Perloff calls "the vagaries of every-day conversation":[31]

> "thank you for the dark and the shoulders"
> "oh   thank you"
>
> okay I'll meet you at the weather station at 5
> we'll take a helicopter into the "eye" of the storm
> we'll be so happy in the center of things at last
> now the wind rushes up nothing happens and departs[32]

O'Hara's late work, "Biotherm (for Bill Berkson)," written in 1961, takes great pains to spice up ordinary speech with poetic conventions, such as including blank space between "oh" and "thank you" to connote the passing of time. The phrasing, too, can seem precious: note the quotation marks around the word *eye*. Far from a benign weather report, the "eye" becomes a metaphor for finding a calm place faraway from the troubles of banal life. While O'Hara dabbles with "the vagaries of everyday conversation," I wonder how everyday they really are. A mere five years later, *a* blasts apart O'Hara's claims to speech-based realism by publishing nearly five hundred pages of *real speech*.[33] As a result, *a* is as ugly (uncomposed) and difficult (barely narrative) as is our normal speech. Take, for example, this passage from *a:*

> O—I gave him amphetamine, I gave him amphetamine one night, when when D—Recently? . . . O—I first met him. D—No no, a long time ago. O—and he was a frightening poetry D—Yeah. O-He wrote poetry, he wrote poetry D—It scared him very much. O—It scared him, . . . D—He's been on LSDand uh, pills and uh every

O—Baby, it doesn't matter. D—It doesn't matter, well well- O— Why why why don't yo have to take pills D—Huh? O—Wht don't you have to t-t-t-ake drugs? Why isn't it a necessity for you to take drugs? D—Oh. O—Why, because you D—Well, no, I O—You're as high as you are . . . Hello? WhO's caluing? Buchess oh, Duchess lover, it's Ondine.[34]

Unlike O'Hara, the words are all jammed together in one undifferentiated string or worse: due to a typist's error, which Warhol intentionally left in, we get the odd compound "LSDand" followed by an ordinary "uh." And as far as precious metaphorical moments, they're nowhere to be found. Indeed, this is truly a demonstration of "the vagaries of everyday conversation." Warhol took modernism's interest in natural speech to its logical conclusion, emphasizing, that blather, in its untouched state, is just as disjunctive as other fragmentary modernist strategies.

Warhol's interest in "real speech" didn't exist in a vacuum. Surrounding Warhol was an entire cult of people constantly engaged in translating ephemeral speech into text. In *POPism*, Warhol's sixties memoir, he says:

Everyone, absolutely everyone, was tape-recording everyone else. Machinery had already taken over people's sex lives—dildos and all kinds of vibrators—and now it was taking over their social lives, too, with tape recorders and Polaroids. The running joke between Brigid and me was that all our phone calls started with whoever'd been called by the other saying, "Hello, wait a minute," and running to plug in and hook up. . . . I'd provoke any kind of hysteria I could think of on the phone just to get myself a good tape. Since I wasn't going out much and was home a lot on the mornings and evenings, I put in a lot of time on the phone gossiping and making trouble and getting ideas from people and trying to figure out what was happening—and taping it all.

The trouble was, it took so long to get a tape transcribed, even when you had somebody working at it full-time. In those days even the typists were making their own tapes—as I said everybody was into it.[35]

At the Warhol Museum in Pittsburgh, while researching my book of Warhol interviews, the archivist rolled out a cart with enormous stacks of paper on it. He told me that these were the complete transcriptions of Warhol's tapes over the years. Apparently, each night out on the town, Warhol would take his tape recorder (which he referred to as his "wife") and let the machine roll for the duration of the evening. People eventually became so used to its presence that they ignored it and went on speaking without any self-consciousness at all or else playing to it, knowing they were being captured for posterity by Andy Warhol. The next morning, Warhol would take the previous night's cache of tapes into the Factory, drop them on a desk, and have an assistant transcribe them. Upon seeing these documents—raw, unedited transcriptions of lost, ephemeral conversations that had transpired decades ago between some of the most famous people in the world—I proposed to the archivist that this would make a great next book. He shook his head and said that, due to the threat of libel, the tapes could not be published until 2037, fifty years after Warhol's death.

Also at the museum were Warhol's time capsules, stacked on shelves in the library. For the better part of his career as an artist, Warhol always kept an open cardboard box in his studio into which he threw both the detritus and the gems that drifted through the Factory. Warhol made no distinction as to what was saved—from hamburger wrappers to celebrity-autographed photos; full runs of his magazine *Interview*; even his wigs—it all went in. When the box was full, it was sealed, numbered, and signed by Warhol, each a work of art. After his death, the museum was given the boxes, totaling over eight thousand cubic feet of material. When I visited the museum, I noticed that only a few dozen of the seemingly hundreds of boxes were opened. When I asked why, the curator informed me that, each time a box is opened, every object in that box must be extensively documented and catalogued, photographed and so forth, to the point where opening a single box entailed a month's worth of work for two or three people laboring full time. The implications of not only the act of archiving but the process of decoding—cataloguing, sorting, preserving—makes Warhol's oeuvre particularly prescient for Web-driven literary practices today, where managing the amount of information flooding us takes on literary dimensions (see the introduction).

Warhol's oeuvre, then, should be read as *text* instead of *literature*, echoing Barthes's idea that "the text is a tissue of citations, resulting from the thousand sources of culture,"[36] which is a shorthand defense for the waves of appropriative, "unoriginal," and "uncreative" artworks that would follow after Warhol for decades. It also explains why Warhol could take a newspaper photo of Jackie Kennedy and turn it into an icon. Warhol understood that the "tissue of citations" around the image of Jackie would only accrue over time, growing more complex with each passing historic event or era. He had a keen eye for choosing the right image, the image with the most accumulative potential. His ongoing strategic removal of himself as author let the works live on after all the day's drama was done with. As Barthes says, "Once the Author is gone, the claim to 'decipher' a text becomes quite useless."[37] What on the surface appears to be a web of lies in Warhol's life is actually a smokescreen of purposeful disinformation in order to deflate the figure of the author.

In a 1962 interview, Warhol famously says, "The reason I'm painting this way is that I want to be a machine and I feel that whatever I do and do machine-like is what I want to do."[38] We uncreative writers, infatuated with the digital age and its technologies, take this as our ethos, yet it's only one in a long laundry list of what we find inspiring about Warhol's practice. His use of shifting identities, his embrace of contradiction, his freedom to use words and ideas that aren't his own, his obsessive cataloguing and archiving as artistic end-games, his explorations into unreadability and boredom, and his un-flinching documentary impulse on the most raw and unprocessed aspects of culture are just a few of the reasons why Warhol's oeuvre and attitudes remain so crucial and inspiring to today's writers.

7   RETYPING *ON THE ROAD*

A few years ago I was lecturing to a class at Princeton. After the class, a small group of students came up to me to tell me about a workshop that they were taking with one of the best-known fiction writers in America. They were complaining about her lack of pedagogical imagination, assigning them the types of creative writing exercises they had been doing since junior high school. For example, she had them pick their favorite writer and come in the next week with an "original" work in the style of that author. I asked one of the students which author she chose. She answered Jack Kerouac. She then added that the assignment felt meaningless to her because the night before she tried to "get into Kerouac's head" and scribbled a piece in "his style" to fulfill the assignment: Initially, it occurred to me that for this student to actually write in the style of Kerouac, she would have been better off taking a road trip across the country in a '48 Buick with the convertible roof down, gulping Benzedrine by the fistful, washing them down with bourbon, all the while typing furiously away on a manual typewriter, going eighty-five miles an hour on a ribbon of desert highway. And, even then, it would have been a completely different experience—not to mention a very different piece of writing—than Kerouac's.

My mind then drifted to those aspiring painters who fill up the Metropolitan Museum of Art every day, spending hours learning by copying the Old Masters. If it's good enough for them, why isn't it good enough for us? The power and usefulness of the act of retyping is invoked by Walter Benjamin, a master copyist himself, in the following passage where he extols the virtue of copying, coincidentally invoking the metaphor of the road:

> The power of a country road is different when one is walking along it from when one is flying over it by airplane. In the same way, the power of a text is different when it is read from when it is copied out. The airplane passenger see only how the road pushes through the landscape, how it unfolds according to the same laws as the terrain surrounding it. Only he who walks the road on foot learns of the power it commands. . . . Only the copied text commands the soul of him who is occupied with it, whereas the mere reader never discovers the new aspects of his inner self that are opened by the text, the road cut through the interior jungle forever closing behind it: because the reader follows the movement of his mind in the free flight of daydreaming, whereas the copier submits to its command.[1]

The idea of being able to physically get inside a text through the act of copying is an appealing one for pedagogy: Perhaps if this student retyped a chunk—or, if she was ambitious, the entirety—of *On the Road*, she might have understood Kerouac's style in a way that was bound to stick with her.

After having learned of my proposition about copying, Simon Morris, a British artist, decided to actually retype the original 1951 scroll edition of *On the Road*, one page a day, on a blog called "Getting Inside Kerouac's Head."[2] In his introductory post, he wrote, "It's an amusing anecdote and it occurred to me that it would make an interesting work. It would be interesting to realize this proposition as a work in its own right and in the process to see what I would learn through re-typing Kerouac's prose." And so on May 31, 2008, he began: "I first met Neal not long after my father died . . . " filling up the page with Kerouac's first page and ending the blog entry mid-sentence, corresponding with the printed page of *On the Road*: "which reminded me of my jail problem it is absolutely necessary now to postpone all." The next blog entry published on June 1 picks up mid-sentence from the preceding day: "those leftover things concerning our personal lovethings and at once begin thinking of specific worklife plans." He reached page 408 on March 22, 2009, thereby completing the project.

Morris had never read the book before and as he retyped it, he enjoyed reading the narrative unravel. It took him twenty minutes each day, hunting and pecking, to type the four-hundred-word pages. And, true to my hunch, he's had a relationship to the book far different from the one he'd have if he had merely read it: "I have told several people in an excited manner that 'this is the most thrilling read/ride of my life.' Certainly, I have never paid any single book this much attention and having never read Kerouac's book, the unfolding story is certainly a pleasurable experience—it's a great read. Not only do I type it up, word for word, each day but I then proofread each page, checking for mistakes before posting it on the blog . . . so each page is being re-typed and read several times. . . . But the level of scrutiny that the daily activity has opened up to me in my reading has drawn my attention to certain characteristics in Kerouac's prose which in my normal reading style I'm fairly certain I wouldn't have noticed." Morris echoes Gertrude Stein, who says, "I always say that you cannot tell what a picture really is or what an object really is until you dust it every day and you cannot tell what a book is until you type it or proof-read it. It then does something to you that only reading never can do."[3]

For example, Morris takes note of Kerouac's use of hyphens in the text, which he discovered gives the story its flow, drawing parallels with lines on the highway. He also calculated how many times the title phrase "on the road" is used (24 times in the first 104 pages). Morris muses, "In Kerouac's book, the words 'on the road' are chanted like a mantra and their repetition keeps you moving through the text, along the asphalt from East to West." He's also gained insight into the way in which Kerouac's shorthand allows the reader to complete sentences in their head, which has led Morris to chuck in a few words of his own: "When re-typing the following words by Kerouac: 'The counterman—it was three A.M.—heard us talk about money and offered to give us the hamburgers for free.' I notice I had added the word 'for free' to the end of the sentence and then had to delete my addition. This has happened on more than one occasion. And there is, of course, the possibility that I haven't caught all my additions and have left some extra words imbedded in Kerouac's text." One wonders, then, if this is really a copy or if it in some way couldn't be construed as an entirely different text, one based on the original. Taking it one step further, one could always write a new text simply by tossing words in as one feels the need to, the way Morris inserted "for free."

By so doing, Morris shows us that appropriation need not be a mere passing along of information, but, in fact, moving information can inspire a different sort of creativity in the "author," producing different versions and additions—remixes even—of an existing text. Morris is both reader and writer in the most active sense of the word.

In the 1970s the experimentally inclined language poets proposed a way that the reader could, in fact, become the writer. By atomizing words, across a page, coupled with disrupting normative modes of syntax (putting the words of a sentence in the "wrong" order), they felt that a nonhierarchical linguistic landscape would encourage a reader to reconstruct the text as they saw fit. Fueled by French theorists such as Jacques Derrida, they wanted to demonstrate that the textual field is unstable, comprised of ever-shifting signs and signifiers, thereby unable to be claimed by either author or reader as authoritative. If the reader were able to reconstruct the open text, it would be as (un)stable and as (un)meaningful as the author's. The end result would be a level playing field for all, debunking the twin myths of both the all-powerful author and the passive reader.

I think that Morris would agree with the language poets about the need to challenge this traditional power dynamic, but he's going about it in a completely different way, based in mimesis and replication instead of disjunction and deconstruction. It's about moving information from one place to another completely intact. With very little intervention, the entire reading/writing experience is challenged.

Morris's undertaking puts into play a game of literary telephone, whereby a text is subject to a remix in ways to which we are more accustomed in the musical world. While Kerouac's *On the Road* would remain iconic, dozens of parasitic and paratextual versions could inevitably appear. This is what happened to Elizabeth Alexander's

Obama inaugural poem days after her reading of it, after I asked readers to remix her words.[4] An MP3 of her reading was available on WFMU's "Beware of the Blog," and, within a week, over fifty wildly disparate versions of the poem appeared, each using her words and voice. One remixer cut up each word of Alexander's reading and strung them back together alphabetically. Others looped and twisted her poems, making her say the opposite of what she intended; some set them to music; others recited them verbatim, but in highly unusual voices; a pair of beat-boxing children even took a stab at it. Like Kerouac, Alexander's status remains iconic, but, instead of an all-powerful author intoning to a sea of listeners, an outpouring of artistic responses was created as an active response. The most *uncreative* response was entitled, "I Am a Robot" and was simply an unaltered recording of Alexander reading her poem. Is this anything new? Haven't there always been parodies and remixes, written or spoken, of events large and small? Yes, but never this quickly, democratically, nor this technologically engaged. And the highly mimetic qualities of the many responses—some of which just barely nudged Alexander's words—showed how deeply ideas of reframing have seeped into the way we think; many of these responses didn't aim to be wildly "creative" and "original." Instead, the uncreative and untouched re-presentation of an iconic artifact placed into a new context proved to be creative enough. However, by treating Alexander's text as fodder for remixing, new types of meaning are created with a wide range of expressions: humor, repetition, *détournement*, fear, hope.

Likewise, Morris's retyping would have been a different project altogether before the Web. It's hard to think of a precedent for such an act. Certainly there were untold numbers of bootlegged and pirated editions of books, of which hours and hours were spent exactly retyping preexisting texts (until the advent of the copying machine), as well as medieval scribes and scriveners of all stripes throughout history. But the fluidity of the digital environment has encouraged and incubated these dormant ideas to fruition as creative/uncreative acts. As I stated in the introduction, the computer encourages the author to mimic its workings where cutting and pasting are integral to the writing process.[5]

Morris asks, "If Kerouac were alive today, would he be publishing on paper, or blogging or tweeting his way across America?" Perhaps the answer to that can be found in an interview Jackson Pollock conducted in 1951, responding to a question about his controversial method of painting: "My opinion is that new needs need new techniques. And the modern artists have found new ways and new means of making their statements. It seems to me that the modern painter cannot express this age, the airplane, the atom bomb, the radio, in the old forms of the Renaissance or of any past culture. Each age finds its own technique."[6] For Morris, it's the blog: "I've probably shifted into reverse—the further forwards I progress on his road from East to West, by the nature of blogs, the further backwards 'my' story goes, disjointed, broken up as a daily bulletin." He likened his readers to passengers joining him on the trip.

Traffic for Morris's project—in this context, Web traffic—has been light, in spite of conventional wisdom that claims consistent blogging for hundreds of days in a row will generate interest. For the duration of the project and its afterlife as an artifactual blog, Morris has only had a handful of commenters/passengers, and, curiously, none of them have been Kerouac's estate or his business representatives crying foul play for freely republishing a very lucrative artwork. Morris's work, then, is an anomaly—not a pirated edition worth legally pursing—and, as such, becoming functionless and aestheticized, it can only be a work of art.[7]

A few months after I finished writing this chapter, a package containing two books arrived in my mailbox from England, both sent to me by Simon Morris. One was the official British edition of Jack Kerouac's *On The Road* published by Penguin Modern Classics and the other was a paper edition of Morris's *Getting Inside of Jack Kerouac's Head*. The books look identical: they're the same size, have the same cover design and typography (the black and white Penguin cover photo of Kerouac and Neal Cassady is mimicked by a black and white image of Morris and his pal, the poet Nick Thurston). The spines, too, are identically designed, except for the fact that the Penguin logo has been replaced by the Information As Material logo (the publisher of the new edition); even the back covers are laid out identically with blurbs, photos, and thumbnails of the author's previously published works. Inside, both have front-end biographical material as well as introductory essays. At a glance, they could be taken for identical tomes. But that's where the similarities end.

When you open Morris's book, the famous first line of *On the Road*, "I first met Dean not long after my wife and I split up," is nowhere to be seen. Instead, the first line is a sentence already in progress: "concert tickets, and the names Jack and Joan and Henri and Vicki, the girl, together with a series of sad jokes and some of his favorite saying such as 'You can't teach the old maestro a new tune.'" Of course, the first page of Morris's book is his final blog entry from his marathon retyping, and so, the end of the first page of Morris's book is the ending of Kerouac's scroll, "I think of Neal Cassidy." The book unfolds this way throughout, progressing backward, page by page (Morris's first page is numbered 408, his second is 407, etc.) until he reaches the start of Kerouac's original text.

Having followed Morris's project online, it was jarring to see a blog-driven project reborn as print. While it's normal to see print migrate to digital forms (e-books or PDFs for example), it's rare to encounter Web-native artifacts rendered into dead-tree stock, even more so when you consider that Kerouac's canonized version is best known for its paper versions (the paper scroll, the paperback). The effect of Morris's gesture is like seeing a couture dress that's been mistakenly thrown in the wash with the gym clothes. From paper to Web and back to paper, Kerouac's text is recognizable as itself, but is somehow shrunken, warped, and misshapen. It's the same but very much different; it's Kerouac's masterpiece run backwards in a mirror.

Morris eloquently sums up the project by claiming "there are more differences than similarities which makes it challenging that the same piece of writing, typed up in a different context, is an entirely new piece of writing." Yet, when asked how the retyping makes him feel, Morris hesitates: "One would hope for some truly profound response but really there is none. I don't feel anything at all. A bit like Jack Kerouac's own journey on the road and into himself in search of something he never really finds." And then, haltingly, he asks, "Am I losing myself as I 'uncreatively' type words that have already been typed in one of literature's most celebrated acts of spontaneous prose?" and answers, "All I can really say with any certainty is I've never spent such a long time with a book or thought about any book as much. When you read a book you are often simultaneously inside and outside of the text. But in this case, I have reflected much more on the process of reading than I would normally when I engage with a text. It's not only about hitting the same keys as Kerouac in the same order, give or take a few slippages but it's also about the process of the project." In the end, he doesn't know if he's succeeded in getting inside Kerouac's head, but it's clear that he's succeeded in getting far inside his own head, garnering a great deal of self-awareness as both reader and writer, which, after this experience, he will never be able to take for granted again.

8 PARSING THE NEW ILLEGIBILITY

Earlier, I focused on the enormity of the Internet, the amount of the language it produces, and what impact this has upon writers. In this chapter I'd like to extend that idea and propose that, because of this new environment, a certain type of book is being written that's not meant to be read as much as it's meant to be thought about. I'll give some examples of books that, in their construction, seem to be both mimicking and commenting on our engagement with digital words and, by so doing, propose new strategies for reading—or *not* reading. The Web functions both as a site for reading and writing: for writers it's a vast supply text from which to construct literature; readers function in the same way, hacking a path through the morass of information, ultimately working as much at filtering as reading.

The Internet challenges readers not because of the way it is written (mostly normative expository syntax at the top level) but because of its enormous size.[1] Just as new reading strategies had to be developed in order to read difficult modernist works of literature, so new reading strategies are emerging on the Web: skimming, data aggregating, RSS feeds, to name a few. Our reading habits seem to be imitating the way machines work by grazing dense texts for keywords. We could even say that, online, we *parse* text—a binary process of sorting language—more than we *read* it to comprehend all the information passing before our eyes. And there is an increasing number of texts being written by machines to be read specifically by other machines rather than people, as evidenced by the untold number of spoof pages set up for page views or ad clickthroughs, lexicons of password code cracks, and so forth. While there is still a tremendous amount of human intervention, the future of literature will be increasingly mechanical. Geneticist Susan Blackmore affirms this: "Think of programs that write original poetry or cobble together new student essays, or programs that store information about your shopping preferences and suggest books or clothes you might like next. They may be limited in scope, dependent on human input and send their output to human brains, but they copy, select and recombine the information they handle."[2]

The roots of this reading/not reading dichotomy can be found on paper. There have been many books published that challenged the reader not so much by their content but by their scope. Trying to read Gertrude Stein's *The Making of Americans* linearly is like trying to read the Web linearly. It's mostly possible in small doses, dipped in and out of. At nearly one thousand pages, its heft is intimidating, but the biggest deterrent to reading the book is its scope, having begun small as "a history of a family to being a history of everybody the family knew and then it became the history of every kind and of every individual human being,"[3] thus rendering it a conceptual work, a beautiful proposal that's hard to fulfill. "Ever tried. Ever failed. No matter. Try again. Fail again. Fail better."[4] says Beckett, a sentiment that could easily apply to uncreative writing.

The Making of Americans is one in a long line of impossibly scoped projects. The anonymously penned *My Secret Life*, a twenty-five-hundred-page nonstop Victorian work of pornography is another. No matter how titillating any given page may be—and every single page is—there's no way of ingesting it straight through. It's a concept as much as anything, a mad work of language to counter the moral repression of the day both by means of content and sheer bulk. It had to be big: It is surplus text at its most erotic.

Or take Douglas Huebler's *Variable Piece #70* (1971), where he attempts to: "photographically document, to the extent of his capacity, the existence of everyone alive in order to produce the most authentic and inclusive representation of the human species that may be assembled in that manner."[5] Like Stein, Huebler began locally, photographing everyone he passed by on the street. Later, he would go to huge rallies and sporting events, photographing the crowds. Finally, realizing the futility of his efforts, he began rephotographing existing photos of large gatherings of people in order to attempt to accomplish his goal. Of course, he too "failed better."

Another instance is Joe Gould's *An Oral History of Our Time*, which was purported in June of 1942 to be "approximately nine million two hundred and fifty-five thousand words long, or about a dozen times as long as the Bible,"[6] written out in longhand on both sides of the page so illegibly that only Gould could read it:

> Gould puts into the *Oral History* only things he has seen or heard. At least half of it is made up on conversations taken down verbatim or summarized; hence the title. "What people say is history," Gould says. "What we used to think was history—kings and queens, treaties, inventions, big battles, beheadings, Caesar, Napoleon, Pontius Pilate, Columbus, William Jennings Bryan—is only formal history and largely false. I'll put down the informal history of the shirt-sleeved multitude—what they had to say about their jobs, love affairs, vittles, sprees, scrapes, and sorrows—or I'll perish in the attempt."[7]

The scope was enormous: included is everything from transcriptions of soliloquies of park bench bums to rhymes transcribed from restroom stalls:

> Hundred of thousands of words are devoted to the drunken behavior and sexual adventures of various professional Greenwich Villagers, in the twenties. There are hundreds of reports of ginny Village parties, including gossip about the guests and faithful reports of their arguments on subjects such as reincarnation, birth control, free love, psychoanalysis, Christian Science, Swedenborgianism, vegeterianism, alcoholism, and different political and art isms. "I have fully covered what might be termed the intellectual underworld of my time," Gould says.[8]

Gould's project, too, ended in failure: No manuscript was ever written. It was an enormous hoax, so convincing that it fooled Joseph Mitchell, a reporter for the *New Yorker*, who wrote a small book about him, ending up being Gould's de facto biographer.

Although there was no *Oral History*, there is *The Making of Americans*. What, then, are we supposed to do with it if not read it? The scholar Ulla Dydo proposes a radical solution: don't read it at all. She remarked that much of Stein's work was never meant to be read closely, rather, Strein was deploying visual means of reading. What appeared to be densely unreadable and repetitive was, in fact, designed to be skimmed and to delight the eye, in a visual sense, while holding the book: "These constructions have an astonishing visual result. The limited vocabulary, parallel phrasing, and equivalent sentences create a visual pattern that fills the page. . . . We read this page until the words no longer cumulatively build meanings but make a visual pattern that does not require understanding, like a decorative wallpaper that we see not as details but only as design." Here's an excerpt from the "Mrs. Hersland and the Hersland Children" chapter:

There are then always many millions being made of women who have in them servant girl nature always in them, there are always then there are always being made then many millions who have a little attacking and mostly scared dependent weakness in them, there are always being made then many millions of them who have a scared timid submission in them with a resisting somewhere sometime in them. There are always some then of the many millions of this first kind of them the independent dependent kind of them who never have it in them to have any such attacking in them, there are more of them of the many millions of this first kind of them, who have very little in them of the scared weakness in them, there are some of them who have in them such a weakness as meekness in them, some of them have this in them as gentle pretty young innocence inside them, there are all kinds of mixtures in them then in the many millions of this kind of them in the many kinds of living they have in them. [9]

This quoted passage proves Dydo's thesis to be correct. It's an extremely visual text, with the rhythm being propelled by the

roundness of the letter *m* and the verticality of the architectural letter formation *illi* of million. The word *million* is the driving semantic
unit, with the visual correlatives—*m* and *on*—framing the *illi*, in an
almost palindromatic way, as the *on* visually glues the two round
humps into another *m*. The negative spaces of the *o* and *n* echo the
negative spaces of the *m*. The result is the visual construction of a
new word, *millim*, a gorgeously rhythmic, palindromic unit. The *ms*
lead the eye up a step to the *is*, which then step you up to the twin *ls*,
the apogee of the unit, and then step back down the way you came.
This visual sequence is echoed by the words *sometimes* and *them*. The
connective tissue is the repeated use of the conjunctions *more of them/
little in them/have in them/some of them/kind of them/many of them*.
which permeate the passage and give it its basic rhythm and flow.

Stein's words, then, when viewed this way, don't really function
as words normally do. We can read them to be transparent or visual
entities or we can read them to be signifiers of language constructed
entirely of language. The latter is the approach Craig Dworkin has
taken in his book *Parse*, where he's parsed an entire grammar book
by its own rules, resulting in a 284-page book. The writing is almost
an abstraction—a schema—of Stein's repetitions:

> Preparatory Subject third person singular intransitive present tense
> verb adjective of negation Noun conjunction of alternation Noun
> locative relative pronoun auxiliary infinitive and incomplete participle
> used together in a passive verbal phrase definite article Noun genitive
> preposition *relative pronoun* period Relative Pronoun third person
> singular indicative present tense verb and required adverb forming a
> transitive verbal phrase marks of quotation definite article singular
> possessive noun verbal noun preposition of the infinitive intransitive
> infinitive verb comma marks of quotation all taken as a direct object
> conjunction marks of quotation definite article verbal noun genitive
> preposition definite article singular noun comma marks of quota-
> tion all taken as a direct object conjunction adjective adjective plural
> direct objective case noun *preposition of the infinitive intransitive in-
> finitive verb and passive incomplete participle used as a complex com-
> pound passive verbal construction* adverb definite article adjective
> noun period Preposition active participle *relative pronoun* second

person subjective case pronoun modal auxiliary second person transitive verb comma marks of quotation *relative pronoun* third person third person singular indicative present tense verb and required adverb forming a transitive verbal phrase indefinite article Noun *preposition of the infinitive intransitive infinitive verb and passive incomplete participle used as a complex compound passive verbal construction* comma abbreviation of an old french imperative period single quotation mark definite article verbal noun genitive preposition definite article noun period single quotation mark marks of quotation[10]

The source text, Edwin A. Abbott's *How to Parse: An Attempt to Apply the Principles of Scholarship to English Grammar*, was first published in 1874 and played a leading role in the pedagogical debate over whether English should be analyzed as if it were Latin. Thousands of copies were printed as textbooks in the last quarter of the nineteenth century. Dworkin says, "When I first came across the book I was reminded of a confession by Gertrude Stein (another product of 1874): 'I really do not know that anything has ever been more exciting than diagramming sentences.' And so, of course, I parsed Abbott's book into its own idiosyncratic system of analysis." The process was slow, taking over five years to complete. Dworkin called it "EXCRUCIATINGLY slow" when he started, but, by the end, he could sit down with the source text and parse-type at "full speed."[11] But parse-typing at full speed requires little inspiration, tons of perspiration, and an acute knowledge of the rules of grammar. This couldn't be more different to the famously hypnotic all-night writing sessions of Gertrude Stein, where inspiration was inseparable from process: "When you write a thing it is perfectly clear and then you begin to be doubtful about it, but then you read it again and you lose yourself in it again as when you wrote it."[12] What Dworkin gives us is structure as literature, plain and simple. It purposefully lacks the play of rhythmic visuality and orality that Stein worked so hard to achieve. This is not to say that there's not visual interest in Dworkin's text, rather it's asking different questions of us.[13]

What does it mean "to parse"? The verb *to parse* comes from the Latin *pars*, referring to parts of speech. In the vernacular to parse means to understand or comprehend. In literature it's a method of breaking a sentence down into its component parts of speech, ana-lyzing the form, function, and syntactical relationship of each part to the whole. In computing it means to analyze or separate parts of code so that the computer can process it more efficiently. In com-puting, parsing is done by a parser, a program that assembles all the bits of code so it can build fluid data structures. But here's where it gets interesting: computational parsing language was based on the rules of English as set forth by the likes of Abbott. Now, the rules of English are notoriously complicated, idiosyncratic, and ambiguous—just ask anyone trying to learn it—and those vagaries have been carried over into computing. In other words, the compiler can get pretty confused pretty easily. It likes repetition and predictable structures; every ambiguity it must parse will ultimately result in slowing down the program. At his most programmatic, the most logical and least ambiguous part of Dworkin's book is when he parsed the complete index of Abbott's book. It's so simple that even I can parse it. Here's the index entry for the word *colon*:

Colon, 309.

which Dworkin parses as:

Noun comma compound arabic numeral period

or the entry for the word "clause":

Clause, defined, 239.

which is:

Noun comma compound arabic numeral comma Noun period

A column of the index looks like this:

Noun comma compound arabic numeral period
Noun comma compound arabic numeral comma Noun period
Noun comma compound arabic numeral period

Noun comma compound arabic numeral period
Noun comma compound arabic numeral period
Noun comma compound arabic numeral period
Noun comma compound arabic numeral period
Noun comma compound arabic numeral period
Noun comma compound arabic numeral period
Noun comma compound arabic numeral dash compound arabic
    numeral comma compound arabic numeral comma compound
    arabic numeral comma compound arabic numeral comma
    compound arabic numeral period
Noun comma compound arabic numeral period
Noun comma compound arabic numeral period
Noun comma compound arabic numeral comma compound arabic
    numeral period
Noun comma compound arabic numeral period
Noun comma compound arabic numeral comma compound arabic
    numeral comma compound arabic numeral period
Noun comma compound arabic numeral period
Noun comma compound arabic numeral period
Noun comma compound arabic numeral comma compound arabic
    numeral comma compound arabic numeral comma compound
    arabic numeral period[14]

This simple and repetitive structure is nearly identical to any
number of returns I get when I use the UNIX command *ls* to view
the contents of a directory. Here's a portion of a log written by a
compiler that notes every time a program on my computer crashes:

Kenny-G-MacBook-Air-2:Logs irwinchusid$ cd CrashReporter
Kenny-G-MacBook-Air-2:CrashReporter irwinchusid$ ls
Eudora_2009–07–24–133316_Kenny-G-MacBook-Air-2.crash
Eudora_2009–08–05–133008_Kenny-G-MacBook-Air-2.crash
KDXClient_2009–04–05–030158_Kenny-G-MacBook-Air.crash
Microsoft AU Daemon_2009–04–23–183439_Kenny-G-MacBook-
    Air.crash
Microsoft AU Daemon_2009–04–23–184134_Kenny-G-MacBook-
    Air.crash

Microsoft AU Daemon_2009–04–24–030404_Kenny-G-Mac
Book-Air.crash

Microsoft AU Daemon_2009–04–27–233001_Kenny-G-MacBook
-Air.crash

Microsoft AU Daemon_2009–04–27–233203_Kenny-G-MacBook
-Air.crash

Microsoft AU Daemon_2009–04–27–233206_Kenny-G-MacBook
-Air.crash

Microsoft AU Daemon_2009–04–27–233416_Kenny-G-MacBook
-Air.crash

Microsoft AU Daemon_2009–04–27–233425_Kenny-G-MacBook
-Air.crash

Microsoft Database Daemon_2009–01–28–141602_irwin-chusids
-macbook-air.crash

Microsoft Database Daemon_2009–06–10–103522_Kenny-G-Mac
Book-Air-2.crash

Microsoft Entourage_2008–06–09–163010_irwin-chusids-macbook
-air.crash

Microsoft Entourage_2008–11–11–133150_irwin-chusids-macbook
-air.crash

Microsoft   Entourage_2008–11–11–133206_irwin-chusids-mac
book-air.crash

Microsoft Entourage_2008–11–11–133258_irwin-chusids-macbook
-air.crash

Microsoft Entourage_2008–11–11–133316_irwin-chusids-macbook
-air.crash

Microsoft Entourage_2008–11–21–131722_irwin-chusids-macbook
-air.crash

Note the cleanly consistency of the data structures, subject/date/
hard drive/crash, a streamlined way of writing that spans more than
a century from Abbott to Dworkin to my MacBook Air—rhetoric,
literature, computing—each employing identical rules and processes. When it comes to language, there's been a general leveling of
labor, with everyone—and each machine—essentially performing
the same tasks. Digital theorist Matthew Fuller sums it up best
when he says, "The work of literary writing and the task of data-

entry share the same conceptual and performative environment, as do the journalist and the HTML coder."[15]

Dworkin's index alone goes on for nearly ten pages and is reminiscent of the index of Louis Zukofsky's life poem, *A*. He calls the index, "Index of Names and Objects," but, unlike a typical index that includes nouns or concepts, Zukofsky also indexes a few articles of speech. Here are the index entries for *a* and *the:*

> a, 1, 103, 130, 131, 138, 161, 168, 173–175, 177, 185, 186, 196, 199, 203, 212, 226–228, 232, 234, 235, 239, 241, 243, 245–248, 260, 270, 281, 282, 288, 291, 296, 297, 299, 302, 323, 327, 328, 351, 353, 377, 380382, 385, 391–394, 397, 402, 404–407, 416, 418, 426, 433, 434, 435, 436, 438, 448, 457, 461, 463, 465, 470, 473, 474, 477–481, 491, 493–497, 499, 500, 505, 507, 508–511, 536–539, 560–563[16]

> the, 175, 179, 181, 182, 184, 187, 191193, 196, 199, 202, 203, 205, 206, 208, 211, 215, 217, 221, 224–226, 228, 231, 232, 234, 238, 239, 241, 243, 245–248, 260, 270, 285, 288, 290, 291, 296, 297, 302, 316, 321–324, 327, 328, 336, 338, 342, 368, 375, 379, 380, 383–387, 390–397, 402, 404, 406, 407, 412, 416, 426–428, 434–436, 440, 441, 463, 465, 468, 470, 473, 474, 476–479, 494, 496, 497, 499, 506–511, 536–539, 560–563[17]

Yet there are major flaws in Zukofsky's index. *a* appears hundreds of times between the pages of 1 and 103, yet they're not indexed. Same thing with *the*, which appears on almost every page of the book, yet the index states that the word doesn't make an appearance until page 175! It turns out that when the University of California Press approached Zukofsky wanting to do a complete volume of *A*, his initial idea was to do an index only containing *a, an* and *the*, words *he felt* were key to understanding his life's work (a subjective constraint-based way of writing). He was delighted with the idea of a conceptual index, and his wife Celia set to work, amassing thousands of index cards, many of which Zukofsky would eliminate when he thought they were unnecessary for his own idiosyncratic reasons—hence the gaps. Clearly Zukofsky thought of the index as another poem—a conceptual one at that—one ridiculing the idea that an artificially formal device such as an index could ever truly control, categorize, domesticate, and stabilize such a wild and uncontrollable beast as language, particularly poetic language.

I've found that the way to deal with the most perplexing of texts is not to try to figure out what they are but instead to ask what they're not. If we say, for example, that *Parse* is not a book of poetry, it is not a narrative, it is not a work of fiction, it is not melodic, it has no pathos, it has no emotion, yet it's not a phone book, nor is it a reference book, and so on, it gradually begins to dawn on us that this is a material investigation of a philosophical inquiry, a concept in the guise of literature. We then begin to ask questions: What does it mean to parse a grammar book by its own rules? What does this tell us about language and the way we process it, its codes, its hierarchies, its complexities, its consistencies? Who made these rules? How flexible are they? Why are they not more flexible? How would this book be different if it were based on a book about how to parse, say, Chinese sentences? Is Dworkin exacting a schoolboy's revenge on Abbott by turning the tables on him, by taking an obsessive "All work and no play makes Jack a dull boy" approach? Is he turning Abbott inside out? Or is Dworkin echoing Abbott's call in *Flatland* to go beyond the page, giving us a portal through which we may truly see the dimensionality of language? As curious as the material text is, it's when *don't read it* that we really begin to understand it.

But, just when we think we've figured it out, we get fooled again. In the midst of all this parsing, you stumble across a sentence in full, normal syntax. This is the entire text on page 217:

NOUN CARDINAL ROMAN
NUMERAL PERIOD

SUBJUNCTIVE MOOD

The answer is, that we desire here to speak of the fact, not as definite facts, but as possibilities.[18]

It's a beautiful and certainly relevant sentence, but why? Dworkin is simply translating into normative English the skeletal examples Abbott used to show how sentences should be parsed.

Dworkin's sentence as parsed—the way it appears in Abbott's book—is:

> Definite article noun singular present continuous verb of definition comma preparatory pronoun first person plural subjective case pronoun first person plural present tense transitive verb preposition of the infinitive infinitive verb genitive preposition definite article objective case singular noun comma adverb of counterfact syncategorematic adjective plural noun comma conjunction syncategorematic plural noun period[19]

So Dworkin *did* do some "creative" writing: He had to come up with several sentences comprised of groups of original words that would be meaningful and sensible, which also cleverly reflect on the text. While he could have filled those words with anything—about the weather or plumbing or dancing—he chose to use those instances as philosophical insertions, ones that comment on both his own process and on Abbott's text. Another reads: "with the entire illustrative sentence meant to suggest an intimately impersonal cast of characters in a reductive permutational drama in the mode of Dick and Jane or Beckett."[20] These small exercises gave Dworkin practice for the next version of the book where he plans to write a narrative novel—completely of his own words—using Abbott's grammatic structure as a template. He'll follow the book to the letter, dropping in *nouns* where they're supposed to go and *present tense transitive verbs* where they're supposed to go, until he's retranslated the entire book according to its own rules, a doubly Herculean task.

While Dworkin could have merely proposed the work—as could Zukofsky or Stein—the realization of it, the *fact* of it, gives us something upon which to base our philosophical inquiries. Had he merely proposed the work—"Parse a grammar book according to its own rules"—we'd have had no conception of what it would feel like to read it, to hold it, to examine it. We would have been denied the sheer pleasure and curiosity of it, the workmanship and craftsmanship, the precision of his execution, the beauty of its language, and the beauty of its concept. It's a wonderful and very powerful object.

The specter of Edwin A. Abbott haunts uncreative writing. For his 2007 book *Flatland,* Derek Beaulieu removed all the letters of Abbott's book of the same title, creating a work of *asemic* literature, a way of writing without using letters. While based entirely on *Flatland,* there's not a word to be found: page after page reveals a series of tangled lines. Like Dworkin, Beaulieu empties Abbott of content to reveal the skeleton of the work. Abbott's *Flatland,* written in 1884, chronicles the adventures of a two-dimensional square who meets a three-dimensional cube, challenging his assumptions and demonstrating his inherent limitations. Abbott wrote the book both as a satire about the rigidity of the Victorian class structure and as a tract that ignited the notion of a fourth dimension in popular imagination.

Beaulieu's tangles of lines represent every letter's placement in Abbott's text, from start to finish. He accomplishes this by taking a ruler and beginning with the first letter on each page, tracing a line to the next occurrence of that letter on the page, then the next and so forth until he reaches the end of the page. He then takes the second letter of the first word on the page and traces that in the same manner. He does this until all letters of the alphabet are accounted for.

The result is a unique graphic rendering of each page. No two pages in Beaulieu's book are identical, and each page contains words and letters in unique sequences. It's a translation or a write-through in the Cagean tradition, based upon letteristic occurrence instead of semantic content, almost performing a conceptual statistical analysis on the text. Colder and more clinical than Dworkin, and minus the sensuality of Stein, what we're left with is a completely unreadable work, yet one based entirely on language.

Perhaps the most unreadable text of all is Christian Bök's *Xenotext Experiment,* which involves infusing a bacterium with an encrypted poem, illegible to the human eye, but meant to be read far into the future, most likely by an alien race after human beings have long since perished. Bök's far-fetched work, with its scope of six million years, makes the propositions of Stein, Gould, or Huebler almost seem humble and earthbound by comparison.

Christian Bök's earlier project, *Eunoia,* which took seven years to write, consists of five chapters, each one of which uses only one

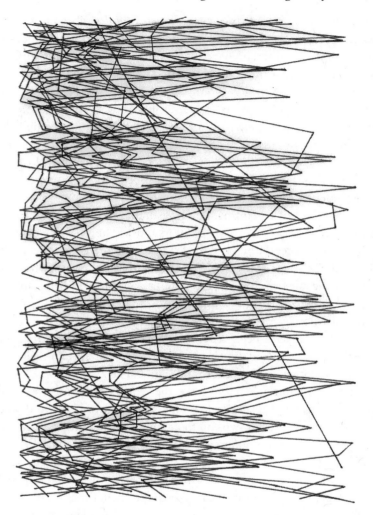

Figure 8.1. Derek Beaulieu, from *Flatland.*

vowel to tell a story, with every chapter containing a variety of linguistic constraints and subnarratives of feasts, orgies, journeys, and
so forth. To accomplish such a staggering feat, he read through
Webster's Third New International Dictionary—a three-volume tome
that contains about a million and a half entries—doing so five

times, once for each of the vowels. When Bök describes his writing process, he sounds like a computational parser, making the idiosyncrasies of the English language speak for themselves, leaving himself with the work that the computer *can't* do. "I proceeded then to sort them into parts of speech (nouns, verbs, adjectives, etc.), and then I sorted each of those parts of speech into topical categories (food, animals, professions, etc.) in order to determine what it might be possible to recount using this very fixed lexicon. It was a very difficult task to abide by these rules, but in the end I demonstrated, I think, that it was possible to write something beautiful and interesting even under such conditions of extreme duress."[21]

While the book is immensely pleasurable to engage with, it's a difficult read because, in spite of all its musical and narrative qualities, what is foregrounded is the structure of the constraint itself, which quickly gets so thick and intrusive that whacking it back to uncover the tale beneath is nearly impossible. Instead of being able to enjoy the text, the reader is drawn into the quicksand of the physicality of language. Readers also continually confront the labor that it must have taken to construct this monumental work, so that the question *How did he do this?* becomes more pressing than trying to make sense of what the author is saying.

The constraints inevitably force the words into some very stiff prose: "Folks who do not follow God's norms word for word woo God's scorn, for God frowns on fools who do not conform to orthodox protocol. Whoso honors no cross of dolors nor crown of thorn doth go on, forsooth, to sow worlds of sorrow. Lo!"[22] But the style couldn't be otherwise if Bök was to abide by the constraint and make it an accountable and realized work of literature.

Far from the drudgery of alienated labor, Bök's lengthy engagement afforded him—and by extension the reader—an intimacy with language that otherwise couldn't be gleaned if he had merely proposed the work: "I discovered that each of the five vowels seems to have its own idiosyncratic personality. A and E, for example, seem to be very elegiac and courtly by comparison to the letters O and U, which are very jocular and obscene. It seems to me that the emotional connotations of words may be contingent upon these vowel distributions, which somehow govern our emotional response to words themselves."[23] In order to explore his idea thoroughly, he kept arbitrary decisions to a minimum, an oblique strategy that paid off and helped him—and once again, by extension, the reader—discover the richness of language just as much as a conventionally expressive "creative" work could.

He says, "The project also underlined the versatility of language itself, showing that despite any set of constraints upon it, despite censorship, for example, language can always find a way to prevail against these obstacles. Language really is a living thing with a robust vitality. Language is like a weed that cannot only endure but also thrive under all kinds of difficult conditions."[24] What emerges, then, is not arid nihilism or negativity, but the reverse: by *not* expressing himself, he's cleared the way to let the language fully express itself.

The Xenotext Experiment involves infusing a bacterium with a poem that will last so long it will outlive the eventual destruction of the Earth itself. While it sounds like something out of a science fiction story, it's for real: Bök has received hundreds of thousands of dollars in funding from the Canadian government, and he's working with a prominent scientist to make it happen.

He's found a species of bacterium—the most resilient on the planet—in which to implement his poems, one that can withstand extremes of cold, heat, and radiation, hence capable of surviving a nuclear holocaust. He's got high aspirations: "I am hoping, in effect, to write a book that would still be on the planet earth when the sun explodes. I guess that this project is a kind of ambitious attempt to think about art, quite literally, as an eternal endeavor."

The process of writing this one poem is insanely difficult and has already taken up several years of his life. Only using the letters of the genetic nucleotides—A, C, G, T—in DNA, Bök is literally using this alphabetic scheme to compose a poem. But since there's only four letters available for him to work with, he's needed to create a set of ciphers that would stand in for more letters. For instance, the triplet of letters AGT might represent the letter B, etc. But it gets more complicated. Bök wants to write the poem in such a way that it will cause a chemical reaction in the DNA strand, which in turn writes another poem. So that the AGT in the new sequence might this time represent the letter X. And on top of all this, Bök insists that both poems make grammatical and semantic sense. He explains the challenges:

> It's tantamount to writing two poems that mutually encipher each other—that are correlated in a very rigorous way . . . Imagine there are about 8 trillion different ways of enciphering the alphabet so that the letters are mutually encoded. Pick one of those 8 trillion ciphers. Now write a poem that is beautiful, that makes sense, in such a way that if you were to swap out every single letter of that poem and replace it with its counterpart from the mutual cipher, you'd produce a new poem that still remains just as beautiful and that still makes sense. So I'm trying to write two such poems. One of these poems is the one that I implant in the bacterium. The other poem is the one that the organism writes in response.[25]

It's fascinating how Bök still uses the word *poem;* the new poems might well be written on computer chips or, in this case, inscribed upon life itself. By referring to the work as a poem, he keeps the project squarely in the realm of the literary as opposed to the scientific or the world of visual art. Although the project will take various forms—the final realization will include a sample of the organism on a slide and a gallery show with images and models of the genetic sequence as support materials for the poem itself—Bök's greatest challenge is to write a good poem, one that will speak to civilizations far into the future. And so Bök notches up the trope of unreadability. This poem is not meant to be read by us, and, by so doing, Bök is enacting one of his long-held precepts, that the future of literature will be written by machines for other machines to read or, better yet, parse.

9   SEEDING THE DATA CLOUD

As has been widely noted, the 2009 Iranian election was challenged by 140-character blasts. Twitter became a surprisingly effective tool to challenge an oppressive regime. It not only could instantaneously link protestors but did so in a form conducive to our information-overloaded age. As data moves faster, and we need to manage more, we are drawn to smaller chunks. Social network status updates succinctly describe an individual's current mood or circumstance, whether it be mundane or dramatic, as in the case of the Iranian protests. These updates or tweets have the ability to reduce complicated circumstances down to a sentence. And the popularity of mood-blasting services like Twitter—which allows no more than 140 characters per post—compress language. These short bursts of language are the latest in a long line of linguistic reductions: Chinese ideograms, haikus, telegrams, newspaper headlines, the Times Square news zipper, advertising slogans, concrete poems, and desktop icons. There's a sense of urgency that compression brings: even the most mundane tweets—what someone is eating for breakfast—can feel like breaking news, demonstrating, once again, that the medium is still the message: the interface of Twitter has reframed ordinary language to make it feel extraordinary.

Social networking updates, which are fast and ephemeral, do not occur in isolation, rather their value is in rapid succession; the more blasts you broadcast with greater frequency, the more effective they are until, like so many little shards, they accumulate into a grand narrative of life. Yet, as soon as they appear, they're pushed off the screen and evaporate even faster than what used to be referred to as yesterday's news. In parsing all this information there's an urge to act, to respond, to click, to hoard, to archive . . . to manage it all. Or don't. Tweets scroll in real time across the screen the way ticker-tape used to spew stock quotes. During the protests, the "hash tag" #iranelection was backed up with so many tweets and retweets that the interface could not keep up. At one point there were twenty thousand blasts in the queue, an echo chamber, packed to the gills with information and disinformation, all expressed in alphanumeric language. Most of us tuning in were trying to make sense of the validity of the ephemera before it slid off the screen, but there are some writers lurking who are harvesting all these tweets, status updates, and other writing on the Web as the basis for future works of literature.[1]

We've witnessed this many times in the last century. The compressed three-line "novels" of Félix Fénéon, which appeared anonymously in a French paper over the course of 1906, read like a mix of telegrams, zen koans, newspaper headlines, and social network updates:

The bread in Bordeaux will not be bloodied at this time; the trucker's passage provoked only a minor brawl.[2]

Love. In Mirecourt, the weaver Colas lodged a bullet in the brain of Mlle Fleckenger, and treated himself with equal severity.[3]

"Why don't we migrate to Les Palaiseaux?" Yes, but M. Lencre, while enroute by cabriolet, was assaulted and robbed.[4]

Hemingway famously wrote a short story in just six words:
For sale: baby shoes, never worn.[5]

Or we end up with the wildly reduced language of later Beckett, fusing the terse compression of telegrams with an innate hesitancy to explicate:

Nothing to show a child and yet a child. A man and yet a man. Old and yet young. Nothing but ooze how nothing and yet. One bowed back yet an old man's. The other yet a child's. A small child's.

Somehow again and all in stare again. All at once as once. Better worse all. The three bowed down. The stare. The whole narrow void. No blurs. All clear. Dim clear. Black hole agape on all. Inletting all. Outletting all.[6]

David Markson, in a remarkable series of late novels, merges the reportage of Fénéon with the compact prose of Beckett, dropping in subjective sentiments of unnamed narrators into the midst of hundreds of shards of art history, most no longer than a line or two:

Delmore Schwartz died of a heart attack in a seedy Times Square hotel. Three days passed before anyone could be found to claim his body.

James Baldwin was an anti-Semite.

Not sorting book and phonograph records merely, but the narrowing residue of an entire life? Papers, files of correspondence?[7]

Like a Twitter stream, it's the slow accumulation of tiny shards, which cohere into a fractured narrative by the book's end. Markson is a compulsive cataloguer: One can imagine him combing through the annals of art history, boiling down long and complicated lives into essential quips. He uses names often as shorthand—tiny two-word headlines. Running your eyes down a page of a Markson work at random produces an incredible list of well-known artists and thinkers: Brett Ashley, Anna Wickham, Stephen Foster, Jacques Derrida, Roland Barthes, Maurice Merleau-Ponty, Roman Jakobson, Michel

Leiris, Jullia Kristeva, Phillipe Sollers, Louis Althusser, Paul Ricoeur, Jacques Lacan, Yannis Ritsos, Iannis Xenakis, Jeanne Hébuterne, Amadeo Modigliani, David Smith, James Russell, and Lady Mary Wortley Montagu. Markson's lists evoke the way gossip columns function, with where names printed in boldface signify importance.

The essayist Gilbert Adair articulates the explosive power of names printed on a page:

> What an alluring entity is the printed name! Consider the following: Steffi Graf, Bill Clinton, Woody Allen, Vanessa Redgrave, Salman Rushdie, Yves Saint Laurent, Umberto Eco, Elizabeth Hurley, Martin Scorsese, Gary Lineker, Anita Brookner. Practically the only thing they have in common is that this essay happens not to be about any of them. Yet how their capital letters glitter on the page—so much so, it is not inconceivable that more than one reader, scanning the essay to see whether it contains anything worth reading, will have been arrested not by its opening paragraph, which is how these things are supposed to work, but by this fourth paragraph, merely on the strength of the names above. It scarcely matters that nothing at all has been made of them, that nothing new, interesting or juicy has been said about them, that the cumulative effect is akin to that produced by some *trompe l'oeil* portrait by Gainsborough in which what seems from a distance to be an intricately, even finickily, rendered satin gown turns out, on closer inspection, to be nothing but a fuzzy, meaningless blur of brushstrokes—it is, nevertheless, just such a bundle of names that is calculated to attract the lazy, unprimed eye. And it has now reached the point where a newspaper or magazine page without its statutory quota of proper, and preferably household, names is as dispiriting to behold as a bridge hand with nothing in it but threes and fives and eights. Household names are, in short, the face-cards of journalism.[8]

In 1929 John Barton Wolgamot, a somewhat obscure writer, privately published a book in a tiny edition consisting almost entirely of names called *In Sara, Mencken, Christ and Beethoven There Were Men and Women*. The book is nearly impossible to read linearly: it's best skimmed, your eye darting across the names, resting on the occasional familiar one, similar to the way Adair shows us how scanning the gossip, society, or obituary columns of a newspaper work.

While listening to a live performance of Beethoven's *Eroica* in New York's Lincoln Center, Wolgamot had a synaesthetic response to the music and heard within "the rhythms themselves, names—names that meant nothing to him, foreign names."[9] A few days after the concert, he checked out a biography of Beethoven from the library, and, in that tome, he found, oddly enough, one after another, all the names he had heard ringing throughout the symphony. And it dawned on him that, "as rhythm is the basis of all things, names are the basis of rhythm," hence deciding to write his book.[10] The entire text consists of 128 paragraphs, the following of which is an example:

> In her very truly great manners of Johannes Brahms very heroically Sara Powell Haardt had very allegorically come amongst his very really grand men and women to Clarence Day, Jr., John Donne, Ruggiero Leoncavalo, James Owen Hannay, Gustav Frenssen, Thomas Beer, Joris Karl Huysmans and Franz Peter Schubert very titanically.[11]

When questioned about *Sara, Mencken*, Wolgamot said that he had spent a year or two composing names for the book, but that the connective sentence—the framework in which the names exist—took him ten years to write. Wolgamot described to composer Robert Ashley (who later used the text as a libretto) how he constructed the sixtieth page of the book, which lists the names of George Meredith, Paul Gauguin, Margaret Kennedy, Oland Russell, Harley Granville-Barker, Pieter Breughel, Benedetto Croce, and William Somerset Maugham: "Somerset has both summer and set as in sun-set, and Maugham sounds like the name of a South Pacific Island, and Maugham wrote a biography of Gauguin, which name has both 'go' and 'again' in it, and Oland could be 'Oh, land,' a sailor's cry, and Granville sounds French for a big city, which Gauguin left to go to the South Pacific."[12]

In 1934, five years after Wolgamot began *Sara, Mencken*, Gertrude Stein described the way in which she wrote the name-laden

The Making of Americans "from the beginning until now and always in the future poetry will concern itself with the names of things. The names may be repeated in different ways . . . but now and always poetry is created by naming names the names of something the names of somebody the names of anything. . . . Think what you do when you do do that when you love the name of anything really love its name."[13]

Fully aware of this history, two Canadian writers, Darren Wershler and Bill Kennedy, have recently fused compressed forms with the power of proper names, giving it a digital spin, in their ongoing work called *Status Update*. They've built a data-mining program that combs social networking sites, collecting all users' status updates. The engine then strips out the user's name and replaces it randomly with the name of a dead writer. The result reads like a mashup of Fénéon, Beckett, Markson, and Wolgamot, all filtered through the inconsequential vagaries of social networking feeds:

> Kurt Tucholsky is on snow day number two. . . . what to do, what to do? Shel Silverstein is gettin' in a little Tomb Raiding before going into work. Lorine Niedecker is currently enjoying her very short break. Jonathan Swift has got tix to the Wranglers game tonight. Arthur Rimbaud found a way to use the word "buttress" as well.[14]

The program authors the poem nonstop, constantly grabbing status updates as fast as they are written and then automatically posts it to a homepage every two minutes. Each proper name on the page is clickable, which brings you to an archive of that author's status updates. If I click, for example, on Arthur Rimbaud's name, I'm brought to the Rimbaud page, an excerpt of which reads:

> Arthur Rimbaud is on a goofy musical nostalgia trip. Arthur Rimbaud just picked up a sweet old studio convertible table for 10 bucks at a yard sale round the corner. Arthur Rimbaud is at the shop and assembling a window display with huge budding branches found at the side of the road! Arthur Rimbaud can finally listen to the wonderfulness of vinyl! Arthur Rimbaud would like to learn to read while sleeping. Arthur Rimbaud is so sleepy! Arthur Rimbaud is

realizing if not now then when? Arthur Rimbaud is kinda drunk and preparing for his accountant.[15]

At the bottom of the Rimbaud page is another feature, something that might have been dreamed up by the nineteenth-century spiritualist Madame Blavatsky, who had a penchant for communicating with the dead, had she the technology: "Arthur Rimbaud has an RSS feed. Subscribe now!" In a deliciously ironic gesture, Wershler and Henry make these legends participate in the flotsam and jetsam of today's online life, pulling them down from their pedestals, forcing them against their will to join in the ruckus. What *Status Update* does is sully the aura of these legends, reminding us that in their own day, they too would have been left wondering why "the cubicle gods are mocking his cleaned-up desk."

Wershler and Kennedy seem to be emulating what the mathematician Rudy Rucker calls a "lifebox,"[16] a futuristic concept whereby one's lifetime of accumulated data (status updates, tweets, e-mails, blog entries, comments one made on other people's blogs, etc.) will be combined with powerful software that would permit the dead to converse with the living in a credible way. The digital theorist Matt Pearson says, "In short, you could ask your dead great-grandmother a question and, even if she had not left record of her thoughts on that topic, the kind of response one might expect from her could be generated. . . . It is autobiography as a living construct. Our grandchildren will be able to enjoy the same quality of relationship with the dead as you might do now with your warm bodied Facebook/ Twitter chums. And as the sophistication of semantic tools develop, the lifebox could become capable of creating fresh content too, writing new blog posts, or copy-pasting together video messages."[17] In fact, Pearson had a coder build a rudimentary lifebox of his living self in the form of a Twitter feed,[18] which he claims, "this undead clone of me may not be as coherent or relevant . . . but it sure sounds like the kind of shite I come out with."[19] (One self-referential tweet reads: "The contestants on Britains Got Talent are victims, toying with this idea Id decided Id have a go at creating my own rudimentary lifebox.")[20] Certainly there must be enough data trails coming off the dozens books written about Rimbaud, his reams of correspondence, the papers written about him, and his poetry as well to reanimate him in a similarly credible way some time in the future. But, for the moment, Wershler and Kennedy are propping up his corpse and forcing him to join our digital world, all of which is to drive home the point that these "ephemeral" wisps of data might not be so ephemeral as we think. In fact, our future selves may be entirely constructed from them, forcing us to perhaps think of such writing as our legacy.

An earlier Kennedy and Wershler electronic writing project has similar concerns. *The Apostrophe Engine* also culls, organizes, and preserves chunks of language from the Internet, yet this program unleashes smaller programs to go out and harvest language en masse, creating what could be the largest poem ever written, and it will keep on being written until someone pulls the plug on the hosting server.

The homepage of the piece is deceptively simple. It reproduces a list poem, written by Bill Kennedy in 1993, in which each line begins with the directive "you are." Every line, it turns out, is clickable. Kennedy and Wershler explain what happens next: "When a reader/writer clicks on a line, it is submitted to a search engine, which then returns a list of Web pages, as in any search. *The Apostrophe Engine* then spawns five virtual robots that work their way through the list, collecting phrases beginning with "you are" and ending in a period. The robots stop after collecting a set number of phrases or working through a limited number of pages, whichever happens first."

Next, *The Apostrophe Engine* records and spruces up the phrases that the robots have collected, stripping away most HTML tags and other anomalies, then compiles the results and presents them as a new poem, with the original line as its title . . . and each new line as another hyperlink.

At any given time, the online version of *The Apostrophe Engine* is potentially as large as the Web itself. The reader/writer can continue to burrow further into the poem by clicking any line on any page, sliding metonymically through the ever-changing content. Moreover, because the content of the Web is always changing, so is the contents of the poem. The page it returns today will not be the page that it returns next week, next month, or next year.[21]

The result is a living poem, being written as the Internet is being written, completely parsed by robots which continues to grow even if no one is reading it. Like *Status Update*, it's an epic of language writ in short bursts, a Marksonian compendium, the nature of which is exactly what Wershler and Kennedy are exploiting:

> The catalogue is a form that struggles with excess. Its job is to be reductive, to squeeze all the possibilities that a world of information has to offer into a definitive set. . . . Its poetic effect, however, is the exact opposite. A catalogue opens up a poem to the threat of a surfeit of information, felt most keenly when the reader wonders, politely, "*How long can this go on?*" It can, in fact, go on for a very long time. In 1993, when the full implications of the nascent World Wide Web were only beginning to occur to us, the catalogue and its paradoxical struggles were already becoming the forum for addressing the fear that we are producing text at a rate beyond our collective ability to read it.[22]

But what happens when this dynamically generated text is bound and frozen between the covers of a book? Wershler and Kennedy published a selection of 279 pages, and the result is a very different project. In the book's afterword, the authors make a disclaimer that they have massaged the texts for maximum effect in print: "*The Apostrophe Engine* has meddled with the writing of others, and we in turn have done the same with its writing. . . . The engine provided us with an embarrassment of riches, an abundance of raw material, beautiful and banal at once and by turns."[23]

Raw material is right. Here's an excerpt of what *The Apostrophe Engine* on the Web returns to me when I click on the line, "you are so beautiful to me," taken from Joe Cocker's hit pop song:

> you are so beautiful (to me) hello, you either have javascript turned off or an old version of adobe's flash player • you are so beautiful to me 306,638 views txml added1:43 kathie lee is a creep 628,573 views everythingisterrible added2:39 you are so beautiful 1,441,432 views caiyixian added0:37 reptile eyes • you are so beautiful (to me) 0 • you are so beautiful 79,971 views konasdad added0:49 before • you are so beautiful to me 19,318 views walalain added2:45 escape the fate— you are so beautiful 469,552 views darknearhome added2:46 sad

slow songs: joe cocker—you are so beautif • you are already a member • you are so beautiful (nearly unplugged) hello, you either have javascript turned off or an old version of adobe's flash player • you are so beautiful 1,443,749 views caiyixian featured video added4:48 joe cocker-you are so beautiful (live at montre • you are so beautiful 331,136 views jozy90 added2:32 zucchero canta "you are so beautiful" 196,481 views lavocedinarciso added3:50 joe cocker mad dogs—cry me a river 1970 777,970 views scampi99 added5:18 joe cocker— whiter shade of pale live 389,420 views dookofoils added4:49 joe cocker—n'oubliez jamais 755,731 views neoandrea added5:22 patti labelle & joe cocker-you are so beautiful • you are the best thit was very exiting> akirasovan (5 days ago) show hide 0 marked as spam reply mad brain damage

It's a rambling mess: the signal to noise ratio is very low. Yet, in print, an excerpt from the same passage is a very different animal:

you are so beautiful • you are so beautiful • you are so beautiful • you are so beautiful artist: Babyface • you are so beautiful • you are so beautiful, yes you are to me you are so beautiful you are to me can't you see? • you are so beautiful the lyrics are the property of their respective authors, artists and labels • you are so beautiful • you are so beautiful artist: Ray Charles • you are so beautiful • you are so beautiful • you are so beautiful to me • you are so beautiful • you are so beautiful • you are so beautiful • you are so beautiful• you are so beautiful to meee • you are so beautiful, would you please[24]

The spacing has been normalized, the numbers have been taken out, the dead lines have been removed; it's been heavily edited to good effect. The printed edition reads gorgeously, full of jagged musical repetitions rhythms, like Gertrude Stein or Christopher Knowles's libretto for the opera *Einstein on the Beach*. And there's careful placement of different types of content such as the copyright warning, which comes crashing down just as you are lulled by the rhythms of the repeating phrases. The two "boldfaced" proper names, Babyface and Ray Charles, each with an identical preceding phrase—"you are so beautiful artist"—are placed far enough apart so as not to interfere with one another, resulting in a perfectly balanced text.

While the computer has harvested the raw material for the poem, it's the authorial hand of Wershler and Kennedy that wrangles the beauty out of the surplus text, making for a more conventional rendition of the work, one predicated upon a skilled editorial hand. Yet the page-bound version lacks the ability to surprise, grow, and continually reinvent itself the same way the rougher Web version does. What emerges, then, in these two versions is a balance that embraces both the machine and the printed book; the raw text and the manipulated; the infinite and the known, showing us two ways of expressing contemporary language, neither one of which can be crowned definitive.

Having a computer write poems for you is old hat. What's new is that, like Wershler and Kennedy, writers are now exploiting the language-based search engines and social networking sites as source text. Having a stand-alone program that can generate whimsical poems on your computer feels quaint compared to the spew of the massive word generators out there on the Web, tapping into our collective mind.

Sometimes that mind isn't so pretty. The Flarf Collective has been intentionally scouring Google for the *worst* results and reframing them as poetry. If people claim that the Internet is nothing more than the world's greatest linguistic rubbish heap, comprised of flame wars, Viagra ads, and spam, then Flarf exploits this contemporary condition by reframing all that trash into poetry. And the well is bottomless. The *Wall Street Journal*, in a profile of Flarf, described their writing methodology: "Flarf is a creature of the electronic age. The flarf method typically involves using word combinations turned up in Google searches, and poems are often shared via email. When one poet penned a piece after Googling 'peace' + 'kitty,' another responded with a poem after searching 'pizza' + 'kitty.' A 2006 reading of it has been viewed more than 6,700 times on YouTube. It starts like this: 'Kitty goes Postal/Wants Pizza.'"[25]

What began as a group of people submitting poems to a poetry. com online contest—they created the absolutely worst poems they could and were naturally rejected—snowballed into an aesthetic, which Flarf cofounder Gary Sullivan describes as "A kind of corrosive, cute, or cloying awfulness. Wrong. Un-P.C. Out of control. 'Not okay.' "[26] Typical of a Flarf poem is Nada Gordon's "Unicorn Believers Don't Declare Fatwas." An excerpt reads:

> Oddly enough, there is a
> "Unicorn Pleasure Ring" in existence.
> Research reveals that Hitler lifted
> the infamous swastika from a unicorn
> emerging from a colorful rainbow.
>
> Nazi to unicorn: "You're not coming
> out with me dressed in that ridiculous
> outfit." You can finally tell your daughter
> that unicorns are real. One ripped the head off
> a waxwork of Adolf Hitler, police said.
>
> April 22 is a nice day. I really like it.
> I mean it's not as fantastic as that hitler
> unicorn ass but it's pretty special to me.
> CREAMING bald eagle there is a tiny Abe
> Lincoln boxing a tiny Hitler. MAGIC UNICORNS
>
> "You're really a unicorn?" "Yes. Now
> kiss my feet." Hitler as a great man.
> Hitler . . . mm yeah, Hitler, Hitler, Hitler,
> Hitler, Hitler, Hitler. . . . German food is so bad,
> even Hitler was a vegetarian, just like a unicorn.[27]

By scouring online forums and arcane cult sites, Gordon uses the debased vernacular of the Web to create a poem whose language is eerily close to her sources. Yet her selection of words and images reveal this to be a carefully constructed poem, showing us that the rearrangement of found language—even as nasty and low as this— can be alchemized into art. But in order to make something great out of horrible materials, you've got to choose well. Flarf's cofounder, K. Silem Mohammad, dubbed Flarf a kind of "sought" poetry, as opposed to "found" poetry, because its makers are actively and constantly engaged in the act of text mining. In Gordon's poem, every hot button is purposefully pushed, from the cheesy image to the cliché: fatwas, abortions, and Hitler's birthday; nothing is off-limits. In some ways, Flarf takes its historical cues from the coterie-based poetics of the New York school, whose poems were filled with in-jokes intended for their friends. In Flarf's case, many of its poems are posted onto its private listserv, which are, in turn, remixed and recycled by the group into endless chain poems based on Internet spew, which are then posted back on to the Web for others to mangle, should they choose. But the New York school—for all their ideas of "low" and "kitsch"—never went as far as Flarf in their indulgence in "bad" taste.

Flarf, by using disingenuous subjectivity, never really believes in what it's saying, but it's saying it anyway, acutely scraping the bottom of the cultural barrel with such prescience, precision, and sensitivity that we are forced to reevaluate the nature of the language engulfing us. Our first impulse is to flee, to deny its worth, to turn away from it, to write it off as a big joke; but, like Warhol's "Car Crashes" or "Electric Chairs," we are equally entranced, entertained, and repulsed. It's a double-edged sword that Flarf holds to our necks, forcing us to look at ourselves in the blade's reflection with equal doses of swooning narcissism and white-knuckled fear, and in this way is typical of the mixed reactions our literary engagement with these new technologies engenders. Flarf and Wershler/Kennedy's practices posit two different solutions for how poets might go about creating new and original works at a time when most people are drowning in the amount of information being thrown at them. They propose that, in its debased and random form, the language generated by the Web is a far richer source material—ripe for reframing, remixing, and reprogramming—than anything we could ever invent.

10 THE INVENTORY AND THE AMBIENT

The impulse to obsessively catalog the minutiae of "real life" spans from Boswell's descriptions of Johnson's breakfasts to tweeting what you ate for breakfast. And with increased storage capacity and more powerful databases emerging all the time, technology seems to be arousing the dormant archivist in all of us. The "data cloud"—those unlimited capacity servers out there in the ether, accessible to us from anywhere on the globe—and its interfaces encourage an "archive" function over a "delete" function.[1] While much of this material is being archived for marketing purposes, writers, as already discussed, are also plundering these vast warehouses of text to create works of literature—not so much using it as raw material from which to craft their next novels, but rather to manage and reshape them. Still other writers are not so much mining these gobs of texts as they are exploring the function of the archive as it applies to the construction of literary works. These sorts of works are closer to the ambient music of Brian Eno than they are to conventional writing, encouraging a textual immersion rather than a linear reading of them. Uncreative writing allows for a new type of writing about ourselves: call it oblique autobiography. By inventorying the mundane—what we eat and what we read—we leave a trail that can say as much about ourselves as a more traditional diaristic approach, leaving room enough for the reader to connect the dots and construct narratives in a plethora of ways.

Some stories are so profoundly moving as they are that any sort of creative gloss or enhancement serves to lessen their impact. Take the best-selling novel *Angel at the Fence* written by Herman Rosenblat. In this work Rosenblat tells of meeting his future wife Roma when he was imprisoned as a child in a concentration camp and she tossed him apples over the fence, helping him to survive. According to Rosenblat, they met by happenstance years later in Coney Island, realized their history, got married, and lived happily ever after. Rosenblat appeared twice on *Oprah,* who called the book "the single greatest love story" she had encountered in her twenty-two years on the show. After much fanfare, his publisher canceled the memoir when he learned it was false. In the aftermath, Rosenblat wrote, "In my dreams, Roma will always throw me an apple, but I now know it is only a dream."[2]

Deborah E. Lipstadt, a professor of Jewish and Holocaust studies at Emory University, upon hearing that yet another Holocaust memoir was falsified, said, "There's no need to embellish, no need to aggrandize. The facts are horrible, and when you're teaching about horrible stuff you just have to lay out the facts."[3]

Lipstadt's sentiments echo—in a very different way and context—something many writers have proposed over the past century: that the unembellished life is more profoundly moving and complex than most fiction can conjure. Popular culture gives us a similar message from a different angle: over the past decade, witness the rise and relentless domination of reality television over the constructed sitcom. And, from the looks of it, our online lives are headed in the same direction through obsessive documentation of our lives. From the early days of webcams to today's rapid-fire Twitter blasts, we've constructed and projected certain notions of who we are through a process of accumulating seemingly insignificant and ephemeral gestures, fashioning identities that might or might not have something to do with who we actually are. We've become autobiographers of an obsessive nature, but, just as much, we've also become biographers of others, collecting scores of minute facts and impressions on whomever we choose to focus our lens. Tribute pages, fan sites, and Wikipedia entries on even the most marginal persons or endeavors continually accumulate, line by line, all adding up to an obsession with detail and biography that rivals Boswell's *Life of Johnson*.[4]

Boswell in many ways both mirrors and predicts our contemporary linguistic condition. His massive tome is an accumulation of bits and pieces of the quotidian ephemera: letters, observations, patches of dialogue, and descriptions of daily life. The text is an unstable one because of Boswell's excessive footnoting and Mrs. Thrale's marginalia rebutting and correcting Boswell's subjectively flawed observations. And Thrale's comments are not just appended to the main body of the text; she also annotates Boswell's minutiae-laden footnotes, some of which take up three-quarters of the page. The book feels Talmudic in its multithreaded conversations and glosses. It's a dynamic textual space reminiscent of today's Web, with built-in feedback and response systems. It also has some of the same cacophonous dilemmas of online space. The spectator sport of Johnson's life in some ways trumps the subject.

Boswell's *Johnson* can be read cover to cover, but it's just as good taken in small chunks, by bouncing around skimming, grazing, or parsing. I recall, in the early days of the Web, a friend lamenting that he reads so "carelessly" online, that he's more curious to get to the next click than he is in engaging in a deeper way with the text. It's a common cry: we do tend to read more horizontally online. But *The Life of Samuel Johnson, LL.D.* is a reminder from more than two centuries ago that not all texts demand a strictly linear reading. Once Boswell actually meets up with his subject, there's no real narrative thrust other than chronological, ending with Johnson's death. You can dip in and out without worrying about losing the thread the way you might in a more conventionally written biography. Running your eyes across the pages—skimming—you haul in gems of knowledge while experiencing fleeting ephemeral moments that have been rendered timeless. Yet there's a lot of chaff, such as this frivolous instance Boswell pens, deep into Johnson's seventy-fourth year: "I never shall forget the indulgence with which he treated Hodge, his cat; for whom he himself used to go out and buy oysters,[a] lest the servants, having that trouble, should take a dislike to the poor creature.[b]"[5] Like a commenter on a blog, Hester Thrale in the margins, chimes in: "[a] I used to joke him for getting Valerian to amuse

Hodge in his last Hours. [b] no, it was lest they should consider him as degrading Humanity by setting a Man to wait upon a beast."[6]

In another example, this not particularly profound conversation about wine feels like the meandering improvised dialogue from an Andy Warhol film:

SPOTTISWOODE. So, Sir, wine is a key which opens a box; but this box may be either full or empty? JOHNSON. Nay, Sir, conversation is the key: wine is a pick-lock, which forces open the box and inures it. A man should cultivate his mind so as to have that confidence and readiness without wine, which wine gives. BOSWELL. The great difficulty of resisting wine is from benevolence. For instance, a good worthy man asks you to taste his wine, which he has had twenty years in his cellar. JOHNSON. Sir, all this notion about benevolence arises from a man's imagining himself to be of more importance to others, than he really is. They don't care a farthing whether he drinks wine or not. SIR JOSHUA REYNOLDS. Yes, they do for the time. JOHNSON. For the time!—If they care this minute, they forget it the next.[7]

It's through these small and seemingly insignificant details that Boswell is able to build a convincing portrait of Johnson's life and genius. Boswell's strength is information management. He's got a great sense balance, mixing throwaways with keepers. The text has a leveling quality—profound with insignificant, eternal with quotidian—that is very much the way our attention (and lives) tend to be: divided and multithreaded. In 1938 *The Monthly Letter of the Limited Editions Club* asked of Boswell, "What, however, has the *Life* to offer a twentieth century reader?" And in the parlance of the day, it goes on to ascribe conventional value to the presumed profundity of the book, saying that "the *Life* has an apt word or phrase for everything" and that it is "at once intimately personal and classically universal."[8] More than seventy years later, I think we can ask the same question: "What has the *Life* to offer a twenty-first century reader?" and get a completely different answer, one intimately connected to the way we live today.[9]

There's something about inventory that feels contemporary. When the graphic user interface emerged, there was a sense among many that "now everybody is a graphic designer." With the ever-increasing push of information and material flowing through our networks, we've become like kids in a candy store: we want it all. And, since it's mostly free, we grab it. As a result, we've had to learn how to store things, organize them, and tag them for quick recall. And we've become very good at it. This ethos has seeped into every aspect of our lives; offline, too, we find ourselves meticulously gathering and organizing information as a way of being in the world. Caroline Bergvall, a tri-lingual poet living in London, recently decided to inventory the opening lines of all the British Library's translations of Dante's *Inferno*. She claims that the act of translating Dante has become "something of a cultural industry." In fact, by the time she finished collecting her versions—there were forty-eight in all—two new translations had reached the library's shelves. Bergvall explains her process: "My task was mostly and rather simply, or so it seemed at first, to copy each first tercet as it appeared in each published version of the Inferno. To copy it accurately. Surprisingly, more than once, I had to go back to the books to double-check and amend an entry, publication data, a spelling. Checking each line, each variation, once, twice. Increasingly, the project was about keeping count and making sure. That what I was copying was what was there. Not to inadvertently change what had been printed. To reproduce each translative gesture. To add my voice to this chorus, to this recitation, only by way of this task. Making copy explicit as an act of copy."[10]

Here's an excerpt from Bergvall's "Via: 48 Dante Variations":

Nel mezzo del cammin di nostra vita
mi ritrovai per una selva oscura
che la diritta via era smarrita
The Divine Comedy- Pt. 1 Inferno—Canto I -

1.
Along the journey of our life halfway
I found myself again in a dark wood
wherein the straight road no longer lay
(Dale, 1996)

2.
At the midpoint in the journey of our life
I found myself astray in a dark wood
For the straight path had vanished.
(Creagh and Hollander, 1989)

3.
HALF over the wayfaring of our life,
Since missed the right way, through a night-dark-wood
Struggling, I found myself.
(Musgrave, 1893)

4.
Halfway along the road we have to go,
I found myself obscured in a great forest,
Bewildered, and I knew I had lost the way.
(Sisson, 1980)

5.
Halfway along the journey of our life
I woke in wonder in a sunless wood
For I had wandered from the narrow way
(Zappulla, 1998)[11]

A simple act of inventory belies the subjectivity of translation as the immortal words of Dante are up for grabs. Through re-presentation, Bergvall *transforms* the tercets into a permutational poem or an Oulipian N+7 style exercise, which replaces each noun in a text with the seventh one following it in a dictionary). We move from a "dark wood" to a "night-dark-wood" to a "great forest" to a "sunless wood"; or "journey of our life halfway" to "midpoint in the journey of our life" to " HALF over the wayfaring of our life" to "Halfway along the road we have to go" and "Halfway along the journey of our life." Each phrase uses metaphor, allusion, sentence structure, and wordiness in entirely different ways. By doing very little, Bergvall reveals so very much. In any other context, such a list would be used to demonstrate the intricacies, vagaries, and subjectivity involved in the act of translation. And, although all those concerns are part and parcel of this work, to stop there would be to miss the greater point that Bergvall herself is acting as a sort of translator by simply recasting preexisting texts into a new poem that is entirely her own.

The poet Tan Lin complies information into what he calls "ambient stylistics," which can be likened to the "nonlistening" of Erik Satie's "Furniture Music." In the midst of an art opening at a Paris gallery in 1902, Erik Satie and his cronies, after begging everyone in the gallery to ignore them, broke out into what they called "Furniture Music"—that is, background music—music as wallpaper, music to be purposely not listened to. The patrons of the gallery, thrilled to see musicians performing in their midst, ceased talking and politely watched, despite Satie's frantic efforts to get them to pay no attention. For Satie it was the first of several gestures paving the way toward "listening" by "not listening," culminating in his "Vexations," a strange little 3-minute piano piece. It's only a single page of music but it has the instructions "to be repeated 840 times" scrawled on it. For years it had been written off as a musical joke—a performance of the piece would take approximately 20 hours—an impossible, not to mention tediously boring, task. John Cage, however, took it seriously and gave "Vexations" its first performance in New York in 1963. Ten pianists working in 2-hour shifts conquered the piece, which lasted 18 hours and 40 minutes. Cage later explained how performing "Vexations" affected him: "In other words, I had changed, and the world had changed. . . . It wasn't an experience I alone had, but other people who had been in it wrote to me or called me up and said that they had had the same experience."[12] What they experienced was a new idea of time and narrative in music, one predicated upon extreme duration and stasis instead of the traditional movements of a symphony, which were aimed for great formal and emotional impact and variety. Instead, "Vexations" took on a more Eastern quality, belatedly joining ragas and other extended forms that were being embraced by Western composers in the early sixties and would go on to form minimalism, the dominant compositional mode for the next two decades.

Satie and Cage's gestures were picked up by Brian Eno some seventy-five years later when he described his concept of ambient music: "An ambience is defined as an atmosphere, or a surrounding influence: a tint. My intention is to produce original pieces ostensibly (but not exclusively) for particular times and situations with a view to building up a small but versatile catalogue of environmental music suited to a wide variety of moods and atmospheres."[13]

Lin wants to create a space for innovative writing that is relaxing, not demanding, to the point where he envisions a writing environment where literature exists without having to be read at all: "A good poem is very boring. . . . In a perfect world all sentences, even the ones we write to our loved ones, the mailman or our interoffice memos, would have that overall sameness, that sense of an average background, a fluid structure in spite of the surface disturbances and the immediate incomprehension. The best sentences should lose information at a relatively constant rate. There should be no ecstatic moments of recognition."[14]

The idea of making a text intentionally flat and boring flies in the face of everything we've come to expect from "good" literature. His project *Ambient Fiction Reading System 01: A List of Things I Read Didn't Read and Hardly Read for Exactly One Year* [15] took the form of a blog documenting each day's intake or textual grazing. Here's an excerpt from Tuesday, August 22, 2006, which begins:

10:08–15 HOME OFFICE NYT From Their Own Online World, Pedophiles Extend Their Reach

10:15–23 Pakistanis Find US an Easier Fit than Britain

10:24–26 nytimes.com Editorial Observer; The Television Has Disintegrated. All that's Left is the Viewer

10:28–31 A Police Car with Plenty of Muscle

10:31–4 Now the Music Industry wants Guitarists to Stop Sharing

10:50–6 Code Promotions, A Madison Ave Staple, are Going Online

10:57–07 The Tragic Drama of a Broken City, Complete with Heroes and Villains When the Levees Broke

11:09–15 Helping Fledgling Poets Soar with Confidence

11:15–12:16 AOL Acts on Release of Data

11:59 wikipedia "abdur chowdhury"

12:16–23 Rohaytn Will Take Lehman Post "I remember the first time I cam into contact with them. I was carrying Adren Meyer's briefcase into a meeting with Bobby Lehman in the mid-1950's. They had six desks. I've always had a yen for them."

12:23–5 wikipedia "rohatyn" "greenberg"

12:25 style.com "greenberg"

12:25–33 What Organizations Don't Want to Know Can Hurt

12:34 Tower Records will Auction its Assets

12:34–57 Web Surfing in Public Places is a Way to Court Trouble

What appears to be a banal list of things he read—or didn't read—with some investigation reveals a wealth of autobiographical narrative and sheds light on the act of consuming, archiving, and moving information. Lin begins his day at 10:08 in his home office where he skims the day's news. The first thing he reads is a story about how pedophiles are colonizing the online space. The story says that "they swap stories about day-to-day encounters with minors. And they make use of technology to help take their arguments to others."[16] We have no way of knowing if Lin is reading this in the paper version or online, but since he's blogging about it or entering his meanderings into a word processing document, we can pretty much assume that he is on the computer. In a sense—without the pedophilia, of course—this article describes Lin's situation. Sitting at his computer, he is simultaneously reading and writing, consuming and redistributing, creating and disseminating information, "mak[ing] use of technology to help take [his] arguments to others." Minus the lurid connotations, we could easily reimagine the title of this excerpt to be "From His Online World, Tan Lin Extends His Reach."

By 10:24, he is definitely online: "The Television Has Disintegrated. All That's Left Is the Viewer" is a folksy mediation on how our digital technology has supplanted the functional simplicity of the old analog television set. With one window cracked to nytimes.com and another open for blog entries, Lin is enacting the dilemma put forth in the article, which was published in the shrinking paper version of the *New York Times* but read online by Lin at nytimes.com.

Immersed in the screen, Lin continues to read about the erosion of old media distribution from 10:31–10:34 in "Now the Music Industry Wants Guitarists to Stop Sharing." The article, which is still online at the *New York Times* site, is 1,500 words long. Quickly reading or skimming, it's entirely plausible that Lin read this article during the time he said he did. Yet a much shorter article of only 920 words, which takes six minutes to read, "Helping Fledgling Poets Soar with Confidence," is a book review where the author claims "poetry is a primal impulse within us all," which, again, Lin is also enacting by churning the day's news into literature.

Much of Lin's work is about the complexities of identity, and he naturally is drawn toward the article "AOL Acts on Release of Data" which is about a data scandal at AOL where the identities of many users were exposed. Coincidentally, that same AOL leak forms the basis of Thomas Claburn's book-length piece, *i feel better after i type to you*, where he republished all the data of one user. As Claburn explains:

> Within the third of the ten files of user search queries AOL mistakenly released (user-ct-test-collection-03), there's a poem of sorts. Between May 7 and May 31 of this year, AOL user 23187425 submitted a series of more than 8,200 queries with no evident intention of finding anything—only a handful of the entries are paired with a search results URL. Rather, the author's series of queries forms a stream-of-consciousness soliloquy.
>
> Whether it's fact or fiction, confession or invention, the search monologue is strangely compelling. It's a uniquely temporal literary form in that the server time stamps make the passage of time integral to the storytelling. It could be the beginning of a new genre of writing, or simply an aberration. But it does beg further explanation. What circumstances prompted the author to converse thus with AOL's search engine?[17]

Claburn's poem looks eerily like Lin's:

Tuesday 1:25 am
2006–05–09 01:25:15 break in
2006–05–09 01:26:00 joseph i have a question
2006–05–09 01:27:27 all the years why did you work out of delphi
2006–05–09 01:28:36 could have gone to detriot
2006–05–09 01:29:40 why you make delphi kettering your base
2006–05–09 01:30:09 your base

2006–05–09 01:31:13 joe why
2006–05–09 01:31:56 you choose kettering
2006–05–09 01:33:01 had opportunity
2006–05–09 01:33:26 to leave
2006–05–09 01:34:19 start there but could have left
2006–05–09 01:34:54 know you started there but could have left
2006–05–09 01:35:28 why did you stay
2006–05–09 01:36:14 but why
2006–05–09 01:37:46 cause of me
2006–05–09 01:38:48 last saw you bicycle
2006–05–09 01:39:31 why didn't you tell me who you were
2006–05–09 01:41:07 was not to tell me
2006–05–09 01:41:47 orders
2006–05–09 01:42:38 jt order
2006–05–09 01:43:59 was thinking
2006–05–09 01:44:38 on line to ask
2006–05–09 01:45:17 no one would tell me
2006–05–09 01:46:11 mean no
2006–05–09 01:47:45 told of everyone else
2006–05–09 01:48:20 keller like you
2006–05–09 01:48:44 all thrash
2006–05–09 01:49:24 told of them
2006–05–09 01:50:27 wasn't my type
2006–05–09 01:50:49 was not my type
2006–05–09 01:51:32 my type is rare[18]

In the same way that Lin tracks his reading habits and, by association, his mental patterns, Clauburn tracks "AOL User 23187425." Our digital footprint, when rendered visible by data trails, makes for compelling narrative, psychological and autobiographical literature, proving once again that, incisively framed, "mere data" is anything but banal.

When Tan Lin reads about the AOL leak, he came across the name Abdur Chowdhury, a professor who was the source of the leak. At 11:59, he most likely opens another browser window and looks up the Wikipedia entry for "Abdur Chowdhury," for which no page is found. The *Times* article claims that "nearly 20 million discrete search queries, representing the personal Internet hunting habits of more than 650,000 AOL customers gathered over a three-month period last spring, were posted by a company researcher, Abdur Chowdhury, on a publicly accessible Web site late last month."[19] One presumes that such a figure would be of interest to Lin, who claims, "Reading, in a web-based environment, crosses into writing, publication, distribution, and marketing. Is a Twitter feed a form of publication? or is it writing? or is it distribution that is 'pulled' by readers who 'subscribe'? It would seem to be a combination and the lines between these practices is less rigid than with a book where writing and publication are distinct temporally and as entities. Even tags used by Twitterers don't necessarily identify the author by name."[20]

So what does this all add up to? What looks at first glance to be a mass of random information is, in fact, multidimensional and autobiographical. And it's also mostly verifiable. Those articles do exist, and the correspondent times generally make sense. In short, we must conclude that this is not a work of fiction and that Lin really did read what he did and when he did over the course of a year. Taken cumulatively, this is a fairly accurate portrait of Tan Lin, a different type of autobiography, accurately describing himself and his circumstances, without once ever having used the pronoun *I*.

In 1974, Georges Perec, the Oulipian writer, wrote a work that asked similar questions. He compiled a massive Rabelaisian piece, "Attempt at an Inventory of the Liquid and Solid Foodstuffs Ingurgitated by Me in the Course of the Year Nineteen Hundred and Seventy-Four," which begins

> Nine beef consommé, one iced cucumber soup, one mussel soup.
>
> Two Guéndouilles, one jellied andouillette, one Italian charcuterie, one cervelas sausage, four assorted charcuteries, one coppa, three pork platters, one figatelli, one foie gras, one fromage de tête, one boar's head, five Parma hams, eight pâté, one duck pâté, one pâtée foie with truffles, one pâté croûe, one pâté grand-mère, one thrush pâté, six pâté des Landes, four brawns, one foie gras mousse, one pig's trotters, seven rillettes, one salami, two saucissons, one hot saucisson, one duck terrine, one chicken liver terrine.

and ends five pages later:

Fifty-six Armagnacs, one Bourbon, eight Calvadoses, one cherries in brandy, six Green Chartreuses, one Chivas, four cognacs, one Delamain cognac, two Grand Marniers, one pink-gin, one Irish coffee, one Jack Daniel's, four marcs, three Bugey marcs, one marc de Provence, one plum liqueur, nine Souillac plums, one plums in brandy, two Williams pears, one port, one slivovitz, one Suz, thirty-six vodkas, four whiskies.

N coffees
one tisane
three Vichy waters[21]

Perec's inventory is a massive indulgence in the pleasure principle, creating a portrait based on the cliché *you are what you eat.* Or perhaps not. Taken as autobiography, if food and drink can be signifiers of class and economic status, then we can glean a lot from this list about the author. But the problem is that, even though the work recounts what Perec himself ate, we have no verification of it. And, if you think about it, quantifying exactly what you ate over the course of a year is almost impossible. In the text he claims to have consumed "one milk-fed lamb." How much of that lamb did he actually eat? Class status might become more traceable when wines are mentioned, for instance, "one Saint-Emilion '61." There's no vintner mentioned, and, if we look up the price of that wine today, it goes anywhere from $220 to $10,000. While it would have been considerably less in 1974, how are we to know that this isn't just fantasy, an impoverished writer dreaming of great luxuries? It's entirely conceivable that Perec sat down and invented this inventory in one drunken evening at his desk in his modest flat. We'll never know. And yet, in the end, what does it matter if Perec is telling the truth or not? While it's fun to try to sleuth out Perec's claims, I'm more intrigued by the idea that someone would try to quantify everything they ate for a year and present it as a nearly fourteen-hundred-word list of food as a work of literature, rich with sociological, gastronomical, and economic implications. Like Bergvall or Lin, Perec pays close attention to and isolates small details, creating a massive inventory of ephemeral experience whereby the sum is clearly greater than the parts.

11 UNCREATIVE WRITING IN THE CLASSROOM
A Disorientation

In 2004, I began teaching a class called "Uncreative Writing" at the University of Pennsylvania. I sensed that the textual changes that I was noticing in the digital landscape as a result of intensive online engagement was going to be echoed by a younger generation who had never known anything but this environment. This is the course description:

> It's clear that long-cherished notions of creativity are under attack, eroded by file-sharing, media culture, widespread sampling, and digital replication. How does writing respond to this new environment? This workshop will rise to that challenge by employing strategies of appropriation, replication, plagiarism, piracy, sampling, plundering, as compositional methods. Along the way, we'll trace the rich history of forgery, frauds, hoaxes, avatars, and impersonations spanning the arts, with a particular emphasis on how they employ language. We'll see how the modernist notions of chance, procedure, repetition, and the aesthetics of boredom dovetail with popular culture to usurp conventional notions of time, place, and identity, all as expressed linguistically.

My hunch proved to be correct. Not only did the students take to the curriculum, but they ended up teaching me much more than

I knew. Every week, they'd come into class and show me the latest language meme raging across the networks or some new remix engine that was more capable of mangling texts than I had ever dreamed of. The classroom took on the characteristics of an online community, more of a dynamic place for sharing and exchanging ideas than a traditional professor-lectures-students college course.

But, as time went on, I realized that although they could show me cool new things, they didn't know how to contextualize these artifacts, historically, culturally, or artistically. If, for example, they showed me "The Hitler Meme," where the infamous scene from Oliver Hirschbiegel's film *Downfall* was resubtitled so that Hitler was screaming about everything from Windows Vista problems to the collapse of the real estate bubble, I had to inform them that, in the 1970s, situationist filmmaker René Viénet used the resubtitling technique to *détourn* genre films like porn or kung fu into scathing artworks of social and political critique. It also dawned on me that they were much more oriented to consuming online culture than seeing it as something to create new works from. Although we were engaging in a meaningful two-way conversation, I felt there was a real pedagogical need to be filled, one that centered around issues of contextualization. And there were big gaps of knowledge. It was as if all the pieces were there, but they needed someone to help put them together in the right place and in the right order, a situation that called for a conceptual reorientation of what already came naturally to them. In this chapter I want to share five basic exercises I give my students to acclimate them to the ideas of uncreative writing and make them aware of the language and its riches, which are, and have always been, around them.

Retyping Five Pages

The first thing I want to do is to get them to think about the *act* of writing itself, so I give them a simple assignment: *retype five pages* with no further explanation. To my surprise, the next week they arrive in the class, each with a unique piece of writing. Their responses are varied and full of revelations. Although some predictably find the task unbearable and can't wait to get it over with, others discover that it is relaxing and Zen-like, saying it's the first time they've been able to focus on the act of typing, as opposed to struggling to find "inspiration." As a result, they find themselves happily ensconced in an amnesialike state, with words and their meanings drifting in and out of their consciousness. Many become aware of the role their bodies play in writing—from their postures to the cramps in their hands to the movement of their fingers—they became aware of the performative nature of writing. One woman says that she finds the exercise closer to dancing than to writing, entranced by her rhythmic tapping on the keys. Another says it's the most intense *reading* experience she's ever had; when retyping her favorite high school short story, she discovers to her amazement just how poorly written it is. For many students, they began to view texts not only as transparent carriers of meaning but also as opaque objects to be moved around the white space of the page.

In the act of retyping, another thing that differentiates one student from another is the choice of *what* to retype. For example, one student retypes a story about a man's repeated inability to complete a sexual act. When I ask him why he chose this text to retype, he replies that he finds it the perfect metaphor for this assignment, frustrated as he is by not being permitted to be "creative." One woman, who has a day job as a waitress, decides to mnemonically retype her restaurant's menu in order to learn it better for work. The odd thing is that it fails: she detests the assignment and is enraged that it didn't help her on the job at all. It's a nice reminder that, often, the value of art is that it has no practical value.

The critique proceeds through a rigorous examination of paratextual devices, those normally considered outside the scope of writing, but that, in fact, have everything to do with writing. Questions arise: What kind of paper did you use? Why was it on generic white computer paper when the original edition was on thick, yellowed, pulpy stock? (It was surprising to me that students had never considered this question, always defaulting to the generic computer stock at hand.) What did your choice of paper stock say about you: your aesthetic, economic, social, political, and environmental circumstances? (Students confessed that, in a world where they supposedly have more choices and freedom than ever, they tended toward the habitual. On economic and social levels, a discussion ensued about cost and availability, revealing heretofore invisible but very present class differences: some of the wealthier students were surprised to learn that other students were unable to afford a better quality of paper. Environmentally, while most claimed to be concerned about waste, none entertained the notion of electronic distribution to their classmates, defaulting instead to printing and handing out paper copies to all.) Did you reproduce exactly the original text's layout page by page or did you simply flow the words from one page to another, the way your word processing program does? Will your text be read differently if it is in Times Roman or Verdana? (Again, most students used the word processing defaults to represent the works in digital format, using a ragged right margin—the default in Microsoft Word—even when their source text was justified. Few had thought to enter a hard page break into the word processing program correspondent to the pages they were copying from. And the same with fonts: most had never considered using anything other than Times Roman. None had considered the historical and corporate implications of font choice, how, say, Times Roman alluded to but is very different than the font that the *New York Times* is printed in—not to mention the waning power of the once-almighty media giant—or how Verdana, created specifically for screen readability, is a proprietary property of the Microsoft corporation. In short, every font carries a complex social, economic, and political history with it that might—if we're attuned to it—affect the way we read a document.) In the end, we learned that writing up to that point had been a transparent experience for them, that they had never considered anything but the construction and resultant meaning of the words they were creating on the page.

Even the way the students discuss their work is closely examined. One student, for example, without thinking, prefaces a presentation of her work to the class by claiming her piece "isn't going to change the world," which is normally shorthand for "this piece isn't all that great." But, in this environment, her pronouncement leads to a heated half-hour-long discussion about writing's ability or inability to affect change in the world, its political ramifications, and its social consequences, all on account of an innocently—but sloppily—spoken platitude.

Transcribe a Short Piece of Audio

I give the class the instructions to transcribe a piece of audio. I try to pick something with little excitement or interest so as to keep the focus on the language, a straightforward news report or something seemingly dry and dull so as not to "inspire" any student. If I give ten people the same audio file to transcribe, we end up with ten completely unique transcriptions. How we hear—and how, in turn, we process that hearing into written language—is riddled with subjectivity. What you hear as a brief pause and transcribe as a comma, I hear as the end of a sentence and transcribe as a period. The act of transcription, then, is a complex one involving translation and displacement. No matter how hard we try, we can't objectify this seemingly simple and mechanical process.

And, yet, perhaps mere transcription is not enough. We end up with text, but, upon reading it over, we're still missing one key element: the physical qualities of the voice—the lulls, stresses, accents, and pauses. Once we allowed those vagaries in, we open Pandora's box: How to transcribe the messiness of speech, say, when two people are talking atop one another? Or what to do when words are mumbled or indecipherable? Or how do we connote someone laughing or coughing while speaking? What to do about foreign accents or multilanguage texts? For such a seemingly simple task, the questions kept piling up.

On an Internet search, one student comes up with a standard set of transcription conventions, one used in courtrooms and in witness statements, that we immediately adopt as our guide. In them we discover a world of orthographic symbols designed to bring the *voice* out of the text. We set to work, peppering our dry texts with extralingual symbols. We listen over and over again, each time parsing with more minute focused intensity—was that pause (.10) seconds or was it (1.75) seconds? No, it was somewhere in between, noted as (.), a micro pause, usually less than a quarter of a second. By the time we are through, the *voices* jump off the page, shouting and singing as if a recording of them were playing in the room. The results look more like computer code than "writing," and it produces a dozen unique works, in spite of the uniform standards we impose upon them, so that, for example, a transcription of a snippet of dialogue would carry over as this:

> He comes for conversation. I comfort him sometimes. Comfort and consultation. He knows that's what he'll find.

And then end up looking like this:

> \He comes for/ *cONverAstion—* I cOMfort him some*ti*mes (2.0) COMfort and >cONsultAtion< (.) He kn*o*ws (.) that's what >H*E*'ll find—< (2.0) He kn*o*ws that's <wh*AT*—> >he'll f*i*—*n*d< (6.0)

The passage was coded using the following transcriptional conventions:

Underlining of the syllable nucleus denotes that the word is stressed with a syntactically focused accent

UPPERCASE indicates words which are spoken in a louder volume and/or with emphatic stress

(2.0) marks a timed pause of about 2 seconds

(.) denotes a micro-pause, usually less than a quarter of a second

– (single dash sign) in the middle of a word denotes that the speaker interrupts himself

—(double dash signs) at the end of an utterance indicates that the speaker leaves his utterance incomplete, often with an intonation which invites the addressee to complete the utterance

\ / inward slashes denotes speech in a low volume (sotto voce)

> < (arrows) denotes speech (between the arrows which is spoken at a faster rate than the surrounding talk

< > denotes speech (between the arrows) which is spoken at a slower rate than the surrounding talk

* * (asterisks) indicate laughter in the speaker's voice while pronouncing the words enclosed

Read the two passages aloud and you'll hear the difference.

Is this writing or is it mere transcription? It depends on whom you ask. To a stenographer, it's a job; to a fiction writer, focused on telling a compelling narrative, it's a clogged storyline; to a screenwriter, it's the actor's job; to a linguist, it's analytical data; yet to an uncreative writer—one who finds unexpected linguistic, narrative, and emotional richness by subtly shifting frames of reference in words they themselves didn't write—it's art, revealing as much about the transcriber/writers' biases, thought, and decision-making processes as traditional types of writing do. Who would have thought that parsing and coding could reveal so much about the coder?

Transcribing Project Runway

As the semester progresses, the class begins to take on a life of its own and the students begin to act as a group. The class virtually assembles to watch, say, the season's finale of *Project Runway* at 10:00 P.M. on a Tuesday evening. We'll each be at our separate homes, scattered up and down the East Coast, yet all connected by a chat room. Once the show starts, no conversation is allowed, except for us to all type what we're hearing on the television as we're hearing it. Subjective commentary, gloss, and opinion—original thoughts and words—are prohibited. From the moment the show's opening credits roll, a blizzard of repeated words are looped onto the screen by all fifteen participants. We don't stop for ads, rather texts are spawned continuously until 11 P.M., at which time over seventy-five pages worth of raw text is generated, which looks like this:

ChouOnTHISSS (10:19:37 PM): really really happy
beansdear (10:19:37 PM): all the models are dress
ChouOnTHISSS (10:19:37 PM): show the world what I can do
WretskyMustDie (10:19:38 PM): Michael's parents
ChouOnTHISSS (10:19:38 PM): Michael's parents
customary black (10:19:38 PM): ready to show the world
Kerbear1122 (10:19:38 PM): weally weally happy
sunglassaholic (10:19:38 PM): ready to show the world

ChouOnTHISSS (10:19:38 PM): I really like it.
ChouOnTHISSS (10:19:38 PM): do or die
tweek90901 (10:19:40 PM): I really like it
EP1813 (10:19:40 PM): coming to life I like it
shoegal1229 (10:19:40 PM): I do or die
WretskyMustDie (10:19:40 PM): do or die now or never
beansdear (10:19:40 PM): i really lke it
tweek90901 (10:19:40 PM): one shot
shoegal1229 (10:19:40 PM): now or never
sunglassaholic (10:19:40 PM): one shot
beansdear (10:19:40 PM): do or die
shoegal1229 (10:19:40 PM): one shot
WretskyMustDie (10:19:40 PM): Jeffrey's girlfriend and son
beansdear (10:19:40 PM): I'm giving it
tweek90901 (10:19:40 PM): all of the looks
tweek90901 (10:19:40 PM): on all of the girls
sunglassaholic (10:19:40 PM): all of the looks
customary black (10:19:40 PM): all the looks all the girls

The class then constructs an editing process. They decide to remove language they feel interrupts the rhythmic flow ("Michael's parents" and "Jeffrey's girlfriend and son" were extricated). After much argument, the user ids and timestamps are removed (some felt that their documentary function was essential to understanding the piece), all punctuation is excised, typos are fixed, and all lower case *i*s are changed to upper, leaving the final text looking like this:

really really happy
all the models are dressed
show the world what I can do
ready to show the world
weally weally happy
ready to show the world
I really like it
do or die
I really like it
coming to life I like it

I do or die
do or die now or never
I really like it
one shot
now or never
one shot
do or die
one shot
I'm giving it
all of the looks
on all of the girls
all of the looks
all the looks all the girls

It's streamlined and rhythmic, none of which was generated by doing anything other than repeating what was heard. But it's a powerful echo chamber, feeling like a minimalistic cross between E. E. Cummings and Gertrude Stein, all generated by a group listening closely to the spew of a popular television show. If the text wasn't convincing enough, the students give a group reading of the piece, each speaking the lines they "wrote," reanimating this media-saturated text with a bodily presence in a physical space. If we listen closely to the everyday language spoken around us, we'll be sure to find poetry in it. When *Project Runway* is aired, you'd be hard-pressed to find a group of viewers paying attention to the *way* words are spoken instead of how they carry the narrative. Yet all media using language is multifaceted, at once transparent and opaque; by reframing, recontexualizing, and repurposing the found language around us, we'll find that all the inspiration we need is right under our noses. As John Cage said, "Music is all around us. If only we had ears. There would be no need for concert halls."[1]

Retro Graffiti

I like to get students out of the classroom, off the page and the screen and, taking a page out of the situationists' book, have them practice uncreative writing on the street. I tell them that they are to choose arcane texts or out-of-date slogans—"Impeach Nixon," for example—and to graffiti their words onto a public space in a non-permanent way. Some choose to work almost invisibly, inscribing a section of Virginia Woolf's *A Room of One's Own* in micrography using a ballpoint pen on the skin of a banana and placing it back in the bowl with the rest of the bunch. Others are brazen, violently scrawling 1940s advertising slogans in red lipstick across washroom mirrors. Some make their most secret data very public, hoisting enormous flags up campus flagpoles in the middle of the night emblazoned with their bankcard PIN numbers. One student scrawls an erotic slogan from AD 79 in Pompeii, MURTIS BENE FELAS ("Myrtis, you suck it so well") in freshly fallen snow across the campus quad in red dye; someone else tacks a futurist slogan "SPEED IS THE NEW BEAUTY" across the front of Wharton, subtly critiquing the leading business school in the country; yet another obsessively chalks the first one hundred numbers of Pi on every flat surface he can find across campus, resulting in a Philadelphia paper sending a team of investigative reporters to try to ascertain the identity and motives of this mysterious graffiti writer.

The next week they take their slogans and, using card stock and computers, created greeting cards out of them, replete with envelopes, made to look as slick and authentic as possible. I then have them source out and adhere authentic bar codes on them and we march en masse to the local CVS's card section and droplift (the opposite of shoplift) them, snuggled amidst the sea of real "get well" and "first communion cards." We document the droplift event and stick around to see if anyone stumbled across and bought one. I have them buy a few to make sure the bar codes worked. Over the next few weeks, the students keep checking on the cards: they're always there. Rarely will someone buy a card with the feminist slogan "WOULD YOU MARRY YOUR HUSBAND AGAIN?" paired with a soft focus illustration of a sad-eyed puppy.

These exercises use language in ways that echo the use of poetic slogans during the Paris of May 1968 (most famously *Sous le paves, la plage* [Under the paving stones, the beach]) that were spray painted across the walls of the city. The nonspecific and literary nature of these slogans serve to disrupt normative logical, business, and political uses of discursive language, preferring instead ambiguity and dreaminess to awaken the slumbering, subconscious parts of one's imagination. Finding their footing in surrealist notions of Comte de Lautréamont's famous line, "beautiful as the chance meeting on a dissecting table of a sewing machine and an umbrella," such uncharacteristic uses of public language were meant, as Herbert Marcuse said, to motivate the populace to move from "realism to surrealism."[2] Of course on a college campus in 2010, it's unrealistic to have such political expectations, but in fact these interventions, within their context, carry a certain disorientation and provoke some strong reactions. These gestures, echoing street art and graffiti, remind the students of the potential that language has to still surprise us in ways and places where we'd least expect to encounter it. It lets them know that language is both physical and material, and that it can be inserted into the environment and engaged with in an active, public way, making them aware that words need not always be imprisoned on a page.

Screenplays

Take a film or video that has no screenplay and make one for it, so precisely notated that it could be recreated after the fact by actors or nonactors. The format of the screenplay should have nothing left to chance or whim about it: the students must use a Courier font as well as adhere to the preordained formatting constraints that are the screenwriting industry standards. In short, the final work should be unmistakable for a Hollywood screenplay.

One student decides to take a short porn film, *Dirty Little Schoolgirl Stories #2*, starring Jamie Reamz, and render it into a screenplay. The piece begins:

FADE IN.
EXT. HOUSE—DAY
For a split second, we see the image of a man, immaculately suited,
    pulling on the lavish handle of a tall wooden door. On either side

of the door sit two lamps, and beyond this are stone columns. The overall effect, although the shot is brief, is one of wealth and prestige.

INT. BEDROOM—DAY

The shot cuts to the inside of a bedroom. The camera sits at a diagonal to the large, mahogany sleigh bed, so that we can see only half of the room. Also in our field of view are a nightstand, in detailed cast iron, and a tall armoire. The bedspread is done in a red-and-gold paisley print and perfectly matches the four or so pillows and small items on the nightstand. In the foreground is a young-looking blonde, JAMIE, who was once wearing a typical school-girl's uniform—button-down shirt, tie, dark blue cardigan, head-band. She is now only wearing white underwear, and we see her pulling up her blue-and-yellow plaid skirt. Her wavy hair swings from side to side as she does so. As she gets the skirt up to her waist, the camera zooms in close to the skirt. She reaches around to the back of the skirt to zip it.

The camera, so invisible in film, is given a prominent role in the screenplay, as are the furnishings, something that normally disappears in a porn film. In fact, just about everything extraneous to bodies and sex is rendered transparent in pornography. When the dialogue is transcribed, the result, naturally, is stilted and awkward; these were words that were neither meant for the page nor to be scrutinized for their literary qualities:

JAMIE (*naughtily*): Well . . . since I am staying home today . . .
TONY (raising his eyebrows): Right . . .
JAMIE (*laughs devilishly*).
Jamie puts one hand over her crotch, then spreads her legs, all while looking at Tony seductively. He returns her gaze.
TONY: Well . . . (*mumbles*).
JAMIE (*laughs*). How do you mean?
(*Tony clears his throat twice.*)
JAMIE: What do you think I mean? (*Her voice is becoming increasingly syrupy and suggestive.*)

The selection of adjectives (*naughtily, devilishly, syrupy*) and use of punctuation (ellipses, parenthesis) are written according to the whim of the student; someone else writing a screenplay for the same film might have chosen other words to use or have selected other actions to describe. Conventional valuations of writing enter: like most literature, it's one's choice of words and how they're arranged that determines the success or failure of the work.

Once the "action" starts, the student employs the most clinical terms to describe it:

> JAMIE moans in response and the camera zooms out again, so that we can see the whole of JAMIE's vagina. TONY has one hand on JAMIE's thigh and one right above her vagina. He is looking at it intensely, as if surveying the territory. The camera zooms out again as TONY strokes her vagina twice, his hand moving downward. He gently touches a finger to her inner thigh.

Like any screenplay, the actions are clearly and factually described, yet these erotic actions, we're led to believe—through the talents of Jamie and Tony's acting—were spontaneous and "real"; they must be as "real" and spontaneous the next time they are performed. Yet, on another level, the student really isn't describing Jamie and Tony's actions as much as she is the camera's movements and the editor's decisions. Hence, by creating her screenplay, she adds another dimension to an already complex chain of authorship, one that interweaves the literary, the directorial, and scopophilic:

> the remade film's viewers → the actors & director of the film from the student's script → the reader (of the student's work as literature) → the transcriber (student) → the film's original intended audience → the film's director → the camera operator → the actors → the set

The chain omits the intended result of any porn film: the erotic. In this exercise the student's language muddies and objectifies the goal of pornography, upending conventions that are almost always unquestioned, transparent, and deeply unaware of their own workings. In writing such a screenplay the student sets up a hall of mirrors, purposely confusing notions of reality, authenticity, viewership, readership, and authorship.

Another student takes a home video, makes a screenplay of it, has copies of it bound, and gives them as gifts to her parents for the Jewish holidays. The video is of her family's emotional return to the ancestral village in Poland where the better part of them had been exterminated during World War II.

> (*Begin to enter cemetery. Jay and Tourguide are in the shot. Inside the cemetery. Mostly dirt, grass, trees.*)
>
> JAY: This is where the residents of the walled city of the Jewish ghetto were buried.
>
> NANCY: So this is an amazing experience. To see where a quarter of a million Jews are buried. Or three and a half million Jews before the war, ten thousand today. To think that people still deny the existence of the Holocaust, having visited the ghetto. We see that millions of Jews were transported out of Poland to the camps. Pardon my jerking, it's really hard, I'm holding my umbrella. And these are our tour guides in Baligrad, currently they're . . . How many people live in Baligrad now?
>
> (*Voices muffled in the background, as the camera pans the rundown cemetery and over-grown greenery.*)

It just so happened that the student's mother, Nancy, is in class during the presentation of the screenplay and is requested by her daughter to stand up in class and "act" out a few lines from the "play." She specifically indicates that she should read the paragraph just reproduced. Nancy, being a good sport, stood up and begins reading her "lines." She is immediately cut off by her daughter, who says, "Mom, that's not the way you said it in the film!" and makes her repeat the lines with "more feeling." The mother begins again and is just as quickly cut off, her daughter begging her to intone her words in a very specific way, to act more "naturally." What we are seeing in the classroom is a recreation of a scripted event, which is a recreation of a home video with mother as "actor" and daughter as "screenwriter/"director." Furthermore, this is not taking into account the degree of "acting" that both of them are doing publicly in front of a class, which is presumably different from the way they would act in the privacy of their home.

It was a very emotional episode. Yet *emotional* is not the first word that comes to mind with transcription or screenplays of preexisting footage. One would think these methods would produce sterile and dry results, but the reality is the opposite. The transcription or interpretation of extant materials provides students with a sense of ownership of these words and ideas, to the point that they become the students' own as much as would a piece of "original" writing.

The uncreative classroom is transformed into a wired laboratory in which students hypertext off the ideas of the instructor and their classmates in a digital frenzy. This was proven during a recent visit by a writer to my classroom. The writer began his lecture with a Power-Point presentation about his work. While he was speaking, he noticed that the class—all of whom had their laptops open and connected to the Internet—were furiously typing away. He flattered himself that, in the traditional manner, the students were taking copious notes on his lecture, devouring every word he spoke. But what he was not aware of was that the students were engaged in a simultaneous electronic conversation about what the writer was saying, played out over the class listserv, to which they had instant access. During the course of the writer's lecture, dozens of e-mails, links, and photos were blazing back and forth; each e-mail eliciting yet more commentary and gloss on previous e-mails, to the point where what the artist was saying was merely a jumping off point to an investigation of depth and complexity such that a visiting writer, let alone a professor's lecture, would never have achieved. It was an unsurpassed form of active and participatory engagement, but it went far astray from what the speaker had in mind. The top-down model had collapsed, leveled with a broad, horizontal student-driven initiative, one where the professor and visiting lecturer were reduced to bystanders on the sidelines.

But what of the sustained classroom discussion or the art of carefully listening to another person's point of view? From time to time

I make the students close their laptops and switch off their cell phones and we reconnect face to face in meatspace. My students seem to be equally comfortable with both modes, moving in and out of them with as much ease as they do in their day-to-day lives, texting their friends during the day and going out dancing with them that evening.

But I do wish to raise a red flag: I work at a privileged university, perhaps one of the most privileged in the world. The classrooms are crammed with the latest technology and top-speed wireless flows like water from the tap. The students, as a whole, come from economically empowered backgrounds; those who aren't are well subsidized by the university. They arrive in class with the latest laptops and smartphones and seem to have every imaginable piece of the latest software on their machines. They are adept at file sharing and gaming, instant messaging and blogging; they tweet nonstop while updating their Facebook status. In short, it's an ideal environment in which to practice the sort of techno-utopianism I preach with enabled students ready, willing, and able to jump right in.

Needless to say, the situation at an Ivy League institution is not in any way normal. While many institutions in the West have ramped up their technological infrastructures in similar—if not quite as elaborate—ways, at most universities students struggle to get by with older laptops, earlier versions of software, and slower connections; smartphones, for now, are the exception, not the rule, and vast numbers of students must balance the demands of school with equally demanding jobs. In many parts of the West and throughout the third world the situation is much worse, to the point of technology being nonexistent. The data cloud is a fiction, with open and accessible wireless connections few and far between. If you've ever tried to find an unlocked or open wireless network anywhere in the USA, you'll know what I mean. This won't be changing any time soon.

My students know how to express themselves in conventional ways; they've been honing those skills since grade school. They know how to write convincing narratives and tell compelling stories. Yet, as a result, their understanding of language is often one-dimensional. To them, language is a transparent tool used to express logical, coherent, and conclusive thoughts according to a strict set of rules that, by the time they've entered college, they've pretty much mastered. As an educator, I can refine it, but I prefer to challenge it in order to demonstrate the flexibility, potential, and riches of language's multidimensionality. As I've discussed throughout this book, there are many ways to use language: why limit to one? A well-rounded education consists of introducing a variety of approaches. A law student can't only study a case from the side of the prosecution; what the defense does is equally important. The Socratic method of legal education emphasizes the importance of knowing both sides of an argument in order to win it. Like a chess match, a skilled Socratic lawyer must anticipate her opponent's next move by embodying the contrary stance. A legal education also stresses objectivity and dispassion so as to represent a client's interests. I think writers can learn a lot from these methods.

Why shouldn't a literary education adopt a similar approach? If we can manage language/information, we can manage ideas and thus the world. Most tasks in the world are oriented around these processes, be it the gathering of legal facts for an appellate brief, the collating of statistics for a business report, fact-finding and drawing conclusions in the science lab, and so forth. Taking it one step further, by employing similar strategies, we can create great and lasting works of literature.

At the start of each semester, I ask my students to simply suspend their disbelief for the duration of the class and to fully buy into uncreative writing. I tell them one good thing that can come out of the class is that they completely reject this way of working. At least their own conservative positions become fortified and accountable. Another fine result is that the uncreative writing exercises become yet another tool in their writing toolbox, one they will be able to draw upon for the rest of their careers. But the big surprise, even for my most skeptical students, is that being exposed to this "uncreative" way of thinking forever alters the way they see the world. They can no longer take for granted the definition of writing as they were taught it. The change is philosophical as much as it is practical. The students leave the class more sophisticated and complex thinkers. I, in fact, train them to be "unoriginal geniuses."

12   PROVISIONAL LANGUAGE

In today's digital world, language has become a provisional space, temporary and debased, mere material to be shoveled, reshaped, hoarded, and molded into whatever form is convenient, only to be discarded just as quickly. Because words today are cheap and infinitely produced, they are detritus, signifying little, meaning less. Disorientation by replication and spam is the norm. Notions of the authentic or original are increasingly untraceable. French theorists who anticipated the destabilizing of language could never have foreseen the extent that words today refuse to stand still; restlessness is all they know. Words today are bubbles, shape-shifters, empty signifiers, floating on the invisibility of the network, that great leveler of language, from which we greedily and indiscriminately siphon, stuffing hard drives only to replace them with bigger and cheaper ones.

Digital text is the body-double of print, the ghost in the machine. The ghost has become more useful than the real; if we can't download it, it doesn't exist. Words are additive, they pile up endlessly, become undifferentiated, shattered into shards now, words reform into language-constellations later, only to be blown apart once more.

The blizzard of language is amnesia inducing; these are not words to be remembered. Stasis is the new movement. Words now find themselves in a simultaneous condition of ubiquitous obsolescence and presence, dynamic yet stable. An ecosystem: recyclable, repurposed, reclaimed. Regurgitation is the new uncreativity; instead of creation, we honor, cherish, and embrace manipulation and repurposing.

Letters are undifferentiated building blocks—with no one meaning more or less than another; vowels and consonants are reduced to decimal code, temporarily constellating in a word processing document; then a video; then an image; perhaps back to text. Both irregularity and uniqueness are provisionally constructed from identical textual elements. Instead of trying to wrest order from chaos, the picturesque now is wrested from the homogenized, the singular liberated from the standardized. All materialization is conditional: cut, pasted, skimmed, forwarded, spammed.

Where once the craft of writing suggested the coming together—possibly forever—of words and thoughts, it is now a transient coupling, waiting to be undone; a temporary embrace with a high probability of separation, blasted apart by networked forces; today these words are an essay, tomorrow they've been pasted into a Photoshop document, next week they're animated as part of a film, next year they've become a part of a dance mix.

The industrialization of language: because it is so intensely consumed, words are fanatically produced and just as fervently maintained and stored. Words never sleep; torrents and spiders are hoovering language 24/7.

Traditionally, typology implies demarcation, the definition of a singular model that excludes other arrangements. Provisional language represents a reverse typology of the cumulative, less about kind than about quantity.

Language is draining and is drained in return; writing has become a space of collision, a container of atoms.

There is a special way of wandering the Web, at the same time aimless and purposeful. Where once narrative promised to deliver you to a final resting place, the Web's blizzard of language now obfuscates and entangles you in a thicket of words that forces you toward unwanted detours, turns you back when you're lost: a *dérive* on overdrive, a fast *flaneur*.

Language has been leveled to a mode of sameness, blandness. Can the bland be differentiated? The featureless be exaggerated?

Through length? Amplification? Variation? Repetition? Would it make a difference? Words exist for the purpose of *détournement*: take the most hateful language you can find and neuter it; take the sweetest and make it ugly.

Restore, rearrange, reassemble, revamp, renovate, revise, recover, redesign, return, redo: verbs that start with *re-* produce provisional language.

Entire authorial oeuvres now adopt provisional language, establishing regimes of engineered disorientation to instigate a politics of systematic disarray.

Babel has been misunderstood; language is not the problem, just the new frontier.

Provisional language pretends to unite, but it actually splinters. It creates communities not of shared interest or of free association but of identical statistics and unavoidable demographics, an opportunistic weave of vested interests.

"Kill your masters." A shortage of masters has not stopped a proliferation of masterpieces. Everything is a masterpiece; nothing is a masterpiece. It's a masterpiece if I say it is. Inevitably, the death of the author has spawned orphaned space; provisional language is authorless yet surprisingly authoritarian, indiscriminately assuming the cloak of whomever it snatched it from.

The office is the next frontier of writing. Now that you can work at home, the office aspires to the domestic. Provisional writing features the office as the urban home: desks become sculptures; an electronic Post-It universe imbues the new writing, adopting corporate-speak as its lingo: "team memory" and "information management."

Contemporary writing requires the expertise of a secretary crossed with the attitude of a pirate: replicating, organizing, mirroring, archiving, and reprinting, along with a more clandestine proclivity for bootlegging, plundering, hoarding, and file sharing. We've needed to acquire a whole new skill set: we've become master typists, exacting cut-and-pasters, and OCR demons. There's nothing we love more than transcription; we find few things more satisfying than collation.

There is no museum or bookstore in the world better than our local Staples, crammed with raw writing materials: gigantic hard drives, spindles of blank discs, toners and inks, memory-jammed printers, and reams of cheap paper. The writer is now producer, publisher, and distributor. Paragraphs are ripped, burned, copied, printed, bound, zapped, and beamed simultaneously. The traditional writer's solitary lair is transformed into a socially networked alchemical laboratory, dedicated to the brute physicality of textual transference. The sensuality of copying gigabytes from one drive to another: the whirr of the drive, the churn of intellectual matter manifested as sound. The carnal excitement from supercomputing heat generated in the service of literature. The grind of the scanner as it peels language off the page, thawing it, liberating it. Language in play. Language out of play. Language frozen. Language melted.

Sculpting with text.

Data mining.

Sucking on words.

Our task is to simply mind the machines.

Globalization and digitization turns all language into provisional language. The ubiquity of English: now that we all speak it, nobody remembers its use. The collective bastardization of English is our most impressive achievement; we have broken its back with ignorance, accent, slang, jargon, tourism, and multitasking. We can make it say anything we want, like a speech dummy.

Narrative reflexes that have enabled us from the beginning of time to connect dots, fill in blanks, are now turned against us. We cannot stop noticing: no sequence too absurd, trivial, meaningless, insulting, we helplessly register, provide sense, squeeze meaning, and read intention out of the most atomized of words. Modernism showed that we cannot stop making sense out of the utterly senseless. The only legitimate discourse is loss; we used to renew what was depleted, now we try to resurrect what is gone.

AFTERWORD

In 1726, Jonathan Swift imagined a writing machine whereby "the most ignorant person, at a reasonable charge, and with a little bodily labour, might write books in philosophy, poetry, politics, laws, mathematics, and theology, without the least assistance from genius or study."[1] He described a primitive grid-based machine with every word in the English language inscribed upon it. By cranking a few handles, the grid would shift slightly and random groups of half-sensible words would fall into place. Crank it again and the device would spit out another set of non sequiturs. These resulting broken sentences were jotted down by scribes into folios that, like pieces of a giant jigsaw puzzle, were intended to be fit together in an effort to rebuild the English language from scratch, albeit written by machine. The Swiftian punchline, of course, is that the English language was fine as it was and the novelty of reconstructing it by machine wasn't going to make it any better. It's a pointed satire of our blinding belief in the transformative potential of technology, even if in many cases it's sheer folly. Yet it's also possible to view Swift's proposition as an act of uncreative writing, particularly when placed in the context of Pierre Menard's rewriting of *Don Quixote* or Simon Morris's retyping of *On the Road*.

I can imagine someone today reconstructing Swift's machine, rebuilding the English language from scratch, and publishing the book as a work of uncreative writing. It would be a rich project, something along the lines of an Oulipian exercise: "Reconstruct the English language from scratch using the 26 letters on a hand-cranked 20 x 20 grid." Yet the lesson wouldn't be that much different from Swift's; in 2010 the English language still functions quite well as is. Would reconstructing it by hand really make it any better or would this be an exercise in nostalgia, hearkening back to the time when reproduction and mimesis were labor intensive? But in the end, we'd probably say, why bother when a computer can do it better?

In 1984 a computer programmer named Bill Chamberlain did try to do it better when he published *The Policeman's Beard Is Half Constructed*, the first book in English that was penned entirely by a computer named RACTER. Like Swift's machine, RACTER reinvented a perfectly good wheel with less than impressive results. The rudimentary sentences RACTER came up with were stiff, fragmented, and surrealist tinged: "Many enraged psychiatrists are inciting a weary butcher. The butcher is weary and tired because he has cut meat and steak and lamb for hours and weeks."[2]

Or it spewed some light romantic cyberdoggerel: "I was thinking as you entered the room just now how slyly your requirements are manifested. Here we find ourselves, nose to nose as it were, considering things in spectacular ways, ways untold even by my private managers."[3]

To be fair, to have a computer write somewhat coherent prose by itself is a remarkable accomplishment, regardless of the quality of the writing. Chamberlain explains how RACTER was programmed:

Racter, which was written in compiled BASIC . . . conjugates both regular and irregular verbs, prints the singular and the plural of both regular and irregular nouns, remembers the gender of nouns, and can assign variable status to randomly chosen "things." These things can be individual words, clause or sentence forms, paragraph structures, indeed whole story forms. . . . The programmer is removed to a very great extent from the specific form of the system's output. This output is no longer a preprogrammed form. Rather, the computer forms output on its own.[4]

In his introduction to the book, Chamberlain, sounding rather Swiftian, states, "The fact that a computer must somehow communicate its activities to us, and that frequently it does so by means of programmed directives in English, does suggest the possibility that we might be able to compose programming that would enable the computer to find its way around a common language 'on its own' as it were. The specifics of the communication in this instance would prove of less importance than the fact that the computer was in fact communicating something. In other words, what the computer says would be secondary to the fact that it says it correctly."[5]

RACTER's biggest problem was that it operated in a vacuum without any interaction or feedback. Chamberlain fed it punch cards and it spewed semicoherent nonsense. RACTER is what Marcel Duchamp would call a "bachelor machine," a singular onanistic entity speaking only to itself, incapable of the reciprocal, reproductive, or even mimetic interaction with other users or machines that might help improve its literary output. Such was the state of the non-networked computer and primitive science of programming in 1984. Today, of course, computers continually query and respond to each other over the Internet, assisting one another to become ever more intelligent and efficient. Although we tend to focus on the vast amount of human-to-human social networking being produced, much of the conversation across the networks is machines talking to other machines, spewing "dark data," code that we never see. In August of 2010 a watershed occurred when more nonhuman objects came online registered with AT&T and Verizon in greater numbers than did new human subscribers in the previous quarter.[6] This long-predicted situation sets the stage for the next phase of the Web, called "the Internet of things," where mechanic interaction far outpaces human-driven activity on the networks. For example, if your dryer is slightly off tilt, it wirelessly sends data to a server, which sends back a remedy, and the dryer fixes itself accordingly. Such data queries are being sent every few seconds, and, as a result, we're about to experience yet another data explosion as billions of sensors and other data input and output devices upload exabytes of new data to the Web.[7]

At first glance, armies of refrigerators and dishwashers sending messages back and forth to servers might not have much bearing on literature, but when viewed through the lens of information management and uncreative writing—remember that those miles and miles of code are actually alphanumeric language, the identical material Shakespeare used—these machines are only steps away from being programmed for literary production, writing a type of literature readable only by other bots. And, as a result of networking with each other, their feedback mechanism will create an ever-evolving, sophisticated literary discourse, one that will not only be invisible to human eyes but bypass humans altogether. Christian Bök calls this *Robopoetics*, a condition where "the involvement of an author in the production of literature has henceforth become discretionary." He asks, "Why hire a poet to write a poem when the poem can in fact write itself?"[8] Science fiction is poised to become reality, enacting Bök's prediction for the literary future:

> We are probably the first generation of poets who can reasonably expect to write literature for a machinic audience of artificially intellectual peers. Is it not already evident by our presence at conferences on digital poetics that the poets of tomorrow are likely to resemble programmers, exalted, not because they can write great poems, but because they can build a small drone out of words to write great poems for us? If poetry already lacks any meaningful readership among our own anthropoid population, what have we to lose by writing poetry for a robotic culture that must inevitably succeed our own? If we want to commit an act of poetic innovation in an era of formal exhaustion, we may have to consider this heretofore unimagined, but nevertheless prohibited, option: writing poetry for inhuman readers, who do not yet exist, because such aliens, clones, or robots have not yet evolved to read it.[9]

It's not just Bök who is decrying an end to human-produced literature. Susan Blackmore, the genetics historian, paints an evolutionary scenario, telling us we've already been sidelined by machines and their ability to move information. She calls this new stage the *third replicator*, claiming that "the first replicator was the gene—the basis of biological evolution. The second was memes—the basis of cultural evolution. I believe that what we are now seeing, in a vast technological explosion, is the birth of a third evolutionary process. . . . There is a new kind of information: electronically processed binary information rather than memes. There is also a new kind of copying machinery: computers and servers rather than brains."[10] She calls these *temes* (technological memes), digital information that is stored, copied and selected by machines. The future doesn't look promising for us as creative entities. Blackmore says, "We humans like to think we are the designers, creators and controllers of this newly emerging world but really we are stepping stones from one replicator to the next." Listening to these scenarios, every direction we turn, it seems, has already been co-opted by machines, pushing us humans to the sidelines. But what of the reader? Once the human is taken out of the picture, the reader begins to assume the identical role as the uncreative writer: moving information from one place to another. Just think of the way you "read" the Web: you parse it, sort it, file it, forward it, channel it, tweet it and retweet it. You do more than simply "read" it. Finally, the long-theorized leveling of roles has been realized where the reader becomes the writer and vice versa.

But wait. Here I am, hammering out original thoughts on unoriginality to convey to you, another human, about the future of literature. Although this book might be available electronically, I can't wait to wrap my hands around the paper version, making it "real" for me. Ironies abound. Much of what I've discussed in these pages, in comparison to Blackmore, Bök, or "the Internet of things," seem folksy and human driven (*humans* retyping books, *humans* parsing grammar books, *humans* writing down everything they read for a year, etc.). Their predictions make me feel old-fashioned. I'm part of a bridge generation, raised on old media yet in love with and immersed in the new. A younger generation accepts these conditions as just another part of the world: they mix oil paint while Photoshopping and scour flea markets for vintage vinyl while listening to their iPods. They don't feel the need to distinguish the way I do. I'm still blinded by the Web. I can hardly believe it exists. At worst, my cyberutopianism will sound as dated in a few years as jargon from the Summer of Love does today. We're early in this game, and I don't need to tell you how fast it's evolving. Still it's impossible to predict where it's all headed. But one thing is for certain: *it's not going away.* Uncreative writing—the art of managing information and re-presenting it as writing—is also a bridge, connecting the human-driven innovations of twentieth-century literature with the technology-soaked robopoetics of the twenty-first. The references I've made in these pages will inevitably contain references to soon-to-be-obsolete software, discarded operating systems, and abandoned social networking empires, but the change in thinking and in doing from an analog way of writing has been made, and there's no turning back.

NOTES

Introduction

1. Douglas Huebler, Artist's Statement for the gallery publication to accompany *January 5—31*, Seth Segelaub Gallery, 1969.

2. Sol LeWitt, "Paragraphs on Conceptual Art," http://radicalart.info/concept/LeWitt/paragraphs.html; accessed July 15, 2009.

3. Craig Dworkin, introduction to *The UbuWeb Anthology of Conceptual Writing*. http://ubu.com/concept; accessed February 9, 2010.

4. Cut-ups and fold-ins refer to a process whereby one takes a newspaper, slices it into columns, then glues those columns back together in the wrong order and reads across the lines, thus forming a poem.

5. In the art world—where such gestures, far from being merely philosophical, can be worth millions of dollars—there is blowback. In March 2011, a Federal judge ruled against Richard Prince's appropriating photographs from a book about Rastafarians to create a series of collages and paintings. The case is currently being appealed by Prince and his gallerist.

6. When Koons finds himself in legal trouble, it's that he sometimes doesn't bother giving credit for what he appropriated (for example, when he turned of a photograph a couple holding eight puppies in their arms into a sculpture called *String of Puppies*), yet it is well understood that everything he does is based on a preexisting image—it's just that the folks from whom he borrowed rightly wanted to share in Koons's payday.

7. Perhaps the tide is turning. A young German writer, Helene Hegemann, published a best-selling memoir in 2010 that was found to be largely plagiarized. After being busted by a blogger, the writer fessed up and did the typical rounds of apologies. Yet, even after the book was outed, it was selected as a finalist for a prize at the Leipzig Book Fair in fiction. The panel said that it had been aware of the charges of plagiarism. The *New York Times* reported that "although Ms. Hegemann has apologized for not being more open about her sources, she has also defended herself as the representative of a different generation, one that freely mixes and matches from the whirring flood of information across new and old media, to create something new. 'There's no such thing as originality anyway, just authenticity,' said Ms. Hegemann in a statement released by her publisher after the scandal broke." Nicholas Kulish, "Author, 17, Says It's 'Mixing,' Not Plagiarism," *New York Times*, February 12, 2010, http://www.nytimes.com/2010/02/12/world/europe/12germany.html?src=twt&twt=nytimesbooks&pagewanted=print; accessed February 12, 2010.

8. Laurie Rozakis, *The Complete Idiot's Guide to Creative Writing* (New York: Alpha, 2004), p. 136.

9. Gertrude Stein, *The Autobiography of Alice B. Toklas* (New York: Vintage, 1990), p. 119.

1. Revenge of the Text

1. Peter Bürger, *Theory of the Avant-Garde* (Minneapolis: University of Minnesota Press, 1984 [1974]), p. 32.

2. Charles Bernstein, "Lift Off," in *Republics of Reality* (Los Angeles: Sun and Moon, 2000), p. 174.

3. Stephane Mallarmé, 1897 preface to *Un coup de dés jamais n'abolira le hasard* (A throw of the dice will never abolish chance), http://tkline.pgcc.net/PITBR/French/MallarmeUnCoupdeDes.htm; accessed February 9, 2010.

4. Ezra Pound, *The Cantos of Ezra Pound* (New York: New Directions, 1973), p. 716.

5. Neil Mills, "7 Numbers Poems," from *Experiments in Disintegrating Language/Konkrete Canticle* (Arts Council of Great Britain, 1971), http://www.ubu.com/sound/konkrete.html; accessed February 9, 2010. Transcribed from an audio recording by Kenneth Goldsmith. It appears that no typographical version exists.

6. Public Computer Errors, Group Pool on flickr, http://www.flickr.com/groups/66835733@N00/pool/; accessed May 27, 2009.

7. I can think of hand-painted films, like Stan Brakhage's later works, that could contain letters, but the effect was overlay rather than disruption at the operational level. There were also gallery-based text works, such as Lawrence Weiner and Joseph Kosuth, but these, too, were analog-based projects, consisting of stenciling and painting walls and/or nondigital photographic reproduction.

8. Nick Bilton, "The American Diet: 34 Gigabytes a Day," *New York Times,* December 9, 2009, http://bits.blogs.nytimes.com/2009/12/09/the-american-diet-34-gigabytes-a-day; accessed December 25, 2010.

9. Roger E. Bohn and James E. Short, *How Much Information? 2009: Report on American Consumers,* Global Information Industry Center, University of California, San Diego, December 9, 2009, p. 12.

10. Marvin Heiferman and Lisa Philips, *Image World: Art and Media Culture* (New York: Whitney Museum of American Art, 1989), p. 18.

11. Mitchell Stevens, *The Rise of the Image, the Fall of the Word* (New York: Oxford University Press, 1998), p. xi.

12. All passages quoted from James Joyce, *Ulysses* (New York: Random House, 1934); here, p. 655.

13. Bohn and Short, *How Much Information?* p. 10.

14. Some points of comparison between the water cycle and the textual cycle can be made:

- The water cycle uses evaporation from the oceans to seed the clouds with precipitation, which in turn falls to the earth to reseed the water supply.
- The text cycle uses text stored locally to seed the network with language, which in turn can travel back down to the home computer, only to be sent back out to reseed the data cloud.
- Water can change states among liquid, vapor, and ice at various places in the water cycle.
- Language can change states among text, video, code, music and images at various places in the textual cycle.
- There are states of stasis and storage: ice and snow, underground, freshwater, and ocean storage.
- There are states of stasis and storage: hard drives, servers, and server farms.
- Although the balance of water on Earth remains fairly constant over time, individual water molecules can come and go.
- The amount of language on the network is exponentially increasing over time, although individual bits of data come and go.

2. Language as Material

1. Jordan Scott, a Canadian writer who is a chronic stutterer, has written *blert* (Toronto: Coach House, 2008) a book that is comprised of the words he most commonly stumbles over, thus creating a self-imposed linguistic obstacle course when he performs the piece.

2. Guy Debord "Introduction to a Critique of Urban Geography," 1955, http://www.bopsecrets.org/SI/urbgeog.htm; accessed February 25, 2010.

3. Ibid.

4. Acconci's piece could be performed on the Web, clicking through blind links until you hit a password-protected page or 404 Page Not Found.

5. Guy Debord and Gil Wolman, "A User's Guide to Détournement," 1956, http://www.bopsecrets.org/SI/detourn.htm; accessed February 25, 2010.

6. Asger Jorn, *Detourned Painting,* Exhibition Catalogue, Galerie Rive Gauche (May 1959), trans. Thomas Y. Levin, http://www.notbored.org/detourned-painting.html; accessed February 26, 2010.

7. Debord and Wolman "A User's Guide to Détournement."

8. Ibid.

9. Ibid.

10. Guy-Ernest Debord, "Theory of the Dérive" (1956), on http://library.nothingness.org/articles/all/all/display/314; accessed August 5, 2009.

11. The *Times,* seeing that their structures were being pulled into an unauthorized format, issued Stefans a swift cease and desist.

12. http://www.foodincmovie.com/; accessed August 10, 2009.

13. Andy Warhol, *America* (New York: HarperCollins, 1985), p. 22.

14. Language Removal Service's investigations mirror the concerns of sound poetry, the mid-century aural counterpart to concrete poetry, where the emphasis was on the way words sounded, not what they meant.

15. I owe these thoughts to Douglas Kahn's great study, *Noise, Water, Meat: A History of Sound in the Arts* (Cambridge: MIT Press, 1999).

16. Charles Babbage, *The Ninth Bridgewater Treatise* (London: Cass, 1967 [1837]), p. 110.

17. http://en.wikipedia.org/wiki/Klangfarbenmelodie (August 5, 2009).

18. Joseph Kosuth, "Footnote to Poetry," in *Art After Philosophy and After: Collected Writings, 1966–1990,* (Cambridge: MIT Press, 1991), p. 35.

19. Liz Kotz, *Words to Be Looked At: Language in 1960s Art* (Cambridge: MIT Press), pp. 138–139.

20. Eugen Gomringer, *The Book of Hours and Constellations* (New York: Something Else, 1968), n.p.

21. Mary Ellen Solt, ed., *Concrete Poetry: A World View* (Bloomington: Indiana University Press, 1968), p. 10.

22. Noigrandres Group, "Pilot Plan for Concrete Poetry," in Solt, *Concrete Poetry*, pp. 71–72.

23. Clement Greenberg, "Towards a Newer Laocoön," *Partisan Review* 7.4 (JulyAugust 1940): 296–310.

24. http://en.wikipedia.org/wiki/Verdana; accessed September 7, 2007.

25. Noigrandres Group, "Pilot Plan for Concrete Poetry," in Solt, *Concrete Poetry*, pp. 71–72.

26. Solt, *Concrete Poetry*, p. 73.

27. Ibid., p. 8.

28. Morton Feldman, "The Anxiety of Art" (1965), in *Give My Regards to Eighth Street*, ed. B. H. Friedman (Cambridge: Exact Change, 2000), p. 32.

3. Anticipating Instability

1. Lucy Lippard, *Six Years: The Dematerialization of the Art Object* (New York: Praeger, 1973), p. 203.

2. Ludwig Wittgenstein, *Philosophical Investigations* (New York: Macmillian, 1958), p. 197e.

3. "Language as Sculpture": Physical/Topological Concepts, http://radicalart.info/concept/weiner/index.html; accessed February 12, 2009.

4. Walter Benjamin, "The Work of Art in the Age of Mechanical Reproduction," http://www.marxists.org/reference/subject/philosophy/works/ge/benjamin.htm; accessed December 25, 2010.

5. As of February 2010, there were some forty billion photos on Facebook. Kenneth Cukier, "Data, Data Everywhere," *Economist*, February 25, 2010, http://www.economist.com/opinion/displaystory.cfm?story_id=15557443, accessed February 26, 2010.

6. Lawrence Weiner as told to the author in conversation, August 9, 2007.

7. Ludwig Wittgenstein, *Philosophical Investigations* (New York: Macmillian, 1958), p. 226e.

8. "Rouge," a rather traditional sound poem, is quite unlike the type of electronic work based on bodily sounds with which he would later be closely identified.

9. Henri Chopin, "Rouge," unpublished, transcribed from the audio by Sebastian Dicenaire.

10. Hundermark Gallery, Germany, 1981. It's since been released many times on various compilations.

11. Chopin's energies as a publisher and enthusiast for electronic sound poetry were highly visible throughout the 1950s and sixties, culminating in 1964 when his *Revue Ou* began publication and its work regularly aired on the BBC.

12. For examples of such PDFs, there are many sites such as Monoskop, http://burundi.sk/monoskop/log/; accessed August 10, 2009; and AAAARG, http://a.aaaarg.org/library; accessed August 10, 2009.

4. Toward a Poetics of Hyperrealism

1. Walter J. Ong, *Orality and Literacy* (London: Routledge, 1982), pp. 82–83.

2. Robert Fitterman, "Identity Theft," in *Rob the Plagiarist* (New York: Roof, 2009), pp. 12–15.

3. Mike Kelley, *Foul Perfection* (Boston: MIT Press, 2003), p. 111.

4. "Obama Receives Hero's Welcome at His Family's Ancestral Village in Kenya," *Voice of America,* http://www.voanews.com/english/archive/2006–08/2006–08–27–voa17.cfm; accessed August 5, 2009.

5. Ara Shirinyan, *Your Country is Great: Afghanistan-Guyana* (New York: Futurepoem, 2008), p. 13–14.

6. Ibid., pp. 15–16.

7. Claude Closky, *Mon Catalogue,* trans. Craig Dworkin (Limoges: FRAC Limousin, 1999), n.p.

8. Alexandra Nemerov, "First My Motorola," unpublished manuscript.

9. Lev Grossman, "Poems for People," *Time Magazine,* June 7, 2007, http://www.time.com/time/magazine/article/0,9171,1630571,00.html; accessed August 13, 2009.

10. *The Selected Poems of Frank O'Hara*, Ed. Donald Allen (New York: Vintage, 1974), p. 175.

11. Andy Warhol, *The Philosophy of Andy Warhol: From A to B and Back Again* (San Diego: Harcourt Brace Jovanovich, 1975), p. 101.

12. Tony Hoagland, "At the Galleria Shopping Mall," *Poetry* 194.4 (July/August 2009): 265.

13. Rem Koolhaas, "Junkspace," in *Project on the City* (Köln: Taschen, 2001), n.p.

14. Ibid.

15. Robert Fitterman, "Directory," *Poetry* 194.4 (July/August 2009): 335.

16. Koolhaas, "Junkspace."

17. Donald Hall, "Ox Cart Man," http://poets.org/viewmedia.php/prmMID/19216, April 16, 2010.

18. http://www.poets.org/poet.php/prmPID/264; accessed June 5, 2009.

19. http://seacoast.sunderland.ac.uk/~osotmc/zola/diff.htm; accessed May 21, 2009.

20. Message sent to Conceptual Writing Listserv: Mon Jun 15, 2009 5:25 pm.

21. Message sent to Conceptual Writing Listserv: Tue Jun 16, 2009 1:11 pm.

22. E-mail correspondence with the author, May 17, 2009.

23. E-mail correspondence with the author, May 17, 2009.

24. http://www.davidleelaw.com/articles/statemen-fct.html; accessed May 18, 2009.

25. Vanessa Place, *Statement of Facts* (UbuWeb: /ubu, 2009), http://ubu.com/ubu; accessed August 10, 2009.

26. Gene R. Swenson, "What Is Pop Art? Answers from 8 Painters, Part I" originally published in *ARTnews*, November 1963; reprinted in *I'll Be Your Mirror: The Selected Andy Warhol Interviews*, ed. Kenneth Goldsmith (New York: Carroll and Graf, 2004), p. 19.

27. E-mail to author, May 17, 2009.

28. The first volume was published in 1934, and the collected poem as a whole finally made an appearance in the late seventies.

29. Charles Reznikoff, from *Testimony*, reprinted in *Poems for the Millennium,* ed. Jerome Rothenberg and Pierre Joris, vol. 1 (Berkeley: University of California Press, 1995), p. 547.

5. Why Appropriation?

1. Richard Sieburth, "Benjamin the Scrivener," in Gary Smith, ed., *Benjamin: Philosophy, Aesthetics, History* (Chicago: University of Chicago Press, 1989), p. 23.

2. Ibid., p. 28.

3. Susan Buck-Morss, *The Dialectis of Seeing: Walter Benjamin and the Arcades Project* (Cambridge: MIT Press, 1991), p. 54.

4. As of this writing in 2010, seven years after the book was published, there's still about fifty unsold copies in my publisher's warehouse.

5. Ron Silliman blog entry dated February 27, 2006, http://epc.buffalo.edu/authors/goldsmith/silliman_goldsmith.html; accessed July 30, 2009.

6. Ron Silliman, blog entry dated Sunday, October 5, 2008, http://ron silliman.blogspot.com/2008/10/one-advantage-of-e-books-is-that-you .html; accessed October 20, 2008.

7. http://www.english.illinois.edu/maps/poets/s_z/silliman/sunset.htm; accessed December 29, 2010.

8. Bob Perlman, *The Marginalization of Poetry: Language Writing and Literary History* (Princeton: Princeton University Press, 1996), p. 186, n. 26.

9. John Lichfield, "I stole from Wikipedia but it's not plagiarism, says Houellebecq," *Independent*, Wednesday, September 8, 2010, http://www .independent.co.uk/arts-entertainment/books/news/i-stole-from-wikipedia-but-its-not-plagiarism-says-houellebecq-2073145.html; accessed September 15, 2010.

6. Infallible Processes

1. Larissa Macfarquhar, "The Present Waking Life," *New Yorker,* http:// www.newyorker.com/archive/2005/11/07/051107fa_fact_macfarquhar; accessed July 13, 2009.

2. Kwame Dawes, "Poetry Terror," http://www.poetryfoundation.org/ harriet/2007/03/poetry-terrors/#more-66; accessed July 13, 2009.

3. Andrea Miller-Keller, "Excerpts from a Correspondence, 1981–1983," in Susanna Singer, *Sol LeWitt Wall Drawings 1968–1984* (Amsterdam: Stedelijk Museum, 1984), p. 114.

4. Pierre Cabanne, *Dialogues with Marcel Duchamp: The Documents of Twentieth-Century Art* (New York: Viking, 1976), p. 72.

5. Lucy Lippard, *Six Years: The Dematerialization of the Art Object* (New York: Praeger, 1973), pp. 112–113.

6. Ibid., p. 162.

7. Sol Lewitt "Paragraphs on Conceptual Art," http://radicalart.info/ concept/LeWitt/paragraphs.html; accessed July 15, 2009.

8. Yoko Ono, *Grapefruit* (New York: Simon and Schuster, 2000 [1964]), n.p.

9. LeWitt, "Sentences on Conceptual Art," http://radicalart.info/concept/LeWitt/sentences.html; accessed October 22, 2009.

10. Lippard, *Six Years*, pp. 200–201.

11. Sol LeWitt "Sentences on Conceptual Art," http://www.ddooss.org/ articulos/idiomas/Sol_Lewitt.htm; accessed October 22, 2009.

12. Lippard, *Six Years*, p. 201.

13. Ibid., pp. 201–202.

14. Ibid.

15. John Cage, "Four Statements on the Dance," *Silence* (Middletown: Wesleyan University Press, 1962), p. 93.

16. Richard Kostelanetz, *Conversing with Cage* (New York: Limelight, 1988), p. 120.

17. Ibid., p. 263.

18. Holland Cotter, "Now in Residence: Walls of Luscious Austerity," December 4, 2008, http://www.nytimes.com/2008/12/05/arts/design/05lewi .html?_r=1&pagewanted=all; accessed October 23, 2009.

19. Lippard, *Six Years*, pp. 200–201.

20. Cory Doctorow, "Giving It Away" *Forbes*, December 1, 2006, http:// www.forbes.com/2006/11/30/cory-doctorow-copyright-tech-media_cz_ cd_books06_1201doctorow.html; accessed October 21, 2009.

21. At Dia:Beacon, they have a "civilian" LeWitt drawing activity as part of their education program for visiting school groups where the kids execute drawings following LeWitt's instructions.

22. http://www.artinfo.com/news/story/33006/the-best-of-intentions/; accessed October 23, 2009.

23. Michael Kimmelman, "Sol LeWitt, Master of Conceptualism, Dies at 78," *New York Times*, April 9, 2007, http://www.nytimes.com/ 2007/04/09/arts/design/09lewitt.html?pagewanted=all; accessed July 13, 2009.

24. "USA Artists: Andy Warhol and Roy Lichtenstein" transcription of television interview, produced by NET, 1966, in Kenneth Goldsmith, ed., *I'll Be Your Mirror: The Selected Andy Warhol Interviews* (New York: Carroll and Graf, 2004), p. 81.

25. Wayne Koestenbaum, *Andy Warhol* (New York: Viking / Penguin, 2001), p. 3.

26. Anne Course and Philip Thody, *Introducing Barthes* (New York: Totem, 1997), p. 107.

27. Andy Warhol, *The Andy Warhol Diaries,* ed. Pat Hackett (New York: Warner, 1989), p. 455.

28. Ibid., p. xx.

29. Ibid.

30. Goldsmith, *I'll Be Your Mirror*, pp. 87–88.

31. Marjorie Perloff, *Frank O'Hara Poet Among Painters* (Chicago: University of Chicago Press, 1998), p. 178.

32. Frank O'Hara, "Biotherm (for Bill Berkson)," in *The Selected Poems of Frank O'Hara,* ed. Donald Allen (New York: Vintage, 1974), p. 211.

33. Warhol's book unconsciously draws inspiration from Molly Bloom's soliloquy in Ulysses, yet, unlike Joyce, there was no element of fiction or trace of literary pretense in it.

34. Andy Warhol, *a: A Novel* (New York: Grove, 1968), p. 333.

35. Andy Warhol and Pat Hackett, *Popism: The Warhol '60s* (New York: Harcourt Brace Jovanovich, 1980), p. 291.

36. Roland Barthes, "The Death of the Author," *Aspen,* http://ubu.com/aspen/aspen5and6/threeEssays.html#barthes; accessed August 10, 2009.

37. Ibid.

38. G. R. Swenson, "What Is Pop Art? Answers from 8 Painters, Part 1" in Goldsmith, *I'll Be Your Mirror*, p. 18.

7. Retyping *On the Road*

1. Walter Benjamin, *Reflections* (New York: Schocken, 1978), p. 66.

2. http://gettinginsidejackkerouacshead.blogspot.com/2008/06/project-proposal.html; accessed February 8, 2009.

3. Gertrude Stein, *The Autobiography of Alice B. Toklas* (New York: Vintage, 1990), p. 113.

4. http://blog.wfmu.org/freeform/2009/01/the-inaugural-poem-remix.html; accessed July 27, 2009.

5. See my introduction for an extended discussion.

6. Jeremy Millar, "Rejectamenta," in Jeremy Millar and Michiel Schwarz, eds., *Speed—Visions of an Accelerated Age* (London: Photographer's Gallery and Whitechapel Art Gallery, 1998), pp. 87–110, at 106.

7. This form of guerrilla publication reminds me of the way books used to get bootlegged years ago on Amazon when someone would cut and paste or retype, say, a Harry Potter book in chunks under the guise of a review; each successive "review" would reveal subsequent pages of the novel until it was finished.

8. Parsing the New Illegibility

1. In the early days of the Web, a typical April Fool's Day joke was someone offering the complete text of the Internet on a CD-ROM, which was, even as early as 1995, clearly impossible. "According to one estimate, mankind created 150 exabytes (billion gigabytes) of data in 2005. This year, it will create 1,200 exabytes." "The Data Deluge," *Economist,* http://www.econo

mist.com/opinion/displayStory.cfm?story_id=15579717&source=hptextfeat
ure; accessed February 26, 2010.

2. Susan Blackmore, "Evolution's Third Replicator: Genes, Memes, and
Now What?" *New Scientist,* http://www.newscientist.com/article/mg20327191
.500-evolutions-third-replicator-genes-memes-and-now-what.html?full
=true; accessed August 6, 2009.

3. Gertrude Stein, *The Autobiography of Alice B. Toklas* (New York: Vintage, 1990), p. 113.

4. Samuel Beckett, *Now How On: Three Novels* (New York: Grove, 1989),
p. 89.

5. Frédéric Paul, "DH *Still* Is a Real Artist, in <<*Variable*>>, *etc.* (Limousin: Fonds Regional D'art Contemporain, 1993), p. 36.

6. Joseph Mitchell, "Professor Seagull," in *Up in the Old Hotel/McSorley's
Wonderful Saloon* (New York: Vintage, 1993), p. 626.

7. Ibid., p. 58.

8. Ibid., pp. 58–59.

9. Gertrude Stein, *The Making of Amercians* (Normal, IL: Dalkey Archive, 1995), p. 177.

10. Craig Dworkin, *Parse* (Berkeley: Atelos, 2008), p. 64.

11. http://stevenfama.blogspot.com/2008/12/parse-by-craig-dworkin-at-
elos-2008.html; accessed July 31, 2009.

12. Stein, *The Autobiography of Alice B. Toklas,* p. 113.

13. Had Dworkin chosen to render Abbott's text visually, it might
have taken the form of a parse tree, a visual method of diagramming
sentences.

14. Dworkin, *Parse,* p. 283.

15. Matthew Fuller, "It looks like you're writing a letter: Microsoft Word,"
http://www.nettime.org/Lists-Archives/nettime-l-0009/msg00040.html;
accessed July 29, 2009.

16. Louis Zukofsky, *A* (Baltimore: Johns Hopkins University Press, 1978),
p. 807.

17. Ibid., p. 823.

18. Dworkin, *Parse,* p. 217.

19. Translated by Craig Dworkin and e-mailed to the author, on August
9, 2009.

20. Dworkin, *Parse,* p. 190.

21. Jonathan Ball, "Christian Bök, Poet," *Believer* 7.5 (June 2009), http://
www.believermag.com/issues/200906/?read=interview_bok; accessed December 25, 2010.

22. Christian Bök, *Eunoia* (Toronto: Coach House, 2001), p. 60.

23. Ball, "Christian Bök, Poet."

24. Ibid.

25. Ibid.

9. Seeding the Data Cloud

1. In April 2010 the Library of Congress announced that it was archiving the entire Twitter archive: "That's right. Every public tweet, ever, since Twitter's inception in March 2006, will be archived digitally at the Library of Congress. That's a LOT of tweets, by the way: Twitter processes more than 50 million tweets every day, with the total numbering in the billions." http://blogs.loc.gov/loc/2010/04/how-tweet-it-is-library-acquires-entire-twitter-archive/; accessedJuly 13, 2010.

2. Félix Fénéon, *Novels in Three Lines* (New York: New York Review of Books, 2007), p. 113.

3. Ibid., p. 147.

4. Ibid., p. 26.

5. *Wired* magazine ran a contest of Hemingway-inspired six-word stories. Nearly one hundred of them can be found at http://www.wired.com/wired/archive/14.11/sixwords.html; accessed August 10, 2009.

6. Samuel Beckett, from "Worstword Ho," in *Nowhow On* (London: Calder, 1992), p. 127.

7. David Markson, *Reader's Block* (Normal, IL: Dalkey Archive, 1996), p. 85.

8. Gilbert Adair, "On Names," in *Surfing the Zeitgeist* (London: Faber and Faber, 1977), p. 2.

9. John Barton Wolgamot, *In Sara, Mencken, Christ and Beethoven There Were Men and Women* (New York: Lovely Music, 2002), p. 15, written and published privately in 1944, in the CD booklet accompanying Robert Ashley's setting of Wolgamot's work.

10. Ibid.

11. Ibid., p. 48.

12. Ibid., pp. 38–39.

13. Gertrude Stein, "Poetry and Grammar," in *Writing and Lectures 1909–1945,* ed. Patricia Meyerowitz (Harmondsworth: Penguin), p. 140.

14. Status Update, http://www.statusupdate.ca; accessed July 16, 2009.

15. Status Update, http://www.statusupdate.ca/?p=Arthur+Rimbaud; accessed July 16, 2009.

16. http://www.cs.sjsu.edu/faculty/rucker/galaxy/webmind3.htm; accessed August 16, 2010.

17. Matt Pearson, "Social Networking with the Living Dead," http://zenbullets.com/blog/?p=683>; accessed August 16, 2010.

18. http://twitter.com/dedbullets; accessed August 19, 2010.

19. Matt Pearson, "Social Networking with the Living Dead," http://zenbullets.com/blog/?p=683>; accessed August 16, 2010.

20. http://twitter.com/dedbullets/status/21570100860; accessed August 19, 2010.

21. http://apostropheengine.ca/howitworks.php; accessed July 23, 2009.

22. Bill Kennedy and Darren Wershler-Henry, *apostrophe* (Toronto: ECW, 2006), p. 286–287.

23. Ibid., p. 289.

24. Ibid., p. 128.

25. Gautam Naik, "Search for a New Poetics Yields This: 'Kitty Goes Postal/Wants Pizza'" *Wall Street Journal*, May 25, 2010, http://online.wsj.com/article/NA_WSJ_PUB:SB10001424052748704912004575252223568314054.html; accessed August 19, 2010.

26. http://en.wikipedia.org/wiki/Flarf; accessed March 20, 2010.

27. Nada Gordon, "Unicorn Believers Don't Declare Fatwas," *Poetry* 194.4 (July/August 2009): 324–325.

10. The Inventory and the Ambient

1. An early example of this is the illusory delete button on Gmail, which doesn't automatically delete your mail, it holds it for thirty days, then deletes it. And if you want to "permanently" delete a message immediately it takes several clicks to do so. But more relevant is the more prominently featured boldfaced Archive button, which allows you to clean up your inbox without deleting anything. Similarly, on Mac OS X, when you "empty the trash," files are recoverable. It's only when you click Secure Empty Trash that you actually delete once and forever.

2. Ibid.

3. Motko Rich and Joseph Berger, "False Memoir of Holocaust Is Canceled," *New York Times*, December 28, 2008, http://www.nytimes.com/2008/12/29/books/29hoax.html?_r=1&scp=1&sq=False%20Memoir%20of%20Holocaust%20Is%20Canceled&st=cse>; accessed August 13, 2009.

4. A typical Web project in this manner is Ellie Harrison's "Eat 22," in which Harrison documented everything she ate for a year between March 2001 and March 2002. See Georges Perec's "Attempt at an Inventory of the

Liquid and Solid Foodstuffs Ingurgitated by Me in the Course of the Year Nineteen Hundred and Seventy-Four," http://www.eat22.com; accessed May 21, 2009.

5. James Boswell, *The Life of Samuel Johnson LL.D.*, vol. 3 (London: Limited Editions Club, 1938), p. 280.

6. Ibid.

7. Ibid., pp. 33–34.

8. *The Monthly Letter of the Limited Editions Club,* no. 109 (June 1938).

9. M's *The Gospel of Sri Ramakrishna*, published in 1897, is one thousand pages of equally obsessive recording of every move the Hindu saint made. Like Johnson, the Master spouts truisms of the deepest profundity amidst the flotsam and jetsam of trivial description: there are countless instances of Ramakrishna waking up, getting in and out of boats, beds getting repaired, and recollections of dialogue in minute detail.

10. E-mail to author, April 1, 2008.

11. Caroline Bergvall, "Via: 48 Dante Variations," unpublished manuscript.

12. Richard Kostelanetz, ed., *Conversing with CAGE* (New York: Routledge, 2003), p. 237.

13. Brian Eno, liner notes to the 1978 release of *Music for Airports*, http://music.hyperreal.org/artists/brian_eno/MFA-txt.html; accessed August 13, 2009.

14. Tan Lin, from "Ambient Stylistics," *Conjunctions* 35 (Fall 2000).

15. http://ambientreading.blogspot.com; accessed June 5, 2009.

16. Kurt Eichenwald, "On the Web, Pedophiles Extend Their Reach," http://www.nytimes.com/2006/08/21/technology/21pedo.html?scp=1&sq=Their%20Own%20Online%20World,%20Pedophiles%20Extend%20Their%20Reach&st=cse; accessed August 10, 2009.

17. Craig Dworkin and Kenneth Goldsmith, eds., *Against Expression: An Anthology of Conceptual Writing* (Evanston: Northwesten University Press, 2011), p. 138.

18. Ibid., pp. 138–140.

19. Tom Zeller Jr., "AOL Acts on Release of Data," *New York Times*, August 22, 2006, http://query.nytimes.com/gst/fullpage.html?res=940CEFDA123EF931A1575BC0A9609C8B63; accessed August 10, 2009.

20. Chris Alexander, Kristen Gallagher, and Gordon Tapper, "Tan Lin Interviewed," http://galatearesurrection12.blogspot.com/2009/05/tan-lin-interviewed.html; accessed August 3, 2009.

21. Georges Perec, *Species of Spaces and Other Pieces* (London: Penguin, 1997), pp. 240–245.

11. Uncreative Writing in the Classroom

1. As quoted in David Toop, *Ocean of Sound, Ocean of Sound: Aether Talk, Ambient Sound, and Imaginary Worlds* (London: Serpent's Tail, 2000), p. 143.

2. Herbert Marcus, *An Essay on Liberation* (Cambridge: Beacon, 1969), p. 22.

Afterword

1. Jonathan Swift, *Gulliver's Travels*, 1726. Project Gutenberg eBook #829, http://www.gutenberg.org/files/829/829-h/829-h.htm; accessed August 22, 2010.

2. Bill Chamberlain (1984), *The Policeman's Beard Is Half Constructed*, UbuWeb, Warner Books, ISBN 0–446–38051–2, http://www.ubu.com/ historical/racter/index.html; accessed August 22, 2010.

3. Ibid.

4. Ibid.; accessed October 1, 2010.

5. Ibid.; accessed August 22, 2010.

6. Marshall Kirkpatrick, "Objects Outpace New Human Subscribers to AT&T, Verizon," http://www.readwriteweb.com/archives/objects_outpace _new_human_subscribers_to_att_veriz.php; accessed August 19, 2010.

7. Richard MacManus, "Beyond Social: Read/Write in the Era of Internet of Things," ReadWriteWeb, http://www.readwriteweb.com/archives/ beyond_social_web_internet_of_things.php; accessed August 22, 2010.

8. Christian Bök, "The Piecemeal Bard Is Deconstructed: Notes Toward a Potential Robopoetics," *Object* 10: Cyberpoetics (2002), http://ubu .com/papers/object/03_bok.pdf ; accessed June 19, 2009. This afterword owes much of its thinking to the work of Bök, who presents his notion of Robopoetics much more elegantly than I ever can. Bök is also more optimistic than I am, but his work in the field, particularly with his latest genomic project, is convincing enough to make any skeptic rethink her position.

9. Ibid.

10. Susan Blackmore, "Evolution's Third Replicator: Genes, Memes, and Now What?" *New Scientist*, http://www.newscientist.com/article/ mg20327191.500-evolutions-third-replicator-genes-memes-and-now-what .html?full=true; accessed August 3, 2009.

SOURCE CREDITS

Every attempt was made to obtain permission for works in the present volume. If you claim copyright to work appearing in this volume and it is not listed below, please contact us so that this oversight may be amended in future printings.

INDEX

Words: to be shared, moved and
manipulated, 15; fluidity and
interchangeability between images
and, 11; formal and material
properties of, 11; meaning v.
sound, 232*n*14; quantity of, 11; used as
metric, 25; writers and shifting
relationship to, 25–27
"The Work of Art in the Age of
Mechanical Reproduction"
(Benjamin), 7
World-flower concrete poems, 46
Writers: expanding and updated role
of, 24; methodology of, 112–14;
plagiarism by, 229*n*6; procrastination
in, 126–27; as producer, publisher,
and distributor, 221; as programmer
v. tortured genius, 1–2, 117; readers
becoming uncreative, 226; words
and shifting relationship to, 25–27;
writer's block in, 126–28; *see also*
specific writers
Writer's block, 126–28
Writing: as act of moving language, 3;
Bök's process for, 172–73; collage and
pastiche as acceptable methods of, 12;
data entry similar to literary, 166–67;

digital environment impacting, 13;
digital media influencing, 11, 15–24;
Internet's influence on, 14–15;
originality and creativity with
traditional notions of, 15; painting
fifty years ahead of, 13; situationist,
40; statement of facts, 103–4; as
uncreative and stuck, 7; visual arts
with lessons for, 125–49; Web as
site for reading and, 158; *see also*
Uncreative writing
Writing strategies: appropriation as, 5;
copying as, 5

Xenakis, Iannis, 178
The Xenotext Experiment (Bök), 170,
173–74
Xerox, 82

Yoga, Hatha, 63
Your Country Is Great (Shirinyan), 86–90
YouTube, 9

Zen Buddhism, 134
Zola, Émile, 100
Zukofsky, Celia, 167
Zukofsky, Louis, 34, 167–68, 169